SEX IN THE LIBRARY

A Guide to Sexual Content in Teen Literature

Mary Jo Heller and Aarene Storms

VOYA Press

an imprint of E L Kurdyla Publishing, LLC

Bowie, Maryland

ISBN 978-1-61751-028-1

Copyright © 2013

Published by VOYA Press, an imprint of E L Kurdyla Publishing LLC

LCCN: 2013934034

The paper used in this publication meets the minimum requirements of the American National Standard for Information Sciences-Permanence of Paper for Printed Materials, ANSI Z39.48-1992.

Printed in the United States of America

Dedication

To sexy librarians everywhere

Acknowledgements

No writing is done without backup and help. We would like to thank our sexy spouses, Aarene's Jim and Mary Jo's Dennis. Thanks for reading, rereading, comments, and beverages served with and without "enhancements."

Thank you to our editor, RoseMary Honnold. Never once did your emails remind us that you had said this before . . . although we did hear a sigh come through once or twice.

Thanks to two separate but very supportive groups of folks: the Shoreline School District and Geneva Norton and Lyn Ching for information and constant book loans. Thank you also to the staff of the Richmond Beach Library, King County Library System, for the same!

Much love to Mary Jo's grandchildren Max and Anna-Maria for support and Anna's lips! Although Archer is a toddler, we have pictures of him helping his Oma write!

We don't have any photos of Aarene's horse Fiddle helping her write, but it's certain that she did. Thanks, Fee!

Finally: Thanks to our many friends in real life and on Facebook who kept making us chuckle, asking what chapter we were on, and encouraging us through the entire project. Without you, it wouldn't have happened.

TABLE OF CONTENTS

Part II
The Good Stuff: Book Reviews

INTRODUCTION

Raised Eyebrows

For nearly a decade, two teen services librarians have been having sex in the library.

It's true!

Well, it's mostly true. What we've been doing is hosting a booktalking program for middle school and high school students, teachers, parents, public library patrons, and librarians about sexual content in books written for teen readers. We call our program "Sex in the Library."

When we have Sex in the Library, we talk about selection policies and mission statements of the school library and the public library. Most importantly, we compare the books available in the public library and the school library, and we talk about *why the collections are different.*

In order to do all that *and* keep the attention of middle school and high school readers, we review and booktalk the newest, hottest titles with sexual content written for teen readers. Teachers sign up weeks in advance to bring their classes to Sex in the Library, because they love to watch their students hear about selection policies, though the students think they are only learning about steamy library books.

A workshop for librarians entitled "A Comparison of Selection Policies and Mission Statements of Public and School Libraries" would be sparsely attended, but everybody wants to have "Sex in the Library" with us.

Our Sex in the Library presentation began because of an incident in 2001: Mary Jo, the librarian at Einstein Middle School, started it. She bought a copy of *Deal with It: A Whole New Approach to Your Body, Brain, and Life as a gURL* by Esther Drill for her middle school library collection. *Deal with It* was on the 2001 Quick Pick list—a list of books that are quick to pick, quick to read—issued by the American Library Association.

Perfect springtime reading for seventh and eighth graders, Mary Jo thought.

A little too perfect, as it turned out. The book got checked out immediately. Then it got renewed. Then it went out on reserve and quickly got a big stack of names on the waiting list. Something about the popularity of the book made Mary Jo's librarian superpowers tingle. She put the book on hold for herself, and took a long, careful look at the contents. It has good, pertinent information. The pink-and-purple pages feature a very hip layout. The illustrations are cartoons, but drawn for accuracy rather than cuteness. Up-to-date resources are referenced for further inquiry by the reader.

So far, so good. It was doing exactly what items from the Quick Pick list are supposed to do when students are yawning, and the days are inviting them outdoors.

Then, Mary Jo got to page 88, which deals with oral sex. That's where her internal alarms began to sound. The book contained, she felt, possibly a little *too* much information for seventh and eighth graders. Just to make sure, Mary Jo showed the book to the school health/sex ed teachers. They liked the information, the layout, the illustrations, and the resources. Then they got to page 88 and handed the book back. "No way," they said. "Parents would *freak.*"

So, Mary Jo pulled the book out of the school library and called Aarene, so she could buy two copies for the public library collection instead. *Deal with It* is a terrific book, full of really pertinent information in an appealing layout that invites reading. Libraries are all about getting information to the students, and there are some teens who need *most* of the information in this book. Our middle school includes many students who are not ready for all of the information in the book, and a few who are ready. There *is* a way to connect the 'ready' group with books like *Deal with It:* Send them to the local public library.

The public library is the perfect vehicle for getting that particular information to the students, but the school library is not.

This incident got us thinking: Maybe there are some other books we should be looking at that we could "share," so that we can get those appropriate-but-too-controversial-for-school books into the hands of the students who need them.

We asked ourselves: What books are appropriate for the middle school? What books are appropriate for the public library? And, most importantly: Why are those books different?

We wanted to spur the students' imaginations, to enable them to think and react in a safe setting, while exploring some necessary social areas to provide them with a knowledge base. We also needed to talk about mission statements. After all, our missions are vastly different, but our goal is the same: helping students through books, whether it is fiction or nonfiction that provides such help.

But mission statements are totally boring. How could we turn a boring topic into an interesting topic?

We wanted to educate students about the mission statements of both the public library and the school library, talk about the books that we love (or hate), and somehow capture and keep the attention and interest of highly-hormonal middle school students.

Let's face it: A lot of teens stop reading in junior high. Sex in the Library is just the presentation to lure them back to books. Now, with the *Sex in the Library* book, we are broadening our audiences still further by inviting our readers to consider having "sex" in their own libraries. This book is a hands-on, try-it-in-your-building-tomorrow manual for teen services librarians—in public schools, private schools, public libraries, or any other kind of library—who want to open up discussions about some great books, especially when the books are a little bit steamy and potentially controversial.

Our booktalks are not just for students, though. Teachers are also a part of our audience. The Common Core Standards are being used by many states to now reflect a national summary of information necessary for today's graduates. The state of Washington joined the initiative in 2009 and adopted the standards in July 2011. The National Governors Association Center for Best Practices (NGA Center) and the Council of Chief State School Officers (CCSSO) combine to further the standards at a national level. Further information can be found at *www.corestandards.org/assets/appendix_A.pdf.*

In presenting any novel in a booktalk, obvious correlations to nonfiction exist. While discussing SITL books to a teen audience, the astute librarian will include the teacher's desire to address Common Core needs. For example, while reading historical fiction, students also check the narrative for accuracy by researching incidents, vocabulary, and cultural references. Teachers can use fiction to illustrate concepts. Students may choose to explore textual evidence, provide an accurate summary of key events, or utilize primary or secondary sources in seeking the reality of a scientifically-based novel.

Teachers working with Common Core standards are looking for complex fictional texts to support a nonfiction curriculum. They want to engage the attention and imagination of students in order to keep them reading. Many SITL books do engage the attention and imagination of students, and *voila*: a silver platter for teachers, students, and administrators.

We'll take you through the process of finding a good sex (in the library) partner, building a list of books, working through "the giggles" (your own and those from the inevitable back row), and presenting for a variety of audiences. Our aim is to help students, teachers, parents, and administrators. We also include lots of sample book reviews and booktalking strategies for a variety of topics and titles. No list could be exhaustive, and neither is ours. We have included a few books that are inevitably out of print because we love them, and have chosen not to incorporate others that might fit because of space. As always, librarians, teachers, and parents think and insert their own ideas while reading. If you find yourself thinking, "Why didn't they include _____?" you are absolutely right—and already preparing your own booktalk.

PART 1

Everything You Always Wanted to Know
about Sex in the Library

CHAPTER 1

Foreplay

Choose a Partner for "Sex in the Library"

Booktalking can be a lonely sport. Many librarians are adept and enthusiastic booktalkers, but most have never had the opportunity or interest to share the fun with another librarian.

Consider this: While you *could* do a Sex in the Library (SITL) presentation on your own (both authors have done so), it really packs a much more powerful punch when two (or more) librarians present SITL booktalks together.

We still remember the eighth grade class that came dragging into the library late one afternoon, sat down, saw the SITL handouts (Bright pink pages, liberally illustrated with our trademark lip prints and labeled "Sex in the Library") still on the table from the previous class. Even the coolest kid in the group sat right up at attention, saying, "Awwl right!"

Our response was, of course, "No. Pass those in to us. That was the last class. This is a class on plagiarism." But for a while we had their full attention!

Solo, it's just another presentation. Maybe it's a great booktalk, and your audience is on the edges of their seats, spellbound and open-mouthed, although this may be not their usual response to you. The novelty of the topic of SITL *and* the tandem-booktalking style can capture and hold the interest of even the "too cool for school" teen audience.

The obvious advantage in working with a partner is not having to read all the books. *We* know you want to read every book in the library, but honestly, do we really have all the time we want to read? Two booktalkers can cover many more titles in a single presentation—and booktalks are all about choices. If you highlight five titles in a booktalk, thirty students suddenly want five titles—not good math. Not good public relations, either. Everybody is dissatisfied, even the librarian, and especially the

3

teacher!

Along with the "whys" of choosing a partner to do booktalks, there are many "whos." The relationship you establish with a partner booktalker will define the style and tenor of your talk. Do you generally try to skitter through as many books as possible as quickly as possible? You might want to find a booktalking partner who feels comfortable delving into the depth of some books in order to reach the less-hasty members of your audience. Do you love historical fiction but hate to talk about reality fiction? Are you generally shy about sensitive topics? Consider partnering with someone who can help you through those titles. Offer a complementary voice and another point of view, in order to appeal to the wide variety of listeners in your audience.

Start off your presentation with a book that one of you loves, but the other dislikes. For example, Mary Jo likes to start SITL by talking about *Tantalize* by Cynthia Leitich Smith:

> Aarene says: In our case, not only does Mary Jo's steadiness balance my ability to flutter several inches off the floor from the excitement of describing a fabulous new book, but she also has vastly different tastes in books—so she will read the books for the list that would bore me to tears. Vampires? She loves the suckers.

> *Quincie Morris has grown up in the family restaurant business. Although both her parents are dead, she runs the restaurant with her uncle. The business is having a difficult time, so they are going through renovations: Sanguini's will reopen soon with a vampire theme: red colors; predator or prey menu; all the staff will wear great costumes . . . and then the chef is murdered. The police suspect that the murderer is a werewolf . . . which makes things awkward between Quincie and her boyfriend, the werewolf.*

Aarene steps in at this point, and asks the audience: "Who is tired of vampires, werewolves, and angels? Wouldn't you prefer a nice dragon and unicorn story ... or better yet, a mixture of re-told fairy tale and science fiction, like *A Long, Long Sleep* by Anna Sheehan:

> *Locked away inside a stasis tube, Rose peacefully slept through the Dark Times that killed millions of people and left her orphaned . . . and heir to the enormous UniCorp fortune. Now that she's been kissed awake by the handsome Brendan, Rose must find her place in a world that is completely different from everything she has ever known.*

It isn't necessary to seek your booktalking *opposite*. Everyone has a different style in booktalking, so find someone with a style that complements yours: someone who can break up the pacing of your presentation and make it more interesting to the audience. The contrast in styles will also serve to keep the presentation from stagnating. Sometimes Mary Jo gets so excited about a category of books (she really does like vampires), that Aarene has to rein her in by working in a title that will throw Mary Jo off topic and leave her with some self-respecting geekiness. Sometimes, Aarene will focus too long on a single book or topic, so Mary Jo will segue into a different book and move the program along.

When seeking a SITL partner, look for a sympatico librarian. Remember that if you are a public librarian, you are seeking a school librarian, and vice versa. If that person isn't your booktalking soul mate, don't despair. Is there a librarian in another type of library who might be a good match? Perhaps a middle school librarian could team up with a high school librarian, or a children's services librarian could pair with a teen services librarian, or a private school librarian could match booktalks with a public school librarian. The key to SITL is to:

- Highlight the *differences* and the *strengths* of each collection; *and*

- Discuss *why* the collections are different; *and*

- Talk about awesome books with sexual content written for teen readers.

A great side-effect of team booktalking is the set of peers associated with your new colleague. They expand your professional network, which creates opportunities for even more future partnerships.

IMPORTANT TIP: You do the choosing. Find someone for all the right reasons and approach them to do a tag-team booktalk. If it doesn't work, drop it. If it does work, you just might find that this quickly becomes the most popular booktalk you do all year. It may also become the start of a beautiful friendship.

Assemble the Booklist

We prepare for each series of SITL booktalks by creating and updating the list of books we want to talk about with each specific audience. Over ten years, we have read hundreds of books and added many to the SITL list of books. Some books stay on the list for only a year or two because people read them, enjoyed them, and then moved on to something else. That was the case with *Angus, Thongs, and Full-Frontal Snogging* by Louise Rennison:

Aarene remembers: The single school library copy of *Forever* that was passed, hand-to-hand, among the seventh graders of Whatcom Middle School back in 1975 was given to me after I was *sworn to silence*. I promised my best friend that I would *never* tell an adult that I knew about the book, and obviously I would never tell an adult that I had actually read it. I couldn't help noticing that if I held the book in my hand in exactly the right way, it would fall open automatically to the page where Michael and Katherine finally have sex. I was thrilled. I stayed in from lunch to read the book and finished it in a single day—which was good, because then the girl whose locker was next to mine demanded to read it as soon as I was done with it.

The humorous journal of a year in the life of a four-teen-year-old British girl who tries to win the love of handsome hunk Robbie.

When the book was new, we *loved* the British slang, the over-the-top dramatic descriptions of events in Georgia's highly dramatic life . . . and we especially loved the kissing lessons. Louise Rennison churned out nine sequels to the original book, but we (and most of our students) lost interest quickly. When circulation of the book dropped to nearly zero at the school library and the public library, we removed the book from the new edition of the booklist. Conversely is the case of *Forever* by Judy Blume:

Katherine and Michael believe their love is so strong that it will last . . . forever.

We have unofficially awarded author Judy Blume the Honorary Golden Condom award for *Forever,* because the book simply will not die. It was originally published in

1975 . . . the year that Aarene was enrolled in the seventh grade. The appeal of *Forever* has never waned. Aarene buys two new copies of *Forever* every year. Within a single year of circulation at a busy public library branch, the covers fall off and the pages wear thin. Even after all these years, if you hold the book in a particular way, it opens automatically to the page where Michael and Katherine finally have sex.

Criteria for Inclusion on the List

We examine each of the titles on our booklist by asking ourselves a few questions:

- Does this book have some kind of sexual content, sexual questioning, or sexual identity seeking? That's why it's called "Sex in the Library." We could broaden the topic to include books about race cars, books about ponies, and books about bathroom remodels, but we think that having a focused list is best.

- Are at least one third of the books on the list available in only *one* of our libraries? These books are key to the discussion about mission statements, and mission statements are secretly what the booktalk is all about.

- Is the book written for, or attractive to, teen readers? No baby books allowed! Books written for adult readers that are appealing to teens are always welcome on our list.

- If the book is new, do we love it? Raving about a new book is one of the best ways to get students to read it.

- Is the book circulating frequently? We check circulation records to see if each title is being checked out in our local libraries as well as in other nearby facilities.

- If the book isn't circulating, does it show signs of wear-and-tear, indicating some unauthorized journeys around the inside—or even outside—the library? We know that some books don't always get officially checked out. Books that teens might be embarrassed to check out sometimes disappear from the library, only to reappear later with dog-eared pages and a slightly rumpled cover—clear signs that the book was kept secretly in a locker or backpack. Books with gay or transgendered characters are frequent anonymous wanderers, as are several of the extremely detailed nonfiction sex-ed books. They stay on the list as long as they show signs of use.

- Does the book include additional themes that are requested by teachers (or students)? If there is a school-wide focus on bullying, an anti-drug campaign, or a need for more attention paid to diversity issues, we will include titles to support those topics.

- Does the book demonstrate a topical trend in publishing that we want to discuss? One year it seemed like every third book was about polygamy. Another year, it was abusive relationships. Recently, we've seen a glut of books about homosexual relationships. We like to point out the trends to our audiences and give them examples of some good (and bad) titles that fit the trend.

Once we're in front of a SITL audience, our organization of events is loosely topical. From the stack of approximately fifty books we bring to each presentation, Aarene will pick up a book she wants to talk about, and that will remind Mary Jo of a similar book, or a book that is the exact opposite, or a book she thinks is a better choice. For example, Aarene likes to talk about *The Fault in Our Stars* by John Green:

Seventeen-year-old Hazel has been surviving cancer for four years when she meets Augustus Waters who lost a leg to osteosarcoma.

The Fault in Our Stars isn't owned by the middle school library. Mary Jo leads a short discussion, focusing on reasons why that the book wasn't selected for purchase. To illustrate some of these reasons, Mary Jo picks up *Cupcake* by Rachel Cohn:

Still pining for her old boyfriend, Cyd moves to New York, finds short-lived new boyfriends, and discovers her worth as a person.

We talk about this third book in the Cyd Charisse novels, noting that the first, *Gingerbread*, has been popular in junior high for several years. We can alert students to the fact that, while the public library stocks all of this author's works, the school library owns only the first in the series . . . and we talk about *why*.

Mission Statements

The discussions about books like *Cupcake* are important to the not-very-secret mission of SITL booktalks: Making the audience aware that our libraries have different mission statements, and therefore, explaining why our collections are not the same! The discussions can happen like this:

- We whet the audience's appetite for the latest book in a series by talking about the earlier books and dropping hints about the new one.

- We tell them that the book is available at one location (the public library, in this case), but not another location (the school library).

- Then, we ask students to name possible reasons for the differences between the two locations.

Students quickly discover that our school library has a significantly smaller budget than the local public library system, so they will easily identify money as a primary reason that the school library does not own a particular title. They soon learn, however, that library selection policies are not merely based on money.

With some guidance from participating teachers and librarians, students determine that the sexual choices the book's character, Cyd, makes is a possible reason the school library declines to carry the second and third book in the series. At this point, a student may notice that the character of Cyd is now twenty-one years old—and no longer an age-mate of the middle school students in the class. That also might make a difference in choices at the school. This is the perfect time to mention the public library and talk about reasons that this part of the series might be found there: differences in budget as well as differences in the mission of the public library as compared to the mission of the school library.

Before you know it, the students have gained a working knowledge of selection policies and mission statements for school and public libraries . . . *and they thought they were just talking about sexy books!*

Much of what we discuss with students is the appropriateness of a particular title for a particular library. The presenters need not always agree! This is always a good conversation for students to witness.

Aarene says: "For example, I couldn't find anything at all in the contents that would make this book inappropriate for a middle-school library: *Sex Kittens and Horn Dawgs Fall in Love* by Maryrose Wood:

Felicia and Matthew research, interview, hypothesize, and test their theories of love attractiveness. But could it be possible that sometimes "Love Just Happens?" And why isn't Matthew falling in love with Felicia?

The book is fluffy, but fun. Felicia and Matthew are fourteen years old and are age-mates to middle-school students. The main character, Felicia, schemes to get closer to a cute boy who seems interested only in his science fair project—something that eighth grade students understand. There are a few, sweet, unexpected kisses, but no cussing, nakedness, or violence. What's not to like?"

Mary Jo responds: "The *title* is what's not-to-like. I know we don't choose a book by its title, but this title just begs for parents to huff into the office, or worse, stomp out without talking. Choose your book battles wisely: Some books might be so wonderful that they are worth fighting for; but frankly, this one isn't. While the story is cute and fun, I don't see the characters as realistic eighth graders. I would rather spend my 'parental credit' on more worthwhile books. True, I could invite a parent to read this, but again, I'd rather have a discussion about a book that I truly love. Teens seem to agree: The book has not held a place on the shelves and is even out of print."

Choosing a partner will allow you to show students that not all adults agree, and that disagreement is okay.

Our SITL Booklist Isn't Necessarily *Your* SITL Booklist

Before you can experience success, you'd better get some books!

Wait . . . *which books????* There are annotated lists of books in Part II, so you are not adrift without a paddle; however, when we do a booktalk for librarians, we always caution them that our lists are *not* "recommended" lists—they are lists to consider.

Examine the lists in Part II. You may not have all the books. You might not want all the books. Most likely you won't, but one book may remind you of another book you *do* have or it will remind you of a book that is available in another library collection. You will combine resources with your booktalking partner. We always put books on the lists that we don't have in both locations, so that the audience will be encouraged to ask for them, and thus, be encouraged to get familiar with both institutions.

As part of the booktalk, we frequently query the audience about whether a particular book (in their opinion) belongs in the school library, the public library, both, or neither. This allows us to expand our discussion about which books belong in which location(s) and why. Our booktalks usually focus on the newest, hottest, and steamiest books with sexual content written for teens. Some books are appropriate for many types of teen library collections. Some are not.

Sex in the Library blogspot (*http://www.sexinthelibrary.blogspot.com/*) has an expanded list of more books, as well as reviews by us and others who have read our reviews. We invite readers to peruse the website, read the reviews, leave comments, and suggest other titles for us to review. SITL is not a "static" performance; indeed, every program is different, depending on the interests of the audience.

The exceptions to the "really new/really popular" guideline are books with controversial themes that are important to discuss, even when your students are not entirely comfortable discussing them. For example: In 2003, we presented SITL to a group of eighth grade students who told us clearly that they didn't think books about homosexuality and homosexual teens were appropriate for a middle school library. We overrode their discomfort and continued to talk about books like *Geography Club* by Brent Hartinger:

> *A group of gay and lesbian teens find mutual support when they form a "Geography Club" at their high school.*

At the end of the class period, when all the other students had left, one teen lingered at the book table, and whispered to Aarene, "I think my brother needs to read that book." If an important book needs to reach a small number of readers in your audience, by all means, include it on your booklist.

Other Booktalking Resources

Don't just take our booklist and consider yourself done for the day. There are many great books on booktalking that offer lists, including those that cover controversial topics. For our current list of recommended favorites, see the Appendix.

The Dreaded Mission Statement

Aarene says: Mary Jo wrote that about castor oil. I'm wayyyy too young to have EVER been told to take castor oil!

Still confused about which books to add to your list? We have come to the "Mission Statement" section of this chapter. This is the "castor oil" section of this book: Just take it, it's good for you.

Don't you wish you could spend more time each day talking about mission statements and selection policies? No? We think you will agree it is difficult to work them into everyday conversation with students. Your mission statement *should* be central to everything you do at your library. If it isn't, perhaps you need to look at the mission statement again to see if you need to adjust *it . . .* or adjust *yourself*.

Here are the few mission statements from our libraries:

- Mission of Einstein Middle School Library: "The mission of the Einstein Middle School library is to create an environment that helps create and foster students as ethical users of a wide range of educational and recreational materials for lifelong learning."

- Mission of Shorecrest High School (a "big sister" school to Einstein): The Shorecrest Library Program provides broad access to information and ideas. We teach our students to seek ideas and discover the power of using information to change their world."

- Mission of King County Libraries: "The mission of the King County Library System is to provide free, open, and equal access to ideas and information to all members of the community."

Your mission statement is probably similar to one or more of these, but how many of your library patrons know what it is? SITL is a tool to help explain your mission by giving concrete examples of materials that *fit* the mission or *do not fit* the mission.

Explaining your mission to others via SITL is also a very good way to keep that mission in front of your own mind, so that you can easily ask yourself, "What am I doing on a daily basis that supports library users who need to expand their thinking, so that they may become independent learners?"

When we show both these statements to teens, their first response is usually, "Golly, what a breathtaking look at your essential work."

BAHHHH-hahahahaha. Don't we wish?

In reality, they look at both statements and initially most can't see any difference at all. Then the nerd in the back row notices that the King County Libraries' mission statement is so very broad as to include most anything and everyone.

Now we can revisit some of the books that posed an earlier quandary. Remember Cyd Charisse in the *Gingerbread* series? Mary Jo can point out that she really likes the character of Cyd, who is a hard worker and has a gift for understanding people; however, Cyd makes a lot of questionable sexual choices. Mary Jo uses this opportunity to ask where this series belongs based on the two mission statements. You won't need the nerd in the back row to remind everyone that the Cyd character fits easily in the "*free, open, and equal access to ideas and information to all members of the community*" realm of the public library, but not the "*educate and foster students as ethical users*" area of the school library.

Students ask why we include *Gingerbread* at all, if we only need "literature" in school libraries. That is the time to mention that author Rachel Cohn won four major awards for *Gingerbread;* students rapidly see that the issue is more complicated than it seems at first glance. Once in a while, a group of savvy students or adults will ask about the school library need to support the curriculum. That's when we bring out the large cardboard cue-cards with the selection policies written on them. Selection policies are more than broad statements hidden on a website or stashed in a forgotten file cabinet. For either institution, we don't bring out the entire policy, which contain pages of dense reading. However, we do highlight important parts of each policy. We show students the policy—in a flapping "look-what-we've-been-up-to" sort of way—and have actually received a few requests to see the entire document. We are always happy to oblige these queries and usually include an application to the University of Washington's iSchool with the packet of papers.

Mary Jo's school district selection policy, in part, is as follows:

- The main objective of our selection procedure is to provide students with a wide range of educational materials on all levels of difficulty and in a variety of formats, with diversity of appeal, allowing for the presentation of many different points of view.

- The objective of the media center is to make available to faculty and students a collection of materials that will enrich and support the curriculum and meet the needs of the students and faculty served.

This contrasts sharply with the selection policy used by Aarene's public library system:

- Library materials selection will develop a broad collection that meets the needs and interests of a diverse community for information, education, and enlightenment. The Library System will be responsive to public suggestions of items and subjects to be included in the library collection. No library materials which meet selection criteria shall be excluded because of the origin, background, or views of those contributing to its creation.

It should be no surprise that school libraries have a vested interest in creating a library to support the curriculum and that the public library doesn't worry about that at all.

Fitting Nonfiction Books in SITL

We do include nonfiction books in our SITL booktalks. In fact, we are always looking for good nonfiction titles, which seem to be much harder to find. Books like *You, the Owner's Manual for Teens: A Guide to a Healthy Body and Happy Life* by Michael F. Roizen, Mehmet C. Oz, and Ellen Rome offer:

> *Straight-up information that teens can use to make smart choices about how to live the good life—and enjoy every second of it . . . starting right now.*

However, questions more often revolve around fiction. As poet Ron Silvern says, "If you want to know what reality is, read fiction." Teens don't just know this, they demand it. They want to understand death, love, war, pregnancy, and kissing. Isn't reading fiction, therefore, a support to the school curriculum?

Mary Jo says: Okay, okay, kissing is not usually in the curriculum.

It just happens that many teens, like many adults, would much rather learn information by reading fiction about people like themselves—characters with emotions, who make bad decisions, and get in trouble with their parents and best friends. Would you rather sit through a health class lecture about the statistics of teen pregnancy, or would you rather read *The First Part Last* by Angela Johnson:

> *Bobby loves his baby daughter Feather. But he's only sixteen—when will he be able to hang out with the guys, eat pizza, and catch up on his sleep?*

Interestingly, the reverse is also true. When teens read a well-crafted and emotional novel about pregnancy, for example, they may want to know if the narrative is realistic. After reading *The First Part Last*, students may want more real-life information about teen pregnancy, at which point we can hand them a nonfiction book like *The Pregnancy Project* by Gaby Rodriguez with Jenna Glatzer:

> *For her senior project, Gaby fakes her own pregnancy to learn more about the experiences of teen mothers.*

It is easy to show that fiction *does* support the curriculum . . . as long as it also supports the other aspects of your mission statement and selection policy.

Resources

Einstein Mission Statement. Available from Einstein School Library Resource Center. 2010.

Einstein Selection Policy. Available from Einstein School Library Resource Center. 2010.

King County Library System Mission Statement. Available from the King County Library System, 2007. *http://www.kcls.org/about/mission/*.

King County Library System Selection Policy. Available from the King County Library System, 2007. *http://www.kcls.org/usingthelibrary/policies/selections.cfm*

Roizen, Michael, Mehmet C. Oz, and Ellen Rome. *You, the Owner's Manual for Teens: A Guide to a Healthy Body and Happy Life.* Free Press, 2011.

Shorecrest Mission Statement. Available from Shorecrest High School Library. 2012. *http://shorecrest-library.blogspot.com/p/mission.html*.

Silvern, Ron. *Imaginary Friend.* Unpublished poetry collection, 2001.

CHAPTER 2

Safe Sex and How to Have It

It's amazing how many parents do *not* freak out when we tell them that their kids' classes are scheduled to have Sex in the Library with us. We like to think the lack of freak-out is related to the amount of trust they have for us as professionals. Of course, it does help that most parents think we're joking. Here are some of the techniques we use to make sure parents and other grown-up types (school principals, for example) want to support SITL, rather than try to undermine it.

SITL Sessions Are Open

Parents are invited and encouraged to attend the SITL sessions. Most don't. That's probably just as well, since some students would be reluctant to participate in the SITL dialog and discussion in front of their parents, and the discussion is the most interesting and important part of the presentation. We also offer special SITL sessions specifically for teacher, librarian, and parent groups. We'll give more specific details about these separate sessions in Chapters 7 and 8. It's important to note here that we adapt our presentation to any group that invites us. We don't treat adults as teens, and we don't treat teens as adults, but we give all groups access to the same key points:

- The *differences* and the *strengths* of each library collection; *and*

- Discussion about *why* the collections are different; *and*

- Booktalks about awesome books with sexual content written for teen readers

Parents and administrators very quickly learn that we aren't trying to hide anything; in fact, we actively seek publicity for the program. We write articles about SITL for professional journals. We insert news items about it in the school and community newsletters. We emphasize the possibly controversial elements in our publicity pieces. We collaborate with the teachers who schedule their classes for the program, so that they can have a pre-discussion. This allows the students to both understand what it is we will be doing or asking, and also to get the giggles out beforehand.

> Rumor has it that someday we will even write an entire book about SITL ...

Booklists

Our booklists are updated for each group. We present a different group of books to seventh graders than to high school-age audiences, not because of censorship concerns, but because their interests are not the same. No matter who the audience is, however, the list contains some books that are *not* included in most school library collections.

Theoretically, we would also include books that aren't included in a public library collection. However, our local public libraries are currently so financially-gifted that we are hard-pressed to find any titles that the public library won't buy, given their broad mission statement and selection policy. As economics change in the public sector, it's possible and entirely likely that this scenario will change.

We understand that this is not the case across the nation, where budgets in some states are being slashed. *School Library Journal*s 2012 budget survey talks about the devastation that is happening to public libraries, especially in Texas and California. When your library is hip-deep in budget cuts, it's difficult to decide that you need to not only *buy* controversial books, you also need to carve out staff time to make public appearances to *talk* about your controversial purchases. And yet, we think that tight times are the best times to inform the public about the mission statement and acquisition policies of their public libraries—and Sex in the Library is a great way to get your public all hot-and-bothered and focused on your library and your budget!

But how does this relate to booklists?

Booklists are slightly problematic, given that a list is a printed page distributed at school. Parents (and some teachers) assume, from years of past experience, that a booklist printed and distributed at school is a list of books that are *recommended* and/or *required* for classroom instruction. Obviously, a SITL booklist is a little different, since it contains books that the school library doesn't even own. Part of the SITL presentation emphasizes verbally that not all books on the list are available in the school library, and indeed, that not all books on the list are recommended for all readers. This is a significant departure from the booklists that students normally get at school, and if parents see the list *without knowing the context* and *without participating in the discussion*, mayhem could result.

> We don't like mayhem. It steams up our little cute reading glasses. And let's not talk about what it does to the hair-bun.
>
> Mary Jo to Aarene: Just which of us has a hair-bun?
>
> Aarene to Mary Jo: It doesn't matter, dear, just tighten the straps on your sensible shoes and move on.

We try to avoid mayhem, but not by being sneaky. We are, rather, un-sneaky in a very careful manner:

- Booklists are distributed in the *middle* of a school program, if at all, *not* at the beginning, before students have had exposure to the "exploration of mission statements" part of the program. They are not distributed at the end, either, when students are most likely to cram the list into a pocket or backpack without regard for where the booklist ends up at the end of the school day. We distribute the lists in the middle of the presentation, when students are fully attentive and participating, and we want to encourage them to ask about specific titles. We have already talked about some books on the list, but by inviting students to seek information about titles we might otherwise skip, we keep them engaged throughout the presentation. Every SITL booktalk is driven by the audience. Because we depend on—and demand—audience participation, each talk travels a slightly different path. This, too, is different from "standard booktalking procedure."

- We don't always hand out the booklists to students. Depending on the group, we may ask the attendees to point to books that are displayed at the front of the room instead. (We'll talk more about this as a booktalking technique in Chapter 6.)

oint Public Library / School Library

ample bibliography

FICTION

Speak by Laurie Halse Anderson

Forever by Judy Blume

Lies Beneath by Anne Greenwood Brown

Gingerbread by Rachel Cohn

Carter's Unfocused One-Track Mind by Brent Crawford

Running Loose by Chris Crutcher

Just Listen by Sarah Dessen

A Northern Light by Jennifer Donnelly

Breathing Underwater by Alex Flinn

The True Meaning of Cleavage by Mariah Fredericks

Geography Club by Brent Hartinger

The First Part Last by Angela Johnson

Stoner & Spaz by Ron Koertge

Blessed by Cynthia Leitich Smith

NONFICTION

Deal with It! by Esther Drill

Changing Bodies, Changing Lives by Ruth Bell

- We have distributed a "tame" list on a bookmark with our trademark lip-print printed on it, with lots of empty space provided. This gives students a place to write down the titles they would like to read. This can also serve as a memory trigger for them later, when they seek a librarian to talk about a topic that they would like to discuss without others present.

- We *do* always hand out booklists to teachers and to administrators. Administrators deserve as much preparation as you can convince them to accept, just in case a concerned parent calls with questions.

- We *do* certainly share our booklists with concerned parents *after* discussing the entire SITL program with them.

- Just as we do with each student group, when we talk to concerned parents and administrators, we discuss the concept of *in loco parentis*—the responsibility of teachers and school librarians to act "in place of a parent" regarding the safety and education of students. We must also consider that the student body is parented by a huge variety of adults, including adoptive parents, same-sex parents, religious parents of many faiths, foster-parents, and grandparents.

In all of our discussions, we emphasize often that the public library, which usually contributes the most controversial titles to the list, *does not* have an *in loco parentis* philosophy. In fact, this responsibility would actually interfere with the *"free, open, and, equal access to ideas and information to all members of the community"* portion of the public library mission statement. This is a tricky concept for parents and other people who don't live their lives thinking about what libraries are and how libraries operate. Don't be afraid to repeat yourself, to restate yourself, and to be redundant (again) if necessary.

Every once in a while, we see the light bulb start to glow in the eyes of a parent or administrator . . . followed by an immediate furrowing of brows as they turn towards Aarene, the public librarian. "But," they sputter, "you don't mean that you would *give* dirty books to kids, do you?"

Sigh. Repeat. Restate. Redundant.

> *The mission of the Public Library is to create free, open, and equal access to ideas and informa-tion to all members of the community regardless of the library user's age (among other things).*

When an adult confronts you about this, proceed with gentle patience. Assume that parents, like you, want their children, and all children, to grow and thrive and learn and become productive members of society. Assume that they have the very best of intentions, and that they *will* agree with you when they completely understand what "free and open access to everyone" actually means.

Do not assume that they will throw rocks at you or try to have you fired, but proceed carefully, kindly, and tactfully, so that they can learn and support your mission—which is, after all, an ethical one.

Emphasize that the differences between the school library and the public library are good and needful. Remind them that, just as *their* reading choices are not restricted in any way by the public library, neither are the reading choices of children and teens restricted. Parents can and should monitor what their teens check out from the school and public library; however, the public library staff cannot act "in place of a par-ent." At the public library, only the parent may restrict a juvenile's choices, and parents may only restrict the choices of their own offspring.

Then play your trump card.

"Of course," you will say, "we encourage parents to actively participate in the reading choices of their own teens. If *you* wish to restrict *your own* teen's reading choices, please feel free to do this." Inform the parent that school libraries may, at the parents' request, restrict *their* child—but not all students—from checking out certain books. Be kind. And, if necessary, be redundant and then be kind again.

We are not nonchalant about queries from concerned parents, administrators, and even other teach-ers and librarians. We know that we are talking about books that can make people in any of these groups uneasy. Sometimes this uneasiness grows into an actual challenge and possible censorship. We cover cen-sorship concerns more thoroughly in Chapter 9. Coping with censorship in any form is an entirely different subject than dealing with an adult concerned over his or her child's reading.

What to Say (or Not) to Administrators

For several years, both of us we were blessed with administrators who thought that the whole concept of presenting Sex in the Library to students was hilarious. Our bosses couldn't believe that anybody would be crazy enough to stand in front of a group of young teens and actually say words like "tits" during a booktalk for *Stoner and Spaz* by Ron Koertge:

> *An unlikely romance blossoms between "Spaz" Ben, who has cerebral palsy and a fascination with classic films, and "Stoner" Colleen who will smoke anything that might smooth out the edges of her life.*

Since we seemed willing to do it, the administrators gave us some tentative encouragement. We always thanked them for their trust. To reward them for their sense of humor, we fed them increasingly shocking examples of our ability to be outrageous. For example, we sent a thank-you email (copied to the administrators) to teachers who participated, entitled: "*Thanks for having SEX with us during third period on Tuesday!*" The subject line made people laugh and made them feel part of an inside joke. But the body of the message was mostly serious, with specific examples of discussion topics for each group, so that the high mucky-mucks would understand that teachers, as well as students, were involved in the important learning process that our SITL program offers.

For example, one ninth grade class really seemed fascinated by the concept of lying and unreliable narrators in fiction. For this group, we focused attention on titles like *Boys Lie* by John Neufeld:

> *Eighth-grader Gina Smith is targeted as easy by some boys in her new school because of her physical development and because of an incident in her past.*

and *After* by Amy Efaw:

> *In complete denial that she is pregnant, straight-A student and star athlete Devon leaves her baby in the trash to die, and after the baby is discovered, Devon is accused of attempted murder.*

These very different books illustrate various aspects and consequences of lying. Both are appropriate for the age group; however, while *Boys Lie* tells a simple, but powerful story, *After* relates events that are more sophisticated and sometimes gruesome. After hearing the reviews and discussion of both titles, students can choose to read one instead of the other, choose to read them both, or leave one or both for later.

Not all the teachers were present for this booktalk, so when we emailed information about the discussion, the ninth grade English department created an entire unit around the concept of lying, even returning for a booktalk just on that topic. "Lying" evolved into the study of truth in historical fiction, lying as a literary device, and the potential virtues of falsification in real life.

A few years later, the leadership changed. The new bosses warily accepted our program, based on rave reviews received from teachers, students, parents, and other administrators. We could, however, see that they had doubts about the appropriateness of our presentation.

Rather than explode the brains of these well-intentioned individuals, we decided to correspond more circumspectly with them. "SITL programs were very successful, thanks for participating" was a better email subject line for these good people than the more in-your-face communication style we used earlier. The body of the message was essentially the same, but the revised subject line was aimed to help adults become comfortable with the concept of the SITL program. As before, we summarized discussion topics and repeated our invitations for administrators to join us at the next presentation.

When Mary Jo informed one principal that we were having Sex in the Library, he nearly jumped out of his shoes. After his heart stopped fibrillating, Mary Jo reassured him that Aarene was just coming to the library to do the annual SITL booktalk. His final response was, "Oh well, just don't let my voicemail get full of parent messages about this."

Trust is what you need, but you will have to earn it. No one can tell their administrators that phone calls won't happen, but you can assure them that you will be caring, careful, and professional with your presentation.

When Administrators Actually *Do* Show Up

Our bosses and administrators are such busy people that they rarely join our booktalking discussions, but when they do show up, we want to engage their participation as well as that of the teachers and students.

One way to do that is to discuss a book that features a "good principal," such as one of the characters in *Games: A Tale of Two Bullies* by Carol Gorman:

> *Boot Quinn and Mick Sullivan fight each other over Tabitha, who keeps score on the bathroom wall. But when the new principal punishes them by having them play games in his office, they see a different side of each other—and Tabitha.*

In the current economic climate, it's hard to take chances that might result in reprisals or even cost you your job. We want to emphasize that creating good, honest discussions about potentially controversial books for teens can actually *save your job*, because the discussions can allow parents and administrators to better understand how important your job is—and how well you do it.

We have seen too many librarian positions eliminated, because administrators sincerely believe that "anybody can check out books to kids." Librarians need to catch—and hold—the attention of busy administrators, and Sex in the Library can help them do that. By partnering school librarians with public librarians in a booktalking presentation like SITL, you can highlight the special skills and knowledge that teens, teachers, and parents want and need in a library professional.

Neither the teen librarian in a public library nor the librarian in a school is exempt from administrators who are trying to balance a very difficult budget. We know first-hand that principals can be hard to educate on the subject of school libraries. How often does your principal observe you working with a class? How many times has someone said to you, "It must be a nice job to sit around and read all day?" Public library administrators need just as much care and feeding. Has a branch manager ever said, "You'll have to cancel your presentation at the school this week, because we need you on the desk," or directed you to spend more time promoting reading programs with elementary-age students instead of teens? No matter where we work or what type of library programs we provide, we want our administrators to both value and wholeheartedly promote teen services.

Have you been reading this to yourself and thinking, "But not *my* administrator?" Take a breathing moment and return to the mission statements. These are not just an exercise—they are here for you to use. It's easy to say that the public library selection policy includes materials for *all* members of the community, but do the actions of the institution reflect priority buying for all, including teens? The school library's selection policy says that "supporting the curriculum" is a priority. Isn't that what you do when you booktalk potentially controversial titles? Your library is ethical, relevant, and fun. You "play well" with teachers and parents. This is what your administrator needs to know!

A study by the Center for Advancing Health shows that education is not enough for teens to fully understand STDs. In fact, "School STD programs have limited influence on teen sexual behavior." What does help? Sex in the Library booktalks! Teens gain understanding of sexual health topics by reading about sexual situations, the consequences of sexual activities, and making connections through feelings. This is the sub-context of SITL booktalks.

Sutton, Amy. "School STD Programs Have Limited Influence on Teens' Sexual Behaviors." *Center for Advancing Health: Health Behavior News Service. 23 February 2010. http://www.cfah. org/hbns/2010/school-std-programs-have-limited-influence-on-teens-sexual-behaviors#.UQ8SgaVi4Zk.*

Resources

Farmer, Lesley. "Brace Yourself." *School Library Journal*, 2012. 58 (3): 38-38.

CHAPTER 3

Slip into Something More Comfortable

Vocabulary and How to Use It

It takes practice to talk about sex, sexual situations, and sexual content of books in front of a large group of people! Even among adults, when speaking in a mature way about sexuality in literature written for teens, at some point somebody is likely to say the "T-word" or the "P-word" or one of the other nearly-taboo words. Sometimes there are more graceful euphemisms that adults (and teens) will appreciate, but seriously, if the book you're discussing uses slang, to give listeners an accurate idea of the book's contents, you need to use some of the vocabulary that the characters use.

For example, in *Stoner and Spaz* by Ron Koertge, Ben is *thrilled* when Colleen offers to show him her "tits" in exchange for a book report due the next day. Colleen doesn't call them "breasts" or any of the other "proper" words that polite people use for mammalian protuberances. If you're going to talk about Colleen, as well as Ben's fascination with Colleen's nonchalant attitude towards bodies in general, you're going to need the word "tits," and that means *somebody* is going to have to say the word out loud.

Here's something they never taught you in library school: If you want the full and undivided attention of teens during a booktalk, say the word "tits" out loud.

21

This might be the #1 reason that SITL is best done with a partner: If you just can't face the "word of the day," there's somebody else in front of the room with you who might be convinced to say it for you. Consider starting out your booktalks with a list of vocabulary words that aren't usually allowed in a classroom context. "Tits" is definitely on the list, as are most of the others on George Carlin's list of the "Seven Words You Can Never Say on Television."

"Penis" and any of the alternative words are also generally shunned. Try asking your teens to generate a list of the forbidden words, while you write them on a whiteboard. Make the exercise short. You don't actually want to create a dictionary of the "Fifty words most likely to get somebody fired or expelled." You may want to limit the list to the first seven words students can generate that aren't normally acceptable in school. Even if you only spend five minutes talking about it, the exercise will accomplish several goals:

The Seven Words You Can't Say On Television

Just in case you don't already know the words, they are: shit, piss, cunt, fuck, cocksucker, motherfucker, and tits. George Carlin's immortal delivery of this skit is on several Youtube.com sites. Although Carlin was actually a very warm and fuzzy guy, teens should view these sites, perhaps, with a parent. "The Seven Words You Can't Say on Television" can also be found on Carlin's album, *Class Clown*.

- You will have the complete, focused attention of the audience (even during first period or right after lunch).

- You will gain a reputation as somebody who really wants to hear what students are saying, even when what they are saying is objectionable to other adults (especially teachers).

- You will get the audience *and yourself* past the giggles that happen when grown-ups say naughty words.

- You may learn vocabulary that you never knew existed.

A cautionary note: This technique works *only* if you know the students in the group, have talked about discussing edgy vocabulary with the teachers beforehand, and have control of your audience. None of us want the principal or branch manager to walk into a booktalk during a free-for-all taboo-word-brainstorming session.

We generally launch our SITL booktalks with the story we related in the Introduction, followed by a double booktalk about *Deal with It!* by Esther Drill:

> The creators of the award-winning website gURL.com present a hip, no-nonsense resource book for girls.

and *Changing Bodies, Changing Lives* by Ruth Bell:

> This book candidly discusses teenage sexuality and the many physical and emotional changes that occur during adolescence.

We begin with these resources, because we want to use a few less-electrically-charged words for body parts in context. This will help us emphasize the concept of getting correct factual information from nonfiction and novels. We are librarians, after all—factually correct information is important to us, and we want our teens to value factually correct information, even when it is presented in a fictional context. We want our realistic fiction to be based on factual reality.

So what do you do when a student asks if what Gretchen saw in E. Lockhart's *Fly on the Wall* is correct? In the novel,

> *Gretchen wishes to be a fly on the wall in the boys' locker room, just so she could figure out what boys are all about. And then, her wish is granted.*

Aarene: (still laughing) "I'll never be able to look at a pickle the same way again!"

Mary Jo: (smiling) "Well, she is a fly after all, eating the mold on the wall. She has no reason to feel smug! But it is so much more descriptive than the 'just the facts, ma'am, of *Changing Bodies* ... "

Gretchen describes the boys' penises as "goofy-looking gherkins." Now, we have to ask: Are you the kind of librarian who can't say that out loud? Or, are you the kind of librarian who laughed uproariously when you read that and couldn't wait to share it? Our student may have asked the question just to see what we would do.

If a student asks because she is really concerned, simply answer the question. If she asks just to see if you would turn red and sputter, you can let her know that you are serious about every book on the list being a good book that you are not afraid to discuss. Students *know* when you are uncomfortable, and it's okay to admit it. As the school librarian, Mary Jo has many reservations about the books on the list and is open with students about what makes her feel "edgy" when those books are featured or requested by students. What you can never, never, *never* do in a SITL booktalk is force yourself to use vocabulary from fiction or nonfiction that makes you feel uncomfortable. Students will spot your unease immediately and either dismiss you as a poseur or challenge you with more ways to make you uncomfortable.

Speaking of nonfiction material, you absolutely want to be sure that the facts presented in novels are correct. When advocating for a novel that presents factual information, especially about an important topic like teen sexuality, do a little homework and make sure that the author isn't just making up information. No matter what the character is dealing with, from teen pregnancy or alcoholism to advanced hangnails and athlete's foot, make sure the medical stuff is accurate and that you are pronouncing all the vocabulary correctly—and be ready to cite your sources.

It is, incidentally, gratifying when other types of fictional details presented as factual really *are* factual. Author Cris Beam is particularly adept at weaving medical information into *I am J*:

> *J's parents think he's a lesbian, his best friend Melissa thinks he's a girl, and his girlfriend Blue is pretty sure he's gay. But J knows that he is a boy, although he was born female.*

J's search for information about his condition and about the medical process of female-to-male transition is imparted bit-by-bit, so that it is much easier to accept and understand than a PowerPoint presentation in a health education class. We'll talk more about the facts-behind-the-fiction in Chapter 9.

Choosing Excerpts

The classic booktalk strategy learned and practiced by many librarians includes a broad smile, a wave of the book to display the cover art, a plot summary, and a brief-but-pertinent excerpt from the book, read aloud by the booktalker.

If you follow this pattern for every booktalk you do for an entire hour, your audience will be asleep after the third or fourth book. We like to break things up in order to keep the program moving. Maybe we'll summarize the plot of the book that's first on the list, then tell a story about the author of a second book, and then ask for a student to choose a book from the list and talk about it. At some point, of course, we will choose a great excerpt from a great book to share with the group. But what, exactly, makes an excerpt *great*?

Here's how we define a "great excerpt:"

- It brings the listeners into the story immediately, through the narrative style, the setting, or the action.

- It's readable, without difficult-to-pronounce names or crazy jargon that requires excessive explanation.

- It summarizes a plot point or problem.

- It leaves listeners in a "cliff-hanging position," eager to learn what happens next in the story.

Practice reading your excerpt aloud several times at home before you read it in front of a group. This will help you with fluency. It will also make the piece familiar enough; so that you can glance up at the audience occasionally and make sure they haven't all walked away or fallen asleep.

The book excerpt need not be the Big Scene on page 69 where the characters finally rip off all their clothes. Remember: Although the sexual content is important in these books, there should be other things going on as well. If you're going to read some excerpts in a SITL presentation, at least a few of them should be steamy . . . but they don't *all* need to focus on sexual situations. For example, in the book *The Fault in Our Stars* by John Green:

> *Seventeen-year-old Hazel has been surviving terminal cancer for four years when she meets Augustus Waters, who lost a leg to the osteosarcoma. Hazel and Gus are smart and witty— they read, they discuss, and they are both very ill.*

You would be doing readers a disservice to read aloud the page where Hazel and Gus have intercourse. To appreciate *that* page, readers need to follow the progression of the characters. Instead, try sharing an earlier scene that invites listeners to hope that, at some point in the book, the two will actually have sex.

Sometimes a great excerpt contains "taboo" words or a phrase that might be awkward for the reader. Do you change the word? Skip over it? Blurt it out? We advocate blurting, if possible, but sometimes that won't work. Another strategy is to warn the audience before you start reading that you plan to change an objectionable word. Announcing this will put them on the edge of their seats, waiting for wickedness. Use this. When you get to the word that you don't intend to say, pause. Look at the students. Smile broadly. Then substitute a humorous and harmless word and finish reading.

Here's an example of a fun excerpt with slightly-racy vocabulary to share with classes from *Swim the Fly* by Don Calame:

> *"Movies don't count," Cooper says. "The Internet doesn't count. Magazines don't count. A real, live naked girl. That's the deal. That's our goal for this summer."*
>
> *"Been there, done that," Sean says.*
>
> *"Taking baths with your sister doesn't count, either, Sean." Cooper snorts.*
>
> *"Screw you, meat stain. I haven't done that since I was, like, two, okay. And that's not what I was talking about," Sean says.*
>
> *. . . "He's talking about Tina Everstone's left boob," I say as we turn onto Maple Drive and walk along the curb.*
>
> *"Oh, please. Not that again." Cooper rolls his eyes.*
>
> *"It's true. I saw the whole thing when she was taking off her sweatshirt during gym. Her T-shirt came up just enough—"*
>
> *"And she wasn't wearing a bra and her left one popped out and you saw the entire thing, nipple and all, and even if I didn't think you were lying to us, it still wouldn't count," Cooper says. "I'm talking totally naked. Not a quick flash, okay?"*
>
> *"Whatever." Sean shrugs and looks off at the rundown ranch houses like he doesn't care what we think.*
>
> *"How are we supposed to see a live naked girl?" I say. "Maybe we better set a more realistic goal for the summer. Like finding Atlantis."*

Swim the Fly. Copyright © 2009 by Don Calame. Reproduced by permission of the publisher, Candlewick Press, Somerville, MA.

This brief excerpt brings the listeners immediately into the situation, it alerts them to the "special language" in the book, it's funny, and it leaves readers wanting to know what happens next.

There are times when promoting a great book might mean *avoiding* excerpts. For example, the works of Sarah Dessen are so widely read by teens in our area that they actually groan when we show one of her books. They don't want to hear a booktalk about any of her books, because most of them have already read them all. Reading aloud from a Dessen book will not make it more appealing. Instead, try revealing fun trivia about the book or the author that will both engage the interest of students who faithfully read every title and also attract the attention of a teen who hasn't yet discovered the author. In the case of Sarah Dessen, the revelation that she frequently takes central characters from older titles and gives them cameo appearances in new books caused a rush for the new book *and* the older novels. All that action and you didn't need to mention sexual content even once!

The Pleasures and Pitfalls of Dual Booktalking

One of the strengths of booktalking as a team is the ability to cover a wider range of books than one busy person could possibly read. This also allows both booktalkers to get "extreme" about what they like and dislike—you don't need to work so hard to balance your booktalking viewpoint, because you know the other librarian will provide another perspective and thus, bring balance to the entire presentation.

The audience will especially enjoy the tension between booktalkers who don't always agree. If one booktalker *loves* a book and the other booktalker *hates* it, listeners are exceptionally motivated to read the book and decide for themselves. For example, Mary Jo absolutely loves *Boys That Bite* by Mari Mancusi:

> *Sunny is bitten by a vampire and must find a cure before the end of the week.*

This is (obviously) a vampire book. Mary Jo will extol the virtues of the characters and the plot and the suspense and the *sex* to anybody who will listen . . . but Aarene disagrees. She's so tired of vampire books. If we *must* talk about fang-fiction, Aarene says, *Boys That Bite* isn't nearly as much fun as *Tantalize* by Cynthia Leitich Smith:

> *Were-wolves. Were-alligators. Were-armadillos. Vampires. And Quincie.*

Students love to watch adults argue. And if any members of the audience have read the book in question, they will soon speak up with their own opinions.

Your partner booktalker will also share the burden of being prepared. It is important to choose someone who loves reading as much as you do. How horrible would it be to have a "hot" topic like Sex in the Library and have a fellow presenter slog through it! It is likely that one of you will be more experienced at booktalking, dealing with students, and dealing with hecklers. When there is back-and-forth patter about books, one can easily slip into a rhythm that creates a comfortable atmosphere for everyone, and keep the booktalk smoothly on track.

If one booktalker focuses on the "silliness" of some books, it is easy for the other teammember to watch the audience and notice that many are squirming in their seats because they expected some serious subjects to be covered. So, for example, when one of us brings up the outrageously "out" character of Tiny in *Will Grayson, Will Grayson* by John Green and David Levithan ...

> *This collaborative novel brings together two people both improbably named Will Grayson.*

... the other partner can insert balance into the discussion by bringing up *Geography Club* by Bret Hartinger—

> *A group of gay and lesbian teenagers finds mutual support when they form the "Geography Club" at their high school.*

—which begins with the silly premise that a Gay/Straight Alliance could be disguised as a boring-sounding "Geography Club." When you share (or perhaps even act out) the scene in which a sweet, bouncy girl enters the club meeting thinking they really are going to talk about maps and mountains, your audience will laugh—and you can segue from the silliness to the serious, because the rest of the book is very serious indeed.

The Art of the Segue

As important as the initial booklist is for your program, we think that the ability to use your partner to move the program along is even more important. There are very many wonderful stories being published for teens. Choose books that you feel comfortable discussing and try not to allow students to hijack your emotions or comfort level.

Sample SITL Program

Aarene begins with a light, fun book, like *How to Get Suspended and Influence People* by Adam Selzer:

> *Leon sarcastically narrates the events that result when he decides to make an avant-garde sex education movie as an assignment for his "gifted and talented" class.*

After a little bit of discussion, Mary Jo offers another book that centers around school: *Misfits* by James Howe:

> *Four students who do not fit in at their small-town middle school decide to create a third political party for the student council elections.*

The discussion about stereotypes that results from that book leads to a comparison with *Memoirs of a Teenage Amnesiac* by Gabrielle Zevin:

> *After hitting her head, resulting in short-term amnesia, Naomi tries to sort out her life, her friends, and two romantic interests.*

From there, we remember that the classic love triangle is found in many books on the SITL list, including *When It Happens* by Susane Colasanti:

> *Sarah wants to find true love and discovers Dave; Toby wants Sarah as his own true love.*

and *Graceling* by Kristin Cashore:

> *In Katsa's world, people who have two differently-colored eyes are endowed with unusual talents, called "graces." Katsa's grace is . . . killing.*

When you are booktalking alone, you might not notice every person in the audience. With a team booktalk, one team member can talk about a book while the other person watches the audience for clues about which book should be discussed next. If Aarene is talking about *Half Brother* by Kenneth Oppel—

> *Ben gets involved with his parents' research project: teaching sign language to a baby chimpanzee. Then, funding for the project fails.*

—Mary Jo might see someone in the audience pointing to the display copy of *Jumpstart the World* by Catherine Ryan Hyde:

> *Frank is a female-to-male transgendered person, and Elle thinks she loves him. When Elle learns the truth about Frank, she is angry, but more importantly, she questions the significance of her crush. Is Elle a lesbian? Or what?*

The two books seem at first to have little in common, but with a bit of verbal stretching, you can connect them through the theme of "understanding someone who is really different." It's a bit of a stretch, obviously, but it will work for students who will cooperate with you in order to hear about the books that make them curious.

There are very few pitfalls in dual booktalking, but those problems can be huge if you aren't ready for them. Be aware of these pitfalls:

- *One partner does everything.* From finding the books to writing reviews to assembling the booklist, be sure to share the burden as equally as possible with your booktalking partner.

- *One partner hogs the stage.* Just as one person cannot do all the preparation, one person cannot do all the talking. Your audience must see this as an equal venture.

- *Booktalkers get focused on talking to each other and forget about the audience.* Remember to *look* at your audience and engage them in conversation, just as you engage your booktalking partner.

- *Booktalkers focus on the contents of* one *library (the public library, for example) and neglect talking about the unique contents of the* other *library.* This is easy to do when one library is vastly better-funded than the other, but one of your goals with a dual booktalking program is to point out the unique virtues of each place!

- *Librarians might slip into stereotypes.* There is sometimes a tendency for the school librarian to appear to be a conservative "school marm" who will not allow any books with sexual content, while the public librarian appears to be a wild woman who will buy anything for the library collection. This can be funny, but beware of pushing it too far.

Choosing Books for a SITL Program

We have some guidelines that we always discuss when we choose the books for our booktalk. We don't take every book on the extended list to every booktalk—baggage fees are expensive, and huge boxes of books are too heavy to lug around. Each time we do a SITL program, we refine the list by replacing older, less-popular titles with newer, hotter books. We have three unchanging rules for choosing SITL books:

- The books must be appropriate for and appealing to teens—and they must have some kind of sexual content. We do include books originally written and marketed to adults on our SITL list, but only when we feel that teens will love them. For example, *After the Golden Age* by Carrie Vaughn:

> *Forensic accountant Celia West is the daughter of superheroes Captain Olympus and Spark, but her only talent seems to be a gift for getting kidnapped and held for ransom.*

This book was written and marketed for adults, but many of the main character's issues are those of adolescence, and the presence of flying-fighting-bursting-into-flame superhero characters makes the story very appealing to teens.

- Each instance of sexual content/longing/kissing, or anything else, MUST contribute to the story. If it doesn't, we rate it in the "prurient" category—those books where sex is thrown in just for effect or to pull in teen readers. If you took the sex out of the book, would the plot still make sense? Would the character's actions change? Would the outcome change?

- The sexual actions can't reach our "ewwww" factor. In our programs, we talk about Mary Jo's threshold for finding something inappropriate, while Aarene will offer her boundaries. The boundaries are not the same; everyone's limits are different. This leads nicely toward a conversation with students about all of their limits being different and knowing what each person's limit is, and how to choose books accordingly.

For example, sometimes we talk about books that deal with sexual abuse, an important subject that is difficult for many people to read about. We find that *Because I Am Furniture* by Thalia Chaltas:

> *Though Anke is ignored by her father, he beats her brother and sexually abuses her sister.*

doesn't freak out readers nearly as often as *Living Dead Girl* by Elizabeth Scott:

> *When Alice was ten, Ray took her away from her family. She learned to give up all power, to endure all pain. She waited for the nightmare to be over.*

Why do different books with similar subjects affect readers so differently? Perhaps the blank-verse poetry format of *Because I Am Furniture* creates distance between the narrator and the reader—distance that feels safe for vulnerable readers—whereas the first-person narrative style of *Living Dead Girl* seems very real, immediate, and alarming.

We frequently tell our audiences: "If this book reaches your "ewwww" threshold, please put it down. Read something else. You can always come back to it. If you have this book at home, and your parent or guardian reads it and finds it inappropriate for you, put it down. They are your parents or guardian. They have that right."

We say this to students, we say it to librarians, we say it to parents, and we even say it to each other: Some books are scary *and* important. Others are just icky. It's up to you, the reader, to decide for yourself and have the emotional maturity to put aside a book that you know is inappropriate for you at this time.

Star Trek Sex and How to Have Some

In direct contrast to books that hit the "ewwww" button for readers are those that are smoothly tactful when dealing with scenes of sexual tension. We refer to these scenes as *"Star Trek* Sex" scenes, because they remind us of 1960s television shows, like when Captain Kirk romanced his way around the universe.

Captain Kirk is making eyes at some alien lady who just wants to suck all the salt out of his blood or turn him into a green-skinned demigod or something.
They get closer, and closer. And closer.
Then the music comes up, the focus goes soft and . . .
/CUT TO COMMERCIAL/

After 180 seconds of commercial interruption:

Captain Kirk is pulling on his boots and the alien lady is brushing her hair.
Pretty soon the red alert will sound, the dilithium crystals will deteriorate, and some guy in a red shirt will disappear mysteriously . . .

That is "*Star Trek* Sex." We all know what happened during the commercial break, but nobody saw a thing.

A lot of teen books contain the literary equivalent of *Star Trek* Sex: It's all romance and soft music leading to the end of a chapter. *Turn the page . . .* and suddenly, the protagonists are passing notes in algebra class.

Television censors' requirements have changed drastically since the old *Star Trek* days, but we still appreciate authors who use *Star Trek* Sex techniques in their books to ensure that their sexually steamy stories can be proudly purchased and displayed, even in very conservative library collections. With *Star Trek* Sex books, the romance and sexual decision-making is kept intact, but the sweaty naked body parts are tactfully taken off-page.

Sometimes the *Star Trek* Sex is so subtle that readers can miss it entirely. Such was the case with *Shiver* by Maggie Steifvater:

Grace is fascinated by the yellow-eyed wolf that saved her when she was a child. Sam, bitten when he was a boy, is that wolf.

"He walks backward, pulling me with him so I stumble. I stumble right out of my shoes. He sits on the edge of the bed and I stand in front of him, and we're finally eye to eye.

He touches my face, covering my cheeks with his hands, sliding his fingertips down my neck, fitting his fingers to the slight curve of my hips.

I can't stop.

I fit my mouth to his, and he tastes like water and smells like fresh air. I drag my hand from his neck to the small of his back, and put it under his shirt. He kisses me harder.

I knew he was strong; I didn't know how strong until I felt the muscles on his back tightening beneath my fingers.

Stop I tell myself.

Suddenly it's as if we're in a hurry, his fingertips brushing my side under my shirt, my hands clutching him, struggling closer but there is no closer. I have never longed for someone this way or this much.

...

Chapter 28

"When he starts to fall asleep, he keeps his arms around me fiercely, a life-preserving prison . . .

Excerpt from *Insurgent* (pages 313-314) by Veronica Roth. Katherine Tegen Books, 2012. *Used by permission of HarperCollins Publishers.*

Mary Jo read and reviewed *Shiver* along with seven other books in a single week. She read so quickly that she completely missed the *Star Trek* Sex, and her review on our SITL blog reported "No sex in this book."

Thankfully, the author alerted us to the mistake via email. ". . . there *is* sex in *Shiver!*" she wrote. She's totally right. It took a while to find it, but there it was, on page 294 (paperback edition): *Star Trek* Sex. Subtle, pretty, and sexy. (It's a terrific read, by the way. We loved this book!) Our apologies, Maggie Stiefvater. There *is* sex in *Shiver*. But no aliens.

We love authors, readers, and tourists on the SITL blog! Visit us online at *http://www.sexinthelibrary.blogspot. com* to read new book reviews and comment on your favorite steamy reads.

Important Points about Booktalking in General and SITL Specifically

As librarians, you are committed to helping teens understand the world around them. If they want to understand how to build a birdhouse, you help them find a book or website to figure that out. If they are trying to understand how a girl can treat them as dirt and still like them, you need to help them figure that out, too. *Many readers enjoy reading fiction because of its ability to explain the emotions behind the facts. Very LeFreak* by Rachel Cohn is one example:

> *Veronica, known as Very LeFreak, enters a rehab facility for the technology-addicted after her professors and classmates stage an intervention.*

Veronica ("Very" to her friends), a self-proclaimed bisexual being, is attracted to, and then rejects Bryce. She makes it very plain that, although she no longer is attracted to him, she sees no reason why they can't be friends. It takes her best friend to actually explain how Very thinks, even if it's not the way that all girls think.

Students may challenge an issue in a fiction book as an authority. You should respond by pointing out a nonfiction reference, like *Our Bodies, Ourselves,* which will provide, perhaps, a dryer understanding of the same topic.

Fiction like *Very LeFreak* can lead to a search for knowledge. Inevitably, one student will ask if Very's tech addiction, or even tech rehab, is real. You have already checked to be sure that any realistic book you use which features scientific references has a legitimate scientific background. Wouldn't you love to help your student find this out in your library later? As librarians, of course we would.

Perhaps the students will ask about Very's attitude toward sex, which is one of the most open in teen literature. She calls herself bisexual. One of you should be able to grab that student's statement (whether made in an open or a challenging way) and explore what it is that teens really want to learn about the character, who is searching for a way to keep from dealing with real issues. Sex is just one of the symptoms. Don't make it a more important part of the book than it was intended, but don't shrink from it either.

When you feel you have extracted all you can from this book (it is a fluff piece, after all), the partner booktalker can move the talk along by pointing out the heart of the book, which is Very's compulsion to constantly plug into technology—the (illegal) flash mobs, the perpetual playmixes, the interminable instant messaging, and finally, the rehab for the computer-addicted—in a very funny way. The book begs you to do this!

From here, you can segue into a book that focuses on using technology in funny ways, but with serious reflections on human emotions and feelings, such as *Girl Parts* by John M. Cusick:

> *David's parents decide to socialize their son through the use of a perfect robot girl— a companion with built-in timing for appropriate levels and times for kissing, touching, etc. If he goes too fast, he receives an electric shock!*

Decide ahead of time which books you are most comfortable discussing with a group. If you think it would be difficult to banter over *Very LeFreak*, but you feel the issues are important enough to keep it on your booklist, display it on the table, but hand-sell it to students who ask about it specifically.

Teens want to connect with other teens on emotional issues. If the people around them don't provide help (or not enough help) when teens are trying to untangle a situation in their own lives, characters in books can provide a "model" in a similar situation to examine. How did that ditzy girl work through an emotion? How could this brilliant guy miss the connection and mess up his life so thoroughly? Fiction provides an opportunity for teens to "experience life" from a safe distance.

Here are some additional SITL booktalking tips

Use your booktalking strengths. If you usually concentrate on plot descriptions when you talk about books, use that as your device to illustrate a point; if your partner really loves to read excerpts, a section read from a book can complement your plot description. You can easily shift toward humor, books by the same author, and even poetry during a Sex in the Library presentation. Your style is what has made you a great booktalker, so don't switch now!

Watch your time! You want students to reflect on a book or a topic, so don't feel that you need to rush through plot descriptions of every book on your booklist. This is what makes Sex in the Library different from any other booktalk. The interactive nature of the discussion allows you to bring issues and books to the students with teacher and parent support. Unfortunately, this process takes more time per book than you might normally allow, so be aware and keep an eye on the clock.

Be honest. If you don't feel comfortable talking about a book, feel free to admit it. On our table we always keep a copy of a book that students often ask about, but Mary Jo doesn't like to discuss, *Doing It* by Melvin Burgess:

> *Three British teen boys confront the confusions, joys, and fears of sexuality.*

Mary Jo simply hands the book to Aarene, who loves talking about the book, even though she didn't actually enjoy reading it (see the book review in Part II for more information). When Aarene finishes the booktalk, Mary Jo might offer her opinion of the book and why she didn't want to talk about it, or she might offer to talk instead about *Peeps* by Scott Westerfeld:

> *When Cal arrived at college, he planned to lose his virginity. He didn't plan to contract vampirism.*

Mary Jo did love this book with a similar theme, so she's happy to bring it up. Doing so also allows her to transition to books about the supernatural.

Talk about books you love . . . and books you don't love. The common advice to booktalkers is to stick to books you really love. We've already mentioned that we don't always love the same books. We agree to disagree, and we are willing to say that out loud in a presentation. Students don't always agree with each other, and during a SITL booktalk, they can discover that adults don't always agree either. Students should be encouraged to express their differing opinions.

Sometimes we are asked about a popular book that isn't on our list (cough, *Twilight,* cough). We give our opinions about the book, including reasons why we didn't put it on our list. If we both hate a title, we don't bother talking about it—even if it's a huge bestseller.

If you are ever asked about a book you haven't read, be honest and confess that you haven't read it—you can always ask to borrow it from the questioner!

The back-and-forth patter about titles is what SITL is all about. When people who are passionate about books actually stand up and argue the virtues or demerits of specific titles, the audience can't help being intrigued. Students are just like everyone else: They want to know what the fuss is all about. By the time they walk out of our booktalks, they know what books they want to read, they know what books they want to avoid, and they had fun.

Our partnership has worked well for us for many years. Your style may be different. Your collection may be different. Your level of comfort with vocabulary may be different. There are endless approaches, and no singular approach is best for everyone. When you find the belief and motivation to have Sex in the Library, you will find a partner.

As with any new relationship, there are always a few awkward moments while both parties adjust to the new situation. Can you imagine going on a first date with your boss scrutinizing everything you say or do? Well, that is what happened to me on my first plunge into Sex in the Library. Aarene and I planned our premiere event, and then my principal decided that would be a great opportunity to conduct an observation for my evaluation. Not only that, but things worked out in such a way that the previous partner (Mary Jo) was there to watch as well. Talk about pressure!

Luckily, there were several things working in my favor. For one, Aarene and I had been working together for almost a year in one way or another. It certainly wasn't anything as extensive as SITL, but I felt like we had good rapport and a feel for each other's personality and style, particularly in regard to working with large groups of middle school students. In addition, as any librarian or teacher can tell you, flexibility is a mandatory job requirement, so we were both able to adapt as necessary throughout the day.

Despite a stiff (pun not intended!) beginning, by the end of the day, Aarene and I had settled into a rhythm complete with witty repartee and dramatic *Star Trek* re-enactments. One benefit of working with a more experienced partner is that you can rely on them a bit more to carry things along until you get the hang of it yourself. This was a fabulous experience, and I look forward to repeating it. The students, as well as the teachers, appreciate the candid look at materials and where to access them. A few weeks after we presented to the eighth grade, they watched a performance of *Romeo and Juliet.* Afterwards, one of the students exclaimed to her teacher "Hey, they just had *Star Trek* sex!" —*Anne Dame, teacher-librarian, Einstein Middle School*

Resources

Stiefvater, Maggie. Blog comment. 10 August 2010. *http://Sexinthelibrary.blogspot.com.*

CHAPTER 4

The Locker Room:
Fiction Books about Sexuality for Guys

"Either you can sleep with any woman—OK? Any woman, at any time. They can't say no. No matter how beautiful and gorgeous, all you have to do is ask. At your disposal. And they have to do whatever you want them to. Anything. But. You ALSO have to be buggered. Once a year for twenty minutes. On the radio."

"On the radio? Why not on telly?" demanded Ben.

"Because on the radio you'd try and keep really quiet so that no one would know it was you, but you wouldn't be able to. Little noises would escape. Oh. Oh. Oo. Ow. You know. Mmm. Ah. Mmm. Woo. Ah. Na-ha. And if you don't, then you get no sex ever. Never. No one. For life."

Dino tried to think about it, but he couldn't. No sex was impossible. So was being buggered.[1]

The first chapter *of Doing It* is full of exerptable vignettes, each one more hormonally slang-driven and socially offensive than the last ... and each one typical of the hyperbolic sexual bluster of insecure teen boys. Not everyone can read this stuff out loud. But if you can, you will have the undivided attention of every person in the room, guaranteed.

---

[1] From *Doing It* © 2004 by Melvin Burgess. Reprinted by permission of Henry Holt Company, LLC. All rights reserved.

Teenaged guys aren't like teenaged girls. They don't look the same, they don't smell the same, they don't act the same, and they don't like the same stuff. Why would anyone expect that teenaged guys would enjoy the same books that teenaged girls enjoy? In fact, studies show that boys entering puberty do not read nearly as much as their female counterparts.

We know of several teachers who include the "male way of learning" in a normal classroom, but we agree that many teachers of teens frequently despair when confronted with boys who will not read. We think that we have an answer to the problem.

Sex.

Studies, such as *Reading Don't Fix No Chevys,* clearly state that boys *will* read when the subject is extremely interesting to them. They *will* read about sports. They *will* read manuals and instruction books to learn the things they want to know. They *will* read action, adventure, and comics. And, if you point them in the right direction, teen boys will happily—although sometimes surreptitiously—read about sex.

Sex is one of the things guys *really* want to know about, and novels about sex can inform them about how it all works. Boys want to know *all* about sex—not only how the plumbing works and how the various parts fit together, but especially how to manage social parts. That's the focus of *Swim the Fly* by Don Calame:

> *Three boys: Matt, Sean, and Coop. One goal: See a live naked girl.*

The readers of *Swim the Fly* and similar "boy books" are primarily boys. The stories and situations in the books are fictional, but they are realistic—the characters *feel* like boys that we all know. The authors convey the characters' triumphs and worries to readers, and readers identify with these characters. It's validating to teen readers to experience the stories of other teen boys with emotions similar to their own. The situations are told in a humorous fashion, but the feelings behind the situations are familiar and real. The situations could happen in a school anywhere in the world.

Gender and Literacy

According to Michael W. Smith and Jeffrey D. Wilhelm in *"Reading Don't Fix No Chevys": Literacy in the Lives of Young Men* (Heinemann, 2002), research on gender and literacy provides some interesting insights:

- Boys take longer to learn to read than girls do.
- Boys read less than girls read.
- Girls tend to comprehend narrative texts and most expository texts significantly better than boys do.
- Boys value reading as an activity less than girls do.

According to a national survey conducted by the Young Adult Library Services Association in 2001, boys of an average age of 14 listed their top obstacles to reading:

- boring/no fun: 39.3 percent
- no time/too busy: 29.8 percent
- like other activities better: 11.1 percent
- can't get into the stories: 7.7 percent
- I'm not good at it: 4.3 percent

Jon Scieszka, author of children's books such as *The Stinky Cheese Man* and the Time Warp Trio series, believes that boys are biologically slower to develop than girls and therefore often have early struggles with reading and writing skills. On his Guys Read website, (*http://www.guysread.com/*), he also says that the male way of learning, which tends to be action oriented and competitive, works against boys in many classrooms.

Sex education textbooks supply some of the basic "body parts" information. However, stories that speak to them of their own lives and situations will not only supply other information they seek, but also serve to inform them that they are not alone on this planet, and their situations are not unique.

Some boys know that they aren't ready for sex, but they still have hormonal urges. These boys might find a friend in Arnold Spirit, Jr., called "Junior" in *The Absolutely True Diary of a Part-Time Indian* by Sherman Alexie:

> *Junior's diary and cartoons chronicle his simultaneously tragic and outrageously funny attempt to escape from life on the Spokane Indian Reservation.*

Junior has a lot going on in his life: He wants an education that will lead him to opportunities off the reservation. He loves his family, but he recognizes that their alcoholism limits their ability to care for him. He wants friends, he wants to be loved by Penelope (a white girl at the rich-kids' school), and he wants to be accepted by both white kids and the tribal members who have no interest in leaving the "rez." Junior takes joy in basketball, in his artwork, in his friendship with his buddy Rowdy, and in masturbation. He doesn't talk a lot to other people, but his diary relates it all—and boys who read the book can experience the life of a kid who is like them in many important ways.

For boys who think that they *are* ready for sex, the question they want answered is more likely *"How can I convince somebody to have sex with me?"* Good and bad answers to that question can be explored through fiction without exposing the reader to health-threatening diseases or situations. Most importantly, as the quote from *Doing It* above illustrates, boys want to know *how* they can have sex: *when, where, how often,* and *with whom.* In *Doing It* by Melvin Burgess:

> *Three British teen boys confront the confusions, joys, and fears of sexuality.*

The three main characters are all frantically interested in sex: they think and talk about it almost all the time. Dino, who seems the smoothest of the group but is actually the most insecure, cannot seem to get pretty-girl Jackie to "put out" for him. Jonathan likes Deborah, whom the other boys call "fat," but whom he sees as "bountiful." Ben is secretly seeing a pretty young teacher, who is overwhelmingly dependent upon him. The obsession with sex and the objectification of women by the three main characters make the book difficult for many adults to read; nonetheless, it is an accurate portrayal of the inside of the boys' heads that some male teens find funny and oddly comforting.

Aarene says: I was really distressed by *Doing It*, because at the time I read it, I was also mentoring two young women who were dating young men, who I thought didn't appreciate the depth and complexity of my girls. The fictional boys' obsessive interest in sex seemed a little too close to reality for me. I gave *Doing It* to a sixteen-year-old boy to read and asked him if he thought that the author was exaggerating the boys' fascination with sex. The young man gave it back to me a week later and told me that he thought the author had gotten things just about right. Desperately, I handed the book to my own spouse, age forty-five, and asked him if he thought that guys outgrow the obsession eventually. He gave the book back to me a week later, saying that he thought the author had gotten things just about right! Finally, I gave the book to the two young women and told them that if they insisted on dating boys, they needed to know how the creatures think and behave. They read it and smiled.

Targeting Boys while Booktalking: Strategies That Will Get (and Keep) Them Interested

Discussing books that boys will love is a great thing, but how can you talk to them so that they will *listen?* Here are some tips:

- *Excerpts work well.* Choose strong narrations with action or an immediate dilemma that will interest the boys in your audience. The dilemma can be sexual or not, as long as it is exciting. Take, for example, this passage from *Tale of Two Summers* by Brian Sloan:

  "When I caught up to him, we were now even higher, maybe fifty feet up. . . As we neared the end of the beams, my pace started to slow up again as the expanse of the river came into view. Henri said that we should walk right out to the edge, and I was like, 'Uh, you're on your own, buddy.' So, as I turned to get out of his way, I of course lost my balance for a sec. As I tottered on the edge of eternity, Henri grabbed me around the waist to keep me from falling. My heart was in my skull by this point, beating so hard that it felt like my eardrums were going to burst. But Henri held on to me, thank God, both his hands tightly gripping my midsection in a way that did serve to stabilize me. But you know what? It also equally served to destabilize me, if you get my meaning here. Translation for the visually impaired: The man had his hands just inches above my manhood. Sure, plunging to my death into the Potomac would not be cute, but getting a boner in broad daylight in front of Henri? Yes, there is a fate worse than death."[2]

- *Summarize the plot with action words.* An example, *Be More Chill* by Ned Vizzini:

  Jeremy can't get a girl to save his soul. Perhaps it's because he hasn't a clue, or perhaps he is just a major, major dork. Technology comes to his rescue: He swallows a a pill with a mini-computer that can talk in his mind to make him more "chill." The computer tells him how to stop looking and acting like a dork. It tells him how to dress, how to talk to girls, and how to finally, finally score with girls!

- *Move around the room*, make lots of eye contact, ask for a male volunteer to help answer questions about things he knows. If your volunteer knows where vampires come from, but doesn't read about them because "they sparkle," he's given you the perfect opportunity to talk about *Peeps* by Scott Westerfeld:

  When Cal arrived at college, he planned to lose his virginity. He didn't plan to contract vampirism.

  There's plenty of action in Peeps, and not much romance. Plus, the book features some exceedingly icky nonfiction chapters interspersed with the plot. These nonfiction chapters are full of gruesome, fascinating facts about real parasites. If your stomach is strong enough,

---

[2] Sloan, Brian. *Tale of Two Summers.* Simon and Schuster, 2005. Reprinted by permission of Simon and Schuster Books for Young Readers, an imprint of Simon and Schuster Children's Publishing Division.

read a portion of the chapter about the worm that eventually burrows out of the host's leg. (See sidebar) You will have to beat boys away from this book with a stick.

- *Point out the common experiences* that your male readers share with fictional protagonists. For example, although not every boy in the audience will have first-hand experience with autism, almost all of them know someone who pushes them to work harder. That common experience will allow readers to relate to Marcelo, the main character of *Marcelo in the Real World* by Francisco X. Stork:

  Marcelo has lots of skills to help him adapt his autism to life in the "real world," but his father continually pushes for more.

- *Talk about books with a variety of male or non-girly female main characters.* If readers don't relate to out-of-the-closet Joe in *Totally Joe* by James Howe,

  Joe has doubts about the classroom assignment to write his "alphabiography," because the project could be ammunition for bullying if it fell into the wrong hands.

  then perhaps they will have something in common with musician *Nick from Nick and Norah's Infinite Playlist* by Rachel Cohn and David Levithan

The natural world is jaw-droppingly horrible. Appalling, nasty, vile.

Take trematodes, for example.

Trematodes are tiny fish that live in the stomach of a bird. (How did that happen? Horribly. Just keep reading.) They lay their eggs in the bird's stomach. One day, the bird takes a crap into a pond, and the eggs are on their way. They hatch and swim around the pond looking for a snail. These trematodes are microscopic, small enough to lay eggs in a snail's eye, as we used to say in Texas.

Well, ok. We never said that in Texas. But trematodes actually do it. For some reason, they always choose the left eye. When the babies hatch, they eat the snail's left eye and spread throughout its body. (Didn't I say this would be horrible?) But they don't kill the snail. Not right away.

First, the half-blind snail gets a gnawing feeling in the pit of its stomach and thinks it's hungry. It starts to eat but for some reason can never get enough food. You see, when the food gets to where the snail's stomach used to be, all that's left down there is trematodes, getting their meals delivered. The snail can't mate, or sleep or enjoy life in any other snaily way. It has become a hungry robot dedicated to gathering food for its horrible little passengers.

After a while, the trematodes get bored with this and pull the plug on their poor host. They invade the snail's antennae, making them twitch. They turn the snail's left eye bright colors. A bird passing overhead sees this brightly colored, twitching snail and says, 'Yum … '

The snail gets eaten, and the trematodes are back up in a bird's stomach, ready to parachute into the next pond over. (pp. 16-17)

Nick just needs a girlfriend for five minutes, so he asks total stranger Norah to step in.

or with the action/adventure heroics of Katniss Everdeen in *The Hunger Games* by Suzanne Collins:

In order to survive, Katniss must win the game, which may mean killing her friends.

- *Ask boys to name the movies and television shows they enjoy*, rather than the titles of books. Then, ask what they like about those programs—and try to match fiction selections to them. A guy who enjoys science stuff may be interested in Ben's description of the scientific process involved in *Half Brother* by Kenneth Oppel:

  Ben gets involved with his parents' research project: teaching sign language to a baby chimpanzee. Then, funding for the project fails.

  A boy who spends hours every day playing computer games is the perfect reader for *For the Win* by Cory Doctorow:

  Teens in China, India, and Southern California fight against the global corporations that run the computer games they love.

- *Ask boys to name books they've read that they* didn't *enjoy* . . . as long as they will identify the reasons they didn't like the book. For example, one eighth grade boy asked us why the guy always gets the unattainable girl in the book— "That doesn't happen in real life." That is the kind of dialog that we encourage, and we are eager to point out books where the unattainable girl really is not attainable. For example, we can point to books like *Flash Burnout* by L.K. Madigan:

  Photographer Blake connects closely with Marissa . . . which creates a problem for Blake and his girlfriend.

  and *Girl Parts* by John M. Cusick:

  David's parents decide to socialize their son through the use of a perfect robot girl— a companion with built-in timing for appropriate levels and times for kissing, touching, etc. If he goes too fast, he receives an electric shock!

  and *Hard Love* by Ellen Wittlinger:

  John and Marisol are both zine writers. John falls in love with Marisol, even though he knows that she is a lesbian.

We want to validate boys' feelings and their reading preferences, and we need to keep them talking. If you know what they don't like, it's easier to find something they do like. Boys who hated the unrealistic nature of a book assigned by a classroom teacher might enjoy the it-could-happen-to-you narrative style of *Seth Baumgartner's Love Manifesto* by Eric Luper

While scheming to get back his girlfriend, Seth starts an anonymous podcast.

or *Don't Let Me Go* by J.H. Trumble:

Nate and Adam have been romantically inseparable for a year ... until Adam moves away.

- *Play to their fears!* Every adolescent is sure that he is the only one—the only one who doesn't know about sex, the only one who is out of touch with girls, the only who stinks, the only one who is *different.* Where we disagreed about vampires before, we love them here. The vampire is the ultimate "guy who only gets the girl because he can overpower her with his mind." Vampires, werewolves, and their ilk really are different and really do need to stay away from everyone. When viewed through this lens, it's possible to sympathize, even with sparkly vampires like Edward Cullen.

- *Don't let them get away with the "I'm cooler than school" attitude.* Many boys will say that they don't read "adolescent" fiction because there is nothing there for them, so they read "adult" books instead. They are really just asking what you have that they could relate to. More quality adolescent literature is being published now than ever before. The books are here. Engage that conversation above and throw your best books at them!

Please note that although all of the books given as examples in this chapter contain scenes with sexual situations, in many of them, the plot focuses on other aspects, with sexual decision-making being a normal part of life. These stories center on the active lives of boys, rather than on the loving relationships that many girls like to read about. By providing boys with a great story that contains some sexual content, you may convince them that reading books won't kill them . . . and their classroom teachers will bless you for the effort.

Resources

Scieszka, Jon. Guys Read. Available: *http://www.guysread.com.*

Smith, Michael W., and Jeffrey Wilhelm. *Reading Don't Fix No Chevys: Literacy in the Lives of Young Men.* Heinemann, 2002.

CHAPTER 5

Not Tonight, Dear

Whenever the title "Sex in the Library" is inserted into a conversation, expectations rise on everyone's part (but ours) on what could possibly be mentioned. It is fair to say most people in the audience do not expect tame books, books on abstinence, or books that include only kissing. One important goal of SITL is to provide literature with themes that speak to teens about their lives, while fitting within the mission and selection statements of the school and public library.

Tying SITL into the School Curriculum

Obviously, a major focus of a school library is to support the academic curriculum. In addition to nonfiction books about the American Civil War, the school library's shelves also contain relevant historical fiction. In addition to nonfiction books about the Pacific Rim, the collection features fiction titles set in Korea, Mexico, Australia, Thailand, and other Pacific Rim countries. And, in addition to nonfiction books about sex education, the middle school and high school library contains many books about teens facing sexual decision-making.

Not all books about sexual decision-making are appropriate for school libraries. The beauty (and the dilemma) of fictional decision-making is that, often, good stories happen when good characters make really unwise choices. An example of this is *A Bad Boy Can Be Good for a Girl* by Tanya Lee Stone:

> *In the blank endpapers of the school library's copy of* Forever, *Josie writes a warning to other girls about the guy who "only wants one thing."*

Josie is flattered by the attention of a handsome older boy and even thinks she might love him, but she hits a sharp learning curve when he dumps her because she won't "put out." Nicolette meets up with the same boy, but she learns a different lesson from her relationship, because her choices were different from Josie's choices. Readers learn that the boy who "only wants one thing" habitually uses girls for sex, and it's up to the girls to stick up for themselves and each other. The three stories together create a much stronger tale than the single abstinence episode tells alone. *Bad Boy* is terrific in terms of presenting different characters and the very different choices they make. Although the *first* girl featured in the narrative says "no," the book contains some cuss words and sex scenes with "details" later in the story, and these might be considered inappropriate for some conservative collections.

As adults, we need to remind ourselves that even though we'd like fictional characters to set good examples for teens by declining unhealthy sexual relationships, we understand that a character (and the reader) will experience a learning experience more fully by making mistakes.

Don't you prefer that teens learn about bad choices vicariously through fiction, rather than making bad sexual choices in real life? We do, too. But when we talk about fiction that supports the sexual education curriculum, we sometimes search for books in which at least one character does something (in a believable way) that comes straight out of the health textbooks.

For a long time, the only books for teens that addressed sexual situations were "cautionary tales" featuring sexually promiscuous teens who came to a Very Bad End: pregnant, diseased, and ostracized from society. In recent years, authors and publishers have sometimes gone to the other extreme. Abstinence and safe sex are topics that few books treat well, and the books that do, deserve to be spotlighted. Here are some strategies for tying "safe-sex" curriculum into SITL booktalks that will thrill health teachers and please many parents.

Teens in the U.S. are:

> 2.5 times as likely to get pregnant as in Canada
>
> 4 times as likely to get pregnant as in Germany or Norway
>
> 10 times as likely to get pregnant as in Switzerland

Mississippi teens are:

> 4 times as likely to get pregnant as in New Hampshire
>
> 15 times as likely to get pregnant as in Switzerland

Kearney, Melissa S., and Phillip B. Levine. 2012. "Why Is the Teen Birth Rate in the United States So High and Why Does It Matter?" *Journal of Economic Perspectives* 26 (2): 141-163, http://www.scribd.com/doc/93928636/Teen-Birth-Study (accessed March 28, 2013).

Books about Saying "NO"

Many tween books aimed at young teens, where the characters do not proceed beyond kissing and longing looks across crowded classrooms, are included on the SITL booklist. Some of these are exceedingly popular, such as *The ABC's of Kissing Boys* by Tina Ferraro:

Sixteen-year-old Parker takes kissing lessons from the freshman across the street as part of her plan to get on the varsity soccer team.

Sources for Christian Fiction Books for Teens

There are many Christian blogs and even Christian fiction sites, but few deal specifically, or even partially, for teens. Here are some we like and have used:

- The YALSA (Young Adult Library Services Association) publishes a list called "Books That Won't Make You Blush" at *http://www.ala.org/yalsa/ booklistsawards/booklists/popularpaperback/ annotations/ppya06#blush.*

- Commonsensemedia.org, while not originally a Christian website, still gives great recommendations for parents on movies, TV shows, books, and more.

- Teen Lit Review: Real Reviews for the Christian Parent at *http://www.teenlitreviewblog.com/* features ratings that include violence, spiritual content (books without spiritual content are included), language, and sexual content. This is geared toward parents, but teens would find it easy to use as well.

- King County's Teen Zone posted a "spiritual" list at *http://www.kcls.org/teens/booklist.cfm? booklistid=61.* Consider developing a list at your library.

It's astonishingly difficult for us to write about teen books that focus on abstinence and saying "no." This is not because we dislike the topic, but rather, because, for reasons known only to catalogers and publishers, the word "no" and the plot consequences that come from it are rarely indexed. It is, quite simply, *really difficult to locate* well-written, mainstream books that deal with the topic of abstinence by using a library or bookseller's catalog. Why this is, we cannot say, but an extensive search in World Cat and similar surveys of the commercial indexes maintained by Amazon.com reveals a lot of nonfiction books about abstinence education (published in the late 1980s) but *no* fiction books, *at all.*

Booklists of religious romances for teens generally avoid the issue of teen sexuality whenever possible. Others lean heavily on a few selected titles like *Crazy in Love* by Dandi Daley Mackall:

> *Mary Jane flirted with Jackson at a party . . . but Jackson already has a girlfriend, the popular and gorgeous Star.*

If you've ever had a parent complain that teen books today are full of smut and sex, how could you disprove the complaint? "Teen sexuality—fiction" is indexed, but "Teen abstinence—fiction" isn't.

Our theory: Publishers recognize that "sex sells" and "no sex" doesn't. To support this theory, we recall our experiences with unfortunately-named books. In these cases, the title alone excludes it from consideration from conservative collections—even when the content is perfectly innocent—especially in a school library, where a parental glance at titles can result in an unnecessary uproar. For example, Mary Jo was confronted by a parent who had a very strong reaction to the title of *Smart Boys & Fast Girls* by Stephie Davis, a book so innocuous that it was never considered for the SITL list. Similarly, no matter how many times we talk to parent groups about *Sex Kittens and Horn Dawgs Fall in Love* by Maryrose Wood,

> *Felicia and Matthew research, interview, hypothesize, and test their theories of love attractiveness. But could it be possible that sometimes "Love Just Happens?" And why isn't Matthew falling in love with Felicia?*

we find it difficult to convince them that the book really doesn't contain any sexual situations! A few kisses, yes. Nakedness? Not even the tactful kind. The moral of this story: Do not judge a book by its title!

We don't want anyone to think that a librarian could avoid controversy simply by choosing only books featured in this chapter. This chapter was not intended to be a Booklist for the Faint of Heart. This is also not The Abstinence Chapter. We don't recommend all of these books for every collection, especially for librarians who are very nervous. Instead, the books mentioned in this chapter are included because they feature decisions that (at some point) include topics that your health teachers want books to include: abstinence, safer sex practices, and disease and pregnancy prevention. Sometimes, of course, these topics are covered because a fictional character makes a poor decision and then must figure out how to proceed.

We also don't necessarily tell our audiences that these books belong in the "responsibility" chapter of SITL. When we are booktalking, we include some of these titles throughout the talk—where they best fit—not in a stand-alone section of the booktalk. We do recognize that some students find "longing and kissing" a safer selection for themselves and want to wait until later to read about "body parts."

Sometimes the longing and kissing can be very intense even without actual sex. Such is the case of *Daughter of Smoke and Bone* by Lain Taylor:

She felt the coarseness of his unshaven throat at her cheek as she tested, against his own, the perfect water-smoothness of her hair ... they were quiet but their blood and nerves and butterflies were not—they were rampantly alive rushing and thrumming in a wild and perfec melody, matched note for note.

Daughter of Smoke and Bone. Laini Taylor, Little, Brown, 2012. p298

"No, I'm Not Ready"

The most well-known celibate characters in recent teen literature are Bella and Edward in *Twilight* by Stephenie Meyer:

> *Bella discovers that Edward and his family are vampires who feed only upon wildlife. But just because Edward doesn't want to drink the blood of humans does not mean that Bella is completely safe with him.*

It must be pointed out that the abstinence between Bella and Edward is strictly Edward's idea. Bella would have happily flopped over to bare her neck by the middle of book one, but Edward prolongs the romance—and the suspense and the sexual tension—by keeping Bella at arm's length until they are "safely" married. In book four of the series, the two *are* married, and the sex isn't just on the page, it's everywhere. Vampiric boyfriends may be the ultimate teaching tool for safe sex! A lady need not fear STDs or pre-marital pregnancy when her favorite guy is (mostly) dead.

For very different reasons, Louie Banks decides to postpone sexual relations in *Running Loose* by Chris Crutcher:

> *Louie, a high school senior in a small Idaho town, learns about sportsmanship, love, and death as he matures into manhood.*

Louie does a lot of growing up in this novel, but nowhere in the story is his learning curve more apparent as in the scene between him and his girlfriend Becky, when he confesses to her that he is just not ready for sex. The scene is tender, but the narrator isn't a sissy, and the story is made stronger by Louie's ability to say "no."

Contrary to what you may have heard or read, teens in real life and teens in fiction *do* say "no" to sex, for some of the same reasons that adults say "no" to sex. That doesn't mean the decision will last throughout the book. People waffle on this momentous decision, or books would not be written with so many variations on that theme. These books exist to help teens (and their parents and the adults in their lives) understand what is at stake and perhaps how to vicariously make that decision.

We are not judging these decisions, but we absolutely want those decisions available for teens to examine. We don't "promote" any one attitude over another. In the same way we demand that the facts surrounding contraception be correct and real, we also demand that situations where characters "say no" be correct and real. The more scenarios readers visit, the more able they will be to examine their own values and make a good decision for themselves. And we aren't judging that decision either.

Sometimes people make bad decisions. So do fictional people. As a plotline develops and the character makes decisions, the reader is forming decisions, as well. Some scenarios just hit closer to home. For example, **"*I think my best friend is having sex, but I don't want to yet.*"** That's the plot in *The True Meaning of Cleavage* by Mariah Fredericks:

> *Jess and Sari, best friends since seventh grade, take very different directions in high school. Will their friendship survive?*

Sari has "developed" in high school, and the quarterback wants to date her but "keep it secret" until he tells his cheerleader girlfriend. The teens meet up after school for sex, and he says he loves her. Sari's best friend Jess watches Sari become increasingly desperate, but tries to deny the situation.

"*I had sex before, but now I don't want to be forced into it. What do I do?*" This is the subject of *Memoirs of a Teenage Amnesiac* by Gabrielle Zevin:

> *Yearbook editor Naomi slips, falls, and suffers amnesia, reducing her last four years to nothing. Everyone wants to help her recover her memory, but Naomi isn't sure she wants to be the girl she evidently was.*

While Naomi is trying to put together a sensible narration of her recent life, which she has forgotten as a result of head trauma, her boyfriend tells her they are going out and they will be having sex, as usual. Naomi's reaction: "I don't know if I am; I'm not sure I would want to; and I am sure that we are not having sex until I know you again and can pull my life together." It's a natural reaction, and a good decision on her part.

"*I told you I would 'go all the way,' but now I don't want to.*" The power to say "no" at any time is a tricky situation for teens in fiction and in real life. Teens in fiction and in real life struggle with the obligations that accompany flirtation, especially when combined with drugs and alcohol. This decision is the focal point of *Crazy in Love* by Dandi Mackall. Mary Jane decides that she really isn't ready for sex, but she might lose Jackson as a result of this decision. This book is rather heavy-handed and message-driven, but there is a segment of the teen population that really wants and needs to read it. *Is it ever too late to say "no"?* Cara must cope with this situation in *Perfect* by Ellen Hopkins.

In this stand-alone sequel to Impulse, *four teens struggle with major issues related to a perception of perfection. Although some issues in the book are less critical, they include dating violence, anorexia, sexual identity, and drug abuse.*

Self-obsessed Cara is struggling with an awakening desire to be with girls instead of with her "perfect" boyfriend. Would having sex with him prove that she really is (or isn't) a lesbian? While leading him on, even urging him on, then changing her mind and saying no at the last minute, Cara demands that the reader faces this question. Teens have discussions about this topic with each other after passing this quick-but-difficult read around. This topic would also make a great lesson in a health class, assuming that a school could teach a Hopkins book, which contains obscenities, drug and alcohol use, and dating violence. Conversations like these are easier when it concerns the emotions of characters, especially when teens feel they actually "know" the person through the novel.

"*I have very specific beliefs that dictate my sexual decisions and behavior.*" In *Does My Head Look Big in This?* by Randa Abdel-Fattah:

Fuck. Fuck. Fuck. What
the hell just happened?
"You wanted this! You
told me so. In fact, you
practically raped me ... "

She sobs, and her entire
body shakes with the force
of it. No. You raped me.
Her voice slices, tempered
steel. I told you to stop.

Perfect. Ellen Hopkins, Margaret McElderry Books, 2011 p. 271. Used by author permission.

Not only does this novel-in-poem-form create an exceptionally intense scene in the book, it also asks readers to examine their own beliefs about saying "no." When (if ever) is it too late to say "no"?

Australian teen Amal has decided to wear the hijab, the Muslim headscarf, full-time.

Amal is very attracted to her friend Adam. She wants to know him better and she wants to spend time with him. When he tries to kiss her at a party, however, Amal chooses her religious beliefs over her sexual attraction to Adam.

It's certainly understandable that teens with strong religious beliefs choose to abstain from sexual relations, but what about when the religious beliefs dictate that a teen *should* have sex and/or marry somebody icky? In *Sister Wife* by Shelley Hrdlitschka:

Celeste knows that when she turns fifteen, she will be assigned to an older member of the community, which means she will have to assimilate into his already-established family and perform the duties of a sister wife.

Celeste has always questioned her faith, but has never known life outside of her small old-fashioned, faith-based polygamous community. Rejecting the husband chosen for her would mean abandoning not only her religious beliefs but also her entire family. At first, Celeste goes along with the expectations of her family. She marries the icky guy, she lives as a sister-wife, and she becomes pregnant. Meanwhile, the young man she truly loves has left the community rather than participate in marriage to wives he does not love.

Only after thoroughly searching her soul and examining her own beliefs does Celeste take steps to leave. The main character in this book eventually says "no" to sexual relations with a man she doesn't love. It is important to note that she isn't a virgin when she makes this choice.

"*No, not with you.*" Religion isn't Elizabeth's problem in *Between* by Jessica Warman:

> *When pretty, popular, and wealthy Elizabeth Valchar wakes up on the morning of her eighteenth birthday, she's dead.*

All of her friends assume that Elizabeth has been having sex with her longtime boyfriend Richie, but they haven't gone all the way yet. Now, somebody knows something bad about Elizabeth and promises not to tell—if she will have sex with him.

"*I want to have sex for the right reasons, not the wrong ones.*" In the award-winning book *A Northern Light* by Jennifer Donnelly,

> *In 1906, sixteen-year-old Mattie works at a summer resort, where she learns the truth about the death of a guest.*

Readers become acquainted with Mattie, who aspires to a college education despite her family's poverty. Mattie could have a life of relative ease by agreeing to marry Royal Loomis, the handsome son of a rich man. After a summer spent working and serving rich people at a resort hotel in upstate New York, she rejects Royal's advances and chooses to attend school instead.

It's not just *sex* that Mattie, Celeste, Elizabeth, and Amal reject: Each of them also, eventually, rejects at least some of the pressure and expectations of others. Sometimes the expectations may seem outrageous to readers; in other instances, rejection seems like doing things the hard way. In each of these stories, the girls affirm their right to determine their own destiny and make their own decisions.

Variations on the theme of choosing sex for the right reasons are explored in *The Sky Is Everywhere* by Jandy Nelson:

> *In the months after her sister dies, seventeen-year-old Lennie falls into a love triangle and discovers the strength to follow her dream of becoming a musician.*

Lennie is attracted to her sister's fiancé but recognizes that they are both grieving; the timing for a relationship is just wrong. The new kid in town is also very attractive, but Lennie feels unable (and unwilling) to make decisions.

"*No, no, no, because I said NO!*" In *Love and Lies* by Ellen Wittlinger,

> *Marisol has taken a year off from her admission to Stanford to "write a novel and fall in love."*

Marisol spurns the advances of her friend Gio, not because she isn't fond of him, but because she is a lesbian. She rejects him gently, but her decision is final, and he is not allowed to argue (although he really tries to).

The main character of *Peeps* by Scott Westerfeld,

> *When Cal arrived at college, he planned to lose his virginity. He didn't plan to contract vampirism.*

has a very powerful reason to abstain from sexual intercourse: He is infected with the sexually-transmitted parasite that turned him into an early-stage vampire, and he doesn't want to infect anyone else, although the parasite greatly enhances his libido. When Lace turns out to be "parasite positive," the rules change.

"*No, not without protection.*" Most modern sex education classes do not focus exclusively on abstinence. In addition to the basic instructions about the configurations of human plumbing and the various ways the pieces can be fitted together, emphasis is placed upon what is now called "safer sex." In the olden days, when Aarene was a blushing middle school student and the hottest new book on the shelves was *Forever* by Judy Blume,

> *Katherine and Michael believe their love is so strong that it will last forever.*

"safe sex" meant "don't get pregnant." In 1975, fictional character Katherine very responsibly goes to Planned Parenthood to get birth control pills. In her introduction to the 2002 edition of *Forever,* Blume reminds new readers that times have changed since the original publication of the book. She writes that although the definition of safe(r) sex now includes protection from sexually transmitted diseases, as well as pregnancy—and urges readers to make good choices and stay safe—the *feelings of falling in love* are eternal ... even when the feelings don't last forever.

As mentioned earlier, sometimes characters (and, dare we say, readers) learn best from bad choices. Even well-educated fictional teen characters make dumb mistakes sometimes. Readers learn valuable lessons along with fictional characters, as long as the message doesn't come across as forced and didactic. Interestingly, in *The Sky Is Everywhere,* it is Lennie's grandmother who questions her about contraception. Lennie rejects contraception, but in *Hooked* by Catherine Greenman:

> *Thea considers herself savvy and spunky, but she throws that all away when she dates Will, who hooks her with his good looks and charm.*

Thea readily accepts it ... and then forgets to take her pills, resulting in pregnancy. Contraception discussions are becoming more common in teen literature, but in our humble opinions, these discussions are not common enough.

Although *one* of the obvious themes in *Every Little Thing in the World* by Nina de Gramont,

> *While Syd and her best friend Natalia spend the summer at a wilderness canoe camp for troubled teens, Syd tries to figure out what to do about her unplanned pregnancy.*

is the consequences of unprotected sex, the characters (just like real teens) deal with several major issues simultaneously. It is the juggling of the fear of pregnancy, the growing attraction for a new love interest, and the concern for a dear friend in crisis that makes the character of Syd seem real to readers.

Unsafe sex is definitely a problem for one of the characters in *Rainbow Boys* by Alex Sanchez:

> *Three high-school boys struggle with family issues, gay bashers, first sex, and conflicting feelings about each other.*

Nelson, the most flamboyant and stereotypically gay character in the book, becomes jealous of the other boys' relationship. He impulsively hooks up with a guy named Brick, and they have unprotected sex. Bad choice? Oh, yes. A potentially life-changing trip to the clinic for Nelson is much more complicated in this novel than Katherine's 1975 encounter with the speculum in *Forever*. Nelson needs a blood test.

"*No, not now (but maybe later).*" Teen literature is good at communicating this message: "It's okay to change your mind when you learn more." Many characters in fiction change their minds. This can be a sign of maturity, devoutly to be wished. The learning process causes some non-appealing characters to become more interesting and likable in the course of a book. This is the case with the main character in *Before I Fall* by Lauren Oliver:

> *In seven "Groundhog Day do-overs" of the day she dies, Sam learns more about her friends, her boyfriend, her teachers, her family, and herself.*

When readers first encounter Sam in the early chapters of the book, there is little to like about her. Sam is shallow, mean-spirited, and nasty. She and her pretty, petty friends rule the school, and they keep score. But there are a few tiny clues that Sam can be redeemed. After a few false starts, Sam changes, grows, and learns ... and she draws readers through the learning process along with her. The book starts as she is planning to have sex with her boyfriend, but on her final day, she makes significantly different choices.

The process of learning and changing opinions about a person, an action, or a situation is one that teens will recognize. Schools spend many years asking students to expand their minds, to learn about the world around them, to imagine the perspective of people whose experiences are very different from the routine and familiar. Teen fiction can be one of the most powerful tools in the education toolbox to broaden minds—and steamy teen fiction can help keep the attention of students on the work without making it *seem* like work.

Resources

Gurl.com. Available: *http://www.gurl.com*.

Kearney, Melissa S., and Phillip B. Levine. "Why Is the Teen Birth Rate in the United States So High and Why Does It Matter?" *The Journal of Economic Perspectives* 26, (2): 141-166.

CHAPTER 6

Kiss and Tell:
Having Sex with Students and Teachers

Losing Your Virginity: Presenting Your First SITL Program to a Group

SITL is unlike any booktalk you've ever presented for a group. It's weird to have another booktalker up there. The subject matter is guaranteed to make the teens in your audience snicker, and the teachers are often no help. If you allow it, they will try to hide their awkwardness by grading papers—in another room!

We recommend that you confront the embarrassing aspects of your program head-on, rather than try to pretend that this booktalk is pretty much the same as your booktalk about 20th century memoirs. It's different, and that's a good thing! Remember the key components of the presentation. You are presenting information about the mission statements and acquisition policies of two very different institutions, by:

- Highlighting the *differences* and the *strengths* of each collection; *and*

- Discussing *why* the collections are different; *and*

- Talking about awesome books with sexual content written for teen readers.

Getting over the Titters

You may wish to start with the "forbidden vocabulary" exercise described in Chapter 4. That will establish your intent to review books honestly, without ducking behind the scientific terminology for body parts like a coward. You weren't intending to do that, *were* you?

Promise your audience that you will use appropriate vocabulary during your booktalks—vocabulary that fits the books you talk about, so that they can use your language as an additional clue about the degree of "saltiness" in each work. There will *still* be a lot of giggling. The topic makes many people—teens *and* adults—nervous, and nerves often manifest as giggling, twittish behavior. How you deal with the situation is up to you. Ignoring the twits is a good first line of defense. Generally, other students will shush the gigglers.

If the behavior persists, sarcasm is a time-honored coping strategy (see sidebar). Threats are often effective: You can threaten to expel miscreants, or even threaten to pull the plug on steamy booktalks and tell them all about the latest books on bathroom remodeling instead. Be prepared to follow through on whatever you threaten or your credibility will be shot.

At some point early in the presentation, we simply state that there are books in the program that are not for everyone. They may be outright objectionable to some. We publicly acknowledge that the language used in some of the books is also the language that, if used in the school hallway, would earn a detention. Ask for a show of hands of those who want to continue. Anyone not raise a hand? Sincerely ask them if they would rather opt out. Of course, you have made arrangements in advance for this possibility and will offer an alternative to those who elect to leave. The last thing you need first thing tomorrow morning is to have parents call the principal because their student was forced to participate in a discussion they thought inappropriate.

These are remarks you should NOT make (but are funny):

"I'm sorry, is this the kindergarten class? I wanted to talk to ninth graders."

"At this rate, we'll never get to page 69!"

"I'm a librarian. Don't make me shush your ass."

Audience Reactions, and How to Use Them Constructively

Next, bring out the poster-sized flashcards with the annual book-buying budget for each institution, so that students can easily see that these are very different. For example, in our local school district, the book budget for some schools one year was (drumroll please) *not one single dime.* Even schools that were allotted money were not given much—sometimes less than $5 per student for the year. Recent budget surveys conducted by *School Library Journal* have indicated declining budgets in school libraries across the country, so perhaps your library has been affected, too.

Here's a great conversation to stage in front of a group:

Mary Jo: "The money allotted to the average high school in our state in 2011 was $5 per student." (*School Library Journal*)

Aarene: So, at $5 for every student, that buys a bunch of books, right?

Mary Jo: Well, that would hardly be right even if all we needed to buy was teen fiction. However, we also have to buy nonfiction books for the curriculum, barcodes, reference books, database access ... "

Aarene: "Ahhhh. Not so many then?"

By contrast, the 2011 teen materials budget for Richmond Beach's medium-sized branch of the enormous King County Library System was about $8,000 just for books. Reference materials, barcodes, and database access, as well as custom-cataloging and processing are coordinated at a system level—and paid out of a completely different budget. Of course, there are forty-eight libraries in the King County Library System, and each of them has a teen budget, so when students ask for a novel at their local branch, they are actually asking forty-eight libraries to find the book for them.

Aarene (aside): "It's good to be the King."

Future math-majors in the crowd will rapidly intuit that $8,000 can purchase a lot more books than $5, which might account for differences in the buying habits of the two institutions. But, there are other, even more significant, reasons for the differences in our collections. The biggest reason is the *mission statement* for each institution.

As we discussed in Chapter 1, we can rarely remember the precise phrasing of mission statements, so we printed them out in big print on a poster-board; the back of the poster with dollar amounts is convenient to use, if not completely ironic as well.

Depending on the class, we will either read our mission statements aloud, or ask a student to read each one aloud to the group. Then we "translate" the fancy wording of the mission statements.

After we've exposed everyone in the room to the differences in budgets and mission statements, we start talking about books. Remember you are talking to students who came to hear a Sex in the Library booktalk. They want to hear about steamy books. They also carry tales home, and we would really love to believe that conversations at dinner might indeed revolve around the library needing money. Don't spend more than ten minutes on the mission statement/budget part of the presentation, though. You want the students to be so excited about books that they will want your budget to increase, so you can buy more steamy titles!

It's important to note that we don't expect most of the student audience to immediately understand the significance between the differences in budget and mission. The rest of the presentation will serve to clarify these differences. How do you start talking about steamy books in relation to mission statements? We do it by starting discussions, which we hope will devolve into arguments.

Discussions, and How to Have Them

Start off the discussion by choosing a great book and giving a quick plot summary and review. For example, *Before I Die* by Jenny Downham:

> *Tessa is dying of leukemia ... but she has a few things she wants to do first.*

Because Tessa is dying, the time left to her is focused on her "bucket list," which includes drugs, sex, and rock and roll. Her list doesn't include falling in love, but it happens anyhow. She engages in behavior that we don't recommend for sixteen-year-olds. In contrast to most sixteen–year-olds that we know, however, Tessa doesn't have much to lose.

Ask audience members to raise hands if, based on this brief summary and review, they think that the middle school library should buy this book, and then ask for a show of hands if the public library should buy this book. If anyone in the audience has already read the book, allow that person to expand your review by asking for one or two sentences of description about it.

Don't allow a student to carry on about the book for too long, or to tell more than half the book. This is the first book you've shown—it should show how your style will help determine which books they want and how the booktalk is paced. If you beat the first novel to death, you will create a drag in the program and certainly lose your audience —and in a program like this, why would you trade away your potential crowd excitement? Pacing is up to you. While we want and encourage discussion, we also need to offer more book choices.

Next, ask somebody to speak *for* the book in each collection, and then ask for a volunteer to speak *against* the book in each collection. (If you don't get volunteers, assign the parts of speaking *for* or *against* the books, even if the students chosen don't agree with their assignment. Tell them they can change places for the next book.)

Finally, reveal the actual purchasing decisions. (In the case of *Before I Die,* the public library bought the book, but the middle school library declined to buy it.) Then, tell them why.

Repeat the exercise. Make the second book an easy decision, one that contains mild *"Star Trek* sex" content and minimal cussing. For example, *How to Get Suspended and Influence People* by Adam Selzer:

> *Fourteen-year-old Leon sarcastically narrates the events that occur when he decides to make an avant-garde sex ed movie as an assignment for his "gifted and talented" class. Leon's video is weird but comforting, irrational but informative, and ... very quickly, banned at school. No violence, some cuss words, a few on-page kisses, and frequent references to nudity and body parts, but everyone stays fully clothed, even when the garage blows up.*

Savvy audience members will note that the protagonist is middle-school aged, like them, and that the characters don't actually get naked. Most audiences will approve this book for school and public libraries, and indeed, it was, budget permitting, deemed an appropriate purchase for both places. Proceed by asking for an audience opinion about books that both institutions can buy and also books that only one library purchased. Allow and encourage discussion. Be thrilled if you can get audience members to argue—if they argue, you know they are sincerely engaged in the topic! Ask the teachers their opinions, too, to keep them from hiding behind those test papers.

It's fun to listen to a discussion about a book, especially when the student consensus is that it *shouldn't* be purchased for the school library collection—and then you show the school library copy. Often this is all you need to get the discussion started again. Once the audience is engaged, you can swing into full-bore booktalking.

The Inevitable Back Row

You can probably predict which students are going to try to side-track your presentation, so bring them into the discussion early. Ask at least one of them to defend the book or to justify not purchasing it. Make these students central to the discussion, so that they can't hijack it later with goofy comments. Even if they respond to your questions with silliness—a frequent occurrence when teens are asked to talk about sexual situations in a classroom group—answer them with respect and seriousness.

Often we ask a back row student to choose a book on the display for us to discuss. After your review, ask that student where s/he would put it: Public library? School library? A student in another part of the room may disagree. Allow some polite discussion and then move on.

You might expect that hecklers are a big problem with a topic like SITL, but they really aren't. We've had our share, however, and you will want to be ready. We don't have all the answers for handling them, but here are a few techniques and tips:

- *Use humor to diffuse a situation.* The student who stood up and shouted, "I don't want to hear about this!" could have been removed by the teacher, but instead, Mary Jo said, "Okay, vampires are maybe soooo last year, so I'll tuck in my fangs and Aarene can suggest a different topic." Aarene quickly found a book that was light and funny and allowed the student to calm down and save face. It's important to note that the one thing to avoid at all costs is making a student the butt of a joke. Humor should be helpful, and if you don't think you can do that without hurting a student's feelings, try something else.

- *Be a teacher.* Most of our booktalks are given to students. The "evil eye" is a time-honored crowd control technique that has been successful for centuries. Use yours. Use your physical proximity as well, if necessary. Stand next to the potential rabble-rouser, lay a gentle hand on his/her shoulder. You know how to do this.

- *Move it!* Simply move yourself, so the focus of the audience changes from looking at the heckler to looking at you. If you can move your body, so that the audience will need to turn all the way around to see the heckler, the movement will also refocus their attention. During one booktalk that contained some strong language, a student objected by standing up and yelling. Mary Jo stepped in with a soft-shoe and said (with apologies to *Stir Crazy*), "The words are bad, yeah, they're bad, so let's drop them and talk about this completely different book instead." Aarene, of course, had already grabbed a book to use.

- *Know your population.* Be aware of the feelings of your community and the individuals in your audience. Tell them about books they will enjoy, books that will challenge them, and books that will make them think.

- *Agree with them.* If a student, parent, or teacher objects to a topic, or to certain words or images, remind them that they have the right to an opinion and the freedom to leave the book on the shelf.

- *Use your best librarian voice.* Sometimes your audience wants to talk about a topic, and rather than talk to the group, they talk to the person next them, or behind them. Believe it or not, this happens a lot more with adults than with teens! Use your shushing skills. You do have the option to pick up on the topic they were discussing. And of course, you can simply request that the student speak with you afterward if he or she has an issue to discuss. Of course, none of these techniques are foolproof. Sometimes, you will simply have to ask a student to leave the room.

- It's important to encourage discussion while maintaining control of the audience. You know the pacing needed to illustrate the number of books that will allow choice at the end of the talk. This booktalk is partly a performance, but it's important that the information you present will allow students to decide which of the books in front of them they might or might not want to read—so pace your performance accordingly.

SITL and Collaboration

We couldn't do this program without teachers who also believe in the program and in the great discussions that occur in their classrooms as a result of it. Don't underestimate the assistance a teacher can bring to this program, even when they'd prefer to lurk in the back of the room grading papers. Many great writing and theme classes have resulted from SITL discussions. Here are a few pointers:

- *Prep the teachers in advance, so they can prepare the students.* Teachers can set parameters of acceptable behavior and establish consequences for unacceptable behavior in advance. Teachers can even help with seating arrangements at the beginning of the program. A pre-lesson in English or Heath Education creates a smoother transition from the classroom to the library.

- *Develop a relationship with teachers to make it easier for them to share concerns with you.* They know their students. We need the teachers' expertise and advice, because we don't know the individual students as well as teachers know them. If the talks are going to be held at the public library, teachers can even give extra credit for participation.

- *Librarians share a mission with teachers: They want great books, with great values that will get students thinking and talking and writing.* We offer quality YA literature. Even reluctant readers will find something appealing in this booktalk. Teachers have been trying to get those kids to read—*you* have the books that even struggling readers will want to read.

- *Be sure to follow up with teachers.* Write those memos and emails! Thank them, and send a booklist and a copy of the message to your principal to relate the wonderful discussions that took place during your program.

No one can sell the SITL library program more effectively than classroom teachers. If they understand that this program can make their own teaching more effective, they will gladly sign up for the booktalk and be your biggest supporters. Teachers don't brag much. You can praise them publicly. Do it.

Resources

Farmer, Lesley. 2012. "Brace Yourself." *School Library Journal* 58, (3): 38-38.

CHAPTER 7

Hearts Beating as One:
Having Sex with the PTA

Things That Parents Want to Know

If you ever suspect that parents don't read messages from the school librarian, insert a note in the next bulletin sent home by your school that students will be scheduled to have Sex in the Library on Thursday and Friday. If your phone rings, you will know that your suspicions were wrong.

In our experience, we've noticed that mostly, the phone doesn't ring. We'd like to suppose that the phone doesn't ring because our reputation as upstanding citizens and outstanding educators precedes us, and that we are awarded *carte blanche* by the parents and PTA of our community. We'd like to suppose that the parents in our community read journals published for professional librarians and are thus familiar with our innovative booktalking program. We'd like to suppose that the adults around us don't think we're kidding when we say stuff.

Instead, we're pretty sure that parents are so busy that a lot of printed and emailed material distributed by the schools just gets ignored, and they don't ever see our cute lip-print clip art and sassy invitation for them to join us.

We refuse to be unnoticed. So, we periodically invite ourselves onto the PTA meeting agenda. Our presentations for adults are similar to the programs for teen audiences. As always we emphasize the main points of SITL:

- Highlighting the *differences* and the *strengths* of the school library collection and the public library collection; *and*

- Discussing *why* the collections are different; *and*

- Talking about awesome books with sexual content written for teen readers.

With adults, however, we spend more time discussing *why* the collections are different.

What Adults Think Librarians Do All Day

Adults, especially those who haven't set foot in a school or public library in twenty years or more, often think they know all about libraries. For many grown-ups, the library is a quiet, studious place ruled sternly by a sensible-shoe and hair-in-a-bun lady who tolerates no nonsense—especially slang, slander, and physical intimacy. The librarian, in the opinion of these well-meaning folks, spends all day reading edifying literature, shushing people, and stamping out due-dates. It's a treat to bring a little reality to this worldview.

Talking about What Librarians Really Do All Day

Depending on the group, it's sometimes appropriate to introduce ourselves with a short description of our experience in library work: our educational background, our number of years working in libraries and working specifically with teen readers, and the various professional groups, conferences, and meetings we attend each year. We always mention that the school librarian has a degree in education and spent some years as a teacher, as well as attaining a master's degree in library science. In Aarene's case, she holds an education degree as well as an MLIS.

This information gently alerts our audience to information that is familiar to librarians but not necessarily familiar to non-librarians: *We are highly-trained, well-educated professionals—educators with qualifications beyond our ability to "shush."* For some parents, this is new information.

What (Some) Librarians Do and *Not* Do (and Why)

Without dwelling too long on our virtues, we proceed to the part of the program where we describe the mission statements of our institutions. We point out the differences between the school library and the public library and hope that somebody will notice that, while the school librarian must act *in loco parentis* as part of the school library mission, the public librarian must *not* do this. We have, on occasion, planted a shill in the audience to speak up about this point.

After the point is made clear, it's often followed by questions and usually some heated discussion. Some adults simply cannot believe that public librarians are not required to act as professionally-responsible parent-like entities. At times, it takes a lot of explanation to clarify this point. The furrowed brows do not clear in unison when we talk about the First Amendment's requirement that free speech be unabridged.

We talk about the difference between child pornography (which is illegal and not permitted in any library) and "regular" pornography (which is legal and protected free speech, and thus accessible in most public libraries *by any patron regardless of age, gender, creed, color, etc.*).

This is a tender and, for some communities, an unwelcome topic of conversation. We keep these discussions respectful, informative, and based on the mission statements of our institutions, rather than our feelings about pornography. We do not avoid the topic; neither do we dwell on it too long. We shift attention, instead, to our central topic for discussion.

Sexual Content in Books Written for Teens

After dropping the bomb that porn is freely available at public libraries, they are ready to learn that sexual content *appropriate for teen readers* is also available. Teen sexual content seems so much tamer and kinder by comparison. That's when we launch into our booktalks.

How to Mention the Budget, Tactfully (or Not)

One topic that we address lightly when talking to students, but emphasize when speaking to groups of adults, is the comparative budgets of the two libraries. Mary Jo's school library is significantly more limited in the number of books appropriate for purchase, because of its more constrictive mission statement; it is also significantly more limited in what it may buy because of a waning book budget.

We like to start this portion of the program with a couple of our most popular booktalks—discussions about books that are cool, exciting, well-written, well-reviewed, and recipients of respectable awards. A good top-of-the-stack choice is *Bloody Jack* by L.A. Meyer:

> *Disguised as a boy, Mary "Jackie" Faber hires onto the HMS Dolphin for adventures on the high seas. Pirates, shipwrecks, and tattoos in a foreign port are only the part of the adventure.*

Bloody Jack is a good choice to lead into the discussions, because it's an awesome, award-winning story that parents would enjoy reading as much as their teens would. *Bloody Jack* features a strong female protagonist who uses her skills to work against injustice. It features action, adventure, intrigue, suspense, and, in the still-growing series, some lovely incidents of *Star Trek* sex (See Chapter 3 for information about *Star Trek* sex). Sex isn't the focus of the stories; it is, rather, an important aspect of Jackie's growing-up process.

We talk about how much we enjoyed reading the Bloody Jack series. We disclose the number of readers on the waiting list for the books at the public library, and we read enticing excerpts that leave listeners wanting to read the rest of the book. Then, we disclose that the school library wouldn't own a single copy of this amazing, incredible, age-appropriate, well-reviewed, award-winning book and its sequels if not for the support of the PTA. This is not because *Bloody Jack* and its sequels don't meet the selection criteria, but rather because the school library budget cannot cover the cost of purchasing the entire series. Parents who thought they knew all about libraries are often taken aback when they learn that school districts and principals sometimes cut school library budgets significantly ... and sometimes cut the book budget entirely.

A small budget is understandable in times of economic stress, but PTA members who hear that the book budget *doesn't even exist* are often incensed, which is a convenient time for librarians to ask the PTA for some book purchasing funds. If you give them something amazing and worthwhile and desirable to fund, the PTA will find the money for you. And if you're lucky, they will also make a few phone calls to the school superintendent and principal to ask why that money isn't budgeted by the school.

Be gentle with this portion of the presentation. You want your audience to feel good about helping you buy books for the library. You don't want them so angry at school administrators that they concentrate on hollering instead of writing checks. It is absolutely okay, however, to provide a tactful pre-written letter or list of useful addresses that interested parents can use to influence budget committees to gain more financial support for your library. A good librarian always has a readily-available wish list that can be immediately printed and distributed.

Discussions and How to Have Them

PTA discussions are often lively once you've broken the ice with the group. Group members want to talk about the books, and they also want to hear what students say about the books presented. In the case of *Tomorrow, When the War Began* by John Marsden,

> *Seven Australian teens return from a camping trip to discover that their country has been invaded and they must hide to stay alive.*

parents are often interested to learn that teens are usually not bothered by the violence perpetrated by the main characters, including one scene of premeditated vandalism that results in death for several enemy soldiers. This book is also good for discussion because, although the first volume in the seven-part Tomorrow series is perfectly acceptable for most school library collections (despite the aforementioned violence), later books in the series are often found only in broader public library collections because of on-page sexual situations that arise between the characters. Because our school library and public library cooperate readily, all of the books in the series, and many others by the author, are available to our readers. It's good to let adults debate the relative merits of character problem-solving and the continuity of story over several books, and we are happy to give them topics like these to discuss.

We also spotlight a few books that may be of interest to the PTA members and their offspring but may only be appropriate for the public library collection. Here are a few books with strong writing that are guaranteed to get cross-generational ethical discussions rolling. *Beauty Queens* by Libba Bray:

> *A plane full of teen beauty pageant contestants crashes on a deserted island. Will they go all* Lord of the Flies*? Will the Sparkle Ponies prevail? Will they survive without straightening irons?*

To say that *Beauty Queens* is a satire is to understate the nonstop, laugh-out-loud comedic social commentary. The book contains on-page sexual situations, LGBTQ characters, feminists, corporation stooges, an insane dictator of a tiny country called ChaCha, and a little bit of cussing, so it is not appropriate for all libraries, but it is highly recommended for teen girls, parents of girls, teachers of girls, and anybody who ever talks to girls (including boys). It is probably impossible to read this book without laughing, and when teens and adults laugh out loud at the same book, a new angel earns a set of wings. *Flash Burnout* by L.K. Madigan:

> *Photographer Blake connects closely with Marissa, which creates a problem for Blake and his girlfriend.*

Blake's parents are wonderful and real and funny (his dad works as a coroner) and rife for jokes. Blake also wants to be a comedian and is constantly trying his one-liners on everyone, often getting a laugh from readers as well.

When aspiring-photographer Blake displays a picture of a homeless woman passed out in an alley, his classmate and friend Marissa reacts with recognition: This is her addict mother. When Marissa's mother is later believed to be dead, Blake and Marissa find that sex is the common connection for dealing with death. This novel sparks discussions about unintended consequences.

Of course, we also feature books owned by the school library, highlighting again the potential discussions that parents can have with their teens after reading these books. Sometimes, this has led to the creation of a lunch-time book discussion group to which parents are invited. Here's a great book for that type of group. *Unwind* by Neal Shusterman:

> *In a future world where those between the ages of thirteen and eighteen can have their lives "unwound" and their body parts harvested for use by others, three teens go to extreme lengths to uphold their beliefs—and, perhaps, save their own lives.*

Parents, no matter what their personal, political, and religious beliefs, have all experienced at least one brief moment in time where they thought to themselves, "I would love to send this kid back to wherever s/he came from." That is the core premise of *Unwind*— that youths can, for a variety of reasons, be legally and ethically "sent back" to be of use to society. It's a scary concept, and the book is excellent for booktalking and discussing in groups of mixed ages.

From Debates to Advocacy

Once parents get the hang of SITL, they enjoy debating the various merits of specific books. They will happily listen to your booktalks and chime in with their opinions about which topics they want to see in each location—and which topics make them uncomfortable.

Relax and enjoy this. They are giving you excellent feedback. Take notes if you like. These are people who are so interested in the education of their offspring that they voluntarily give up an evening or two each month (or more) to help improve that education. You want these people working *with* you. Within a single sixty-minute presentation, it is possible for thirty or more adults in your community to learn so much about the mission statements and selection policies of your institutions that they will become a rolling advocacy group for these policies.

These parents are the adults who are interested in what their students read. Their kids might roll their eyes, but they do listen when parents talk to each other and their offspring about books, even (and especially) books with sexual content. Parents can't always keep up with every single book that their kids want to read, so you want them to feel confident that they can ask you for guidance. SITL booktalks offer the perfect opportunity to build trust between your library and their home.

The public library also benefits from an involved PTA group. Because of the public library's broader mission statement, it can provide professional books written for parents on topics such as teen pregnancy, abstinence, and other teen health issues. The public library also offers larger religious fiction collections, as well as access to a wide variety of community resources. PTA parents value a personal introduction to the public library's teen services specialist, so use this opportunity to shine and get to know the active adult voters in your area.

Invite parents to your library! Your invitation needs to be sincere—you *do* need volunteers, don't you? If you have tasks for them, invite them and they will come. Some parents have admitted to Mary Jo that they volunteer to shelve books during the school lunch period in order to politely eavesdrop on teens, so that they can better understand the lives of their children and their children's peers. At times, parent volunteers will want to discuss the books they see while shelving. Make time for these discussions—they are worth gold.

More than once after meeting with parent groups, Aarene has been shyly approached in the vegetable aisle of the grocery store by parents who want to talk about what their kids are reading. Hold onto your carrots, and listen!

Understanding leads to agreement. It's likely that not everyone will agree with all of your purchasing choices, but once parents understand the decision-making process, they will be much more comfortable with it. And when they come across a book that makes them really uncomfortable, they will be much more likely to ask questions than throw rocks. Even better, they will bring some of the energy (and money) from those monthly PTA meetings to your library.

Chapter 8

Just Do It: Having Sex with Librarians

Things That Librarians Want to Know

We have presented Sex in the Library programs to groups of librarians for many years at conferences and conventions. Our focus for this audience is slightly different than for other groups, because, for the most part, librarians already know that a school librarian and a public librarian have different responsibilities. We do hit the three main points, as always:

- Highlighting the *differences* and the *strengths* of each collection; *and*

- Discussing *why* the collections are different; *and*

- Talking about awesome books with sexual content written for teen readers.

We sometimes spend a little more time talking about our specific mission statements when speaking to other librarians, and we certainly bring up the topic of budgets early-on. Librarians who come to our presentations want to know about the books: the newest, the hottest, and the books that might get them fired.

We are always careful to tell all of our audiences that the SITL booklist is not a "recommended for all readers and all institutions" list of books, but this point is especially important when speaking with other teen services librarians from a variety of institutions.

Lots of librarians who attend a conference have limited time and even more limited budgets, so they want to get the most information out of their experience. They cruise each session room at the beginning of each presentation, grab all the handouts, and move on to the next session room. This is standard practice and a good way to pick up a lot of "recommended reading/purchasing lists" in a short period of time.

Our booklist is *not* a recommended reading/purchasing list. It is, rather, a starting point for discussions, a list of titles that we consider worthwhile, but not necessarily appropriate for everyone. There are, in fact, books on the list neither of us recommend, a big reason not to appropriate our list as your recommended list. There is, to paraphrase a T-shirt sold by the National Coalition Against Censorship, "*Something on our list to offend everyone.*" That includes *you*. It also includes *us*.

Collection Development: Rinse and Repeat

We aren't going to cover the hows or whys of collection development from Chapter 1, but you will find us bringing them up again and again. If you don't have your selection policies to bolster your decisions, you will find yourself floundering when faced with additions to this most sensitive material.

Although we make light of the public library's decision to add these books through their, admittedly, rather broad selection policy, public librarians do not automatically draw a "free pass" card. Even with the broader mission of the public library, librarians are responsible to taxpayers to purchase books that are appropriate for the community. Some communities are incredibly diverse and need a library collection that reflects their diversity. Other communities are more homogeneous and need a library collection to support the interests and curiosities of the local residents.

No matter what type of institution a librarian works for, if the budget is limited (and whose budget is unlimited these days?), it is especially imperative that purchases be made with the support of the library selection policy and mission statement. Admittedly, school librarians often have a tougher job. Many see their job as "curriculum first." This is the unique role of the school library—the need to balance support of the constantly-morphing curriculum with the ongoing task to help students become responsible citizens by enabling them to develop the skills and absorb the knowledge necessary to evaluate their lives and the world around them.

Just as a health curriculum is a basic part of a good education, so is the fictional counterpart to that healthful existence. Reading fiction is integral to the learning process, and the school librarian is a teacher who works to help develop special skills, values, and attitude. Librarians work with teachers and administrators to ensure that library materials support the academic lessons, as well as the social growth of students. While the public librarian isn't directly charged with curriculum support, s/he often collaborates with teachers to ensure that the public library supports student needs whenever possible. When talking to librarians, we always try to highlight one of the Sarah Dessen books, like *Along for the Ride*:

> *Over the course of the summer, Auden tackles many new projects: learning to ride a bike, making real connections with peers, facing the emotional fallout of her parents' divorce, distancing herself from her mother, and falling in love with Eli.*

Sarah Dessen's books are all about decision-making, and we highlight her books, because every single student in a class will face many of the same decisions in their own lives. Dessen's characters face divorce, broken homes, new siblings from blended families, loss of friends, and making new friends. In other words, the characters are normal teens who confront issues common to the process of growing-up. By reading one of Sarah Dessen's books, teens are able to explore life choices through someone else's eyes and see how those choices play out. We admit that the romance helps.

It's good to know that Sarah Dessen has stated that she won't include on-page sexual situations in her stories. Almost any library institution can feel safe buying a Dessen book. (We do wish she would include more contraception conversations, though).

With a "safe" book like Dessen's on your shelf, why seek out controversy? Because controversial fiction books are as important to the well-being of students heading toward adulthood and adult decisions as any nonfiction curriculum-supporting book. Both needs are ongoing and must be supported if the library is to be a dynamic and current collection. Consider including a title like *Bumped* by Megan McCafferty:

> *In this up-tempo dystopian novel, teen pregnancies are not only normal, they are vital.*

Dystopic novels are traditional targets for socially-conservative groups, and the social commentary embedded in *Bumped* is certain to raise some eyebrows. Despite the narrative focus on pregnancy and sex, there is no on-page intercourse. The twist on social expectations in this story are so interesting that it's easy to overlook the important embedded messages about teen sexuality, sibling rivalry, religious tolerance, and the difficulty of living a life different from the one parents and society expect.

Both public and school libraries need balance. The nonfiction needs are important; the fiction needs are equally important. Controversial fiction is as important as "safe" fiction. It requires a balancing act. As much as we love her books, Sarah Dessen would never tackle the messages addressed by *Bumped*. Fortunately, many librarians are good at assessing the needs of library users and at providing a well-balanced collection. If you plan to advance fiction as well as nonfiction in your collection, make sure that you include a statement of this nature in your selection policy.

Of course, both the public and the school librarian need to gain the confidence of the teachers and administrators of their institutions if they are to be successful. We discussed this topic in Chapters 2 and 7, but it bears repeating: These relationships should clearly reflect the authority and responsibility of those roles. You need support and endorsement to have a successful library—not just with SITL, but in every program with which you are involved.

Just the Books, Ma'am

We all want to be the first librarian on the block to have chosen the latest greatest books for our collections. We want immediate street cred from the kids. But how do we get there when book reviews lack the specificity that we need?

In talking to groups of librarians at conferences, we display the books as we do for teens and parents. Many of the display books have already been read by the librarians at the workshop, because librarians love books. We ask our audiences if they have read the book we are currently displaying and may change the workshop accordingly. Because librarians want to budget their time effectively, we want to talk about the books they want to discuss, which are often books they haven't read yet. As conference participants ourselves, we understand the time constraints and need to find the workshop that fits our audience's needs.

We all read reviews and have our own trusted sources, online and printed. However, reviews alone cannot give you the in-depth analysis of the book *for your collection needs.* Only you can make that professional decision. Reading negative or even mediocre reviews can easily winnow out books. It is the good reviews that force you to make difficult choices with your ever-shrinking budget. Rather than relying on reviews or even blogs that can't give you the exact information you need, hearing two librarians discuss the pros and cons of a title can make the difference. There is a different level of understanding, for example, when a librarian who is willing to purchase LGBTQ books also wants to understand and prepare for the parents who might oppose those purchases.

Of course we recommend workshops like SITL in order to learn more about potentially controversial books, but to meet your immediate needs, we urge you to pick up the phone and call your counterpart's number: If you are a school librarian, introduce yourself to the local public librarian. Public librarians, call the school librarian at the end of the school day to get her undivided attention.

Public librarians read different books than school librarians read. By comparing notes, you will learn more about books that you probably wouldn't seek out unaided. Our local public teen services librarians meet with the secondary school librarians in our area once a year. Even if you aren't already partnered, an event like this is a great way to exchange needs and book reviews. There may be librarian groups in your area who meet and deeply discuss books. In Northwest Washington, we have WASHYARG (Washington Young Adult Reviewer's Group) that meets quarterly for school and public librarians to talk about books, give their honest opinions, and even (spoiler alert!) discuss the ending and whether it fits with the story. Don't have groups like this? Organize one!

Read the dreaded catalogs! At least page through them and look at the pretty pictures. If you have questions about suitability, check another library's holdings to borrow and read a copy before purchasing. If the book isn't available locally, try posting a query on a teen library services listserv like PUBYAC (*http://www.pubyac.org/*), emailing or Facebooking a colleague, or sending a note to the SITL blog (*http://www.sexinthelibrary.blogspot.com*).

Choosing a SITL (or any fiction) book is different for librarians, because we *don't* want an unbiased review! Publishers' catalogs are very good at dividing the nonfiction by subject area, but dreadful when adding teen fiction, often lumping them together no matter the subject of the novel, and often burying or eliminating controversial titles. You are tapping your foot, looking at your watch, and considering your inevitable time-to-guilt ratio—and are already feeling behind! Realistically, you can read only so many reviews and blogs. Like Facebook, it can be a time-sink. See a list of our favorite online resources in the Appendix.

Just as our SITL list is not your SITL list, our review sources and blogspots are not necessarily the ones you will want to read regularly (other than—blatant plug— our blogspot of course!) It is important to choose several that you will want to read regularly. You will know them when you find them. We don't have all the answers, and we are still looking (and lurking) ourselves. If you find any great ones, let us know!

Local independent bookstores may be another source of wisdom ... and a source for Advance Reader Copy (ARC) editions of books that you want to consider for your collection.

Remember the "cautionary tale" of Mary Jo's ordering the Quick Pick books in the Introduction? Librarians do not have time or money to waste. Consult lists like the Quick Picks with caution, do your homework, and offer to let parents or teachers pre-read new acquisitions before adding them to your collection.

In a recent WLMA (Washington Library Media Association) session, author Kimberly Derting complained about teen covers all looking alike a windswept (white) girl looking sad or pensive. Look at your shelf: It's true, isn't it? Yes we all do judge a book by its cover. Do you really have the budget for a book you know will take a booktalk to get it checked out?

Mary Jo says: *"How I Live Now* had a number of problems for me. We have all found a cousin to crush on. Then we grow up and move on. In this book, the character of Daisy is simultaneously thrown into the cousin-crush and a war, suddenly and powerfully. Rosoff writes the first-person narrative as though she were really living this. Daisy and Edmund have a bond 'so close' they can feel each other even when apart—except when they can't. The psychic connection falls flat for me, and because the ending depends on that bond, the storyline falls apart, as well. In the U.S., marrying your first cousin is illegal in more than half of the states, because crossing genes that closely can produce problems. In some cases, our audiences are thirteen years old, and I feel that the character of fourteen-year-old Edmund hit my 'ewwww' button. Talking about my reaction with students encourages them to also treat it seriously, to think deeply about how they see this relationship and perhaps pass the book by at this stage in their lives."

Aarene says: "I recognize that the book *Sold* is well-written, because if it were poorly written, it probably wouldn't bug me. The author did a ton of research, visited Katmandu and a village in the Himalayas, and interviewed not only girls who had been sold as prostitutes, but also village people, parents, and the people who took girls and sold them.

The entire book was very difficult for me to read. Before reading the book, I could not imagine what the lives of those girls must be like. After reading it, I can imagine their lives all too easily, and it haunts me. I would never keep this book out of my library and will recommend it to teens and adults, but I am not shy about admitting that it gave me nightmares."

Part II is our complete list of SITL books, with our unique (and sometimes opposing) reviews. This list is continually growing and constantly changing: To see the most up-to-date version of the list, visit the website: *http://www.sexinthelibrary.blogspot.com.* The blog format allows our readers to weigh in with their own opinions and experiences. Join us there and take part in the conversation.

Self-censorship

Mary Jo isn't shy about telling people how much the incestuous relationship between Daisy and Edward in *How I Live Now* by Meg Rosoff:

> *In a not-distant-future, Daisy is sent off to England to live with relatives and falls into a sexual obsession with her cousin Edmund. Separated by war, the two family members must survive and find their way home again.*

totally squicks her out, even though she is not usually very squeamish. Aarene isn't bothered by this book, although she's not as thrilled with the final chapters as the Michael L. Printz Award committee, which awarded *How I Live Now* their medal in 2005.

By contrast, Aarene had a hard time reading *Sold* by Patricia McCormick:

> *Lakshmi is thirteen years old when her stepfather sells her into a life of sexual slavery in an Indian brothel.*

How can you avoid self-censorship? And *should* you avoid it? It would be difficult to avoid buying a Printz award-winner like *How I Live Now*, especially since the parts that Mary Jo doesn't like are mostly *implied*—the sex occurs off-page. Teachers, parents, and students expect to find award-winning books in their library, and if you don't buy a particular one, prepare to defend your reasons.

"I don't like it" isn't part of a professional acquisition policy, obviously, but it *is* a perfectly valid opinion. Your library patrons value your judgment and they often want to know what you actually think of a particular book. In the case of the award-winning books that you don't care for, a good response to queries might be to hand over the book with a smile and a suggestion: "Read this for yourself, and then come back and tell me what you think of it. I'd love to talk about it with you."

Don't let fear cause you to censor your collection unnecessarily. In talking with teens about books with sexual content, we have noted repeatedly that they often censor their reading much more strongly than most adults will. If students aren't comfortable with a book because of the theme, the characters, the setting, or the sexual content, *they do not want to read it.*

As we were conducting a booktalk with a high-school class, for example, the subject of sexual abuse arose. We asked the students if they thought that the book *Living Dead Girl* by Elizabeth Scott,

> *When Alice was ten, Ray took her away from her family. She learned to give up all power, to endure all pain. She waited for the nightmare to be over.*

should be placed in the school library or the public library. This is a horror story of sexual perversion that reaches the "ewwww" factor in a hurry. Though never graphic, the obvious sex is both beyond horrible and very believable. We told the class that we would recommend it only for a high school class. One girl raised her hand and said, "Well, obviously it is in the school library, because I see our school barcode on it, but it shouldn't be here." We asked her for more details, and she told us that none of her friends could handle this particular book (her friends were in the class, too), although the theme would be okay in other books (that we had discussed). She thought perhaps we could put it "behind the counter" where students would have to ask for it.

A lively discussion ensued with students taking both sides on whether to include it or hide it. The conclusion for many of them: The book definitely belonged in the public library. Most of those who opposed the book in the school library conceded that they could ignore it on the shelves and not read it, so that the students with the opposite opinion could have access to it.

At this presentation—and at all others—we reminded the students that if a book doesn't meet their needs, they can and should return it to the library without reading it or without finishing it. This statement is empowering for students—and liberating as well.

The teachers were standing open-mouthed, and the librarian at the school was listening intently. The students noticed this. The adults in the room scored points for showing tenth graders that their opinions are valuable. The book was an instant hot item for *some students*, with readers offering their opinions to the librarian later.

Obviously, when we talk to librarians, they mostly want to know about the books: Which books are well-written? Which books are too steamy for my school or for my conservative community? Which books will all the kids be demanding by this time next month? Which books will blow the kids out of the sky? Often they ask Mary Jo: "Do you have this book in your school library now?" Our response is always, "Would YOU?" We aren't hedging; rather, we want decisions made locally. In doing that, you need to read these books yourself. Only *you* can make those decisions for your library. But if you mostly want to know about the books, make your next stop Part II.

Resources

WASHYARG. 960 Newport Way NW, Issaquah, WA. email: washyarg@kcls.org

CHAPTER 9

Morning After Pills:
The Reality of Fiction

Reasons to Include Fiction in the Library and the Curriculum

Teachers know that fiction can be a terrific way to impart *real* and current information about people, cultures, and events. Sometimes realistic fiction can also be frightening—to teens, to parents, and to members of the community. Research supports the use of fiction in the classroom. This chapter focuses on that research for the schools, as well as arguments for the inclusion of fiction with sexual content in libraries and classroom curricula.

There is nothing new about reading fiction in classrooms. Literature circle discussions are commonly used to enable students to read, query, and discuss a wide variety of selected books in small and large groups. Teachers also know that enthusiasm for a factual topic can be generated when students are first introduced to concepts through the experiences of fictional characters.

Much More Than "Just the facts, Ma'am"

Students are social creatures; they want to interact with each other in the classroom, the cafeteria, on their phones, and online. It is not surprising, therefore, that teens might view a character in a book as a "person"—one whose fictional experiences of joy and sorrow, triumph and adversity, accomplishment and failure, affect them deeply. Literature allows readers to feel intimately acquainted with brand-new experiences, cultures, and emotions—and for teens, these connections are vital to the learning process.

Young adults understand the virtual world. For many teen readers, book characters are friends. Mary Jo recalls an eighth grade student who was excited to visit Forks, Washington, "where Bella lives!" When Mary Jo asked her gently if she realized Bella was only a character in a book, M_____ exasperatingly said of course she did. However, when she returned from the trip, M_____ airily informed the entire library that, "Dr. Cullen had his own reserved parking spot at the Forks Hospital!"

It is important to make sure that the "facts" in works of fiction are accurate. In the *Roeper Review*, Gail N. Herman writes about the opportunities for cultural understanding and laments the fact that inaccuracies exist in many children's books. When choosing fiction books for social studies curriculum support, she seeks out novels written by "insiders," or those based on first-hand accounts, in order to allow students to see accurately inside a culture and allow readers to experience daily life alongside the characters. With fiction, a class can focus on ideas in depth by exploring a person's thoughts and actions through the narrative lens of a novel. We absolutely love *The Absolutely True Diary of a Part-Time Indian* by Sherman Alexie.

Photo credit: Mary Jo Heller

Research Supporting the Use of Fiction in the Classroom

Boyd, Josh. 2004. "A Different Kind of [Text]Book: Using Fiction in the Classroom." *Communication Education* 53, (4): 340-347. *http://ezproxy.kcls.org/docview/214119104?accountid=46* (accessed January 29, 2012).

Herman, Gail N. "Using Multiethnic Literature in the K-8 Classroom." 1999. *Roeper Review* 22, (1): 67-67, *http://ezproxy.kcls.org/docview/ 2066961 32?accountid=46*. (accessed January 29, 2012).

McCall, Ava L. "Teaching Powerful Social Studies Ideas through Literature Circles." *The Social Studies,* 101(4), 2010. p152-159. *http://ezproxy.kcls.org/ docview/759963365?accountid=46*. (accessed January 29, 2012).

Paul, Annie Murphy, "Your Brain on Fiction," *New York Times Sunday Review,* 17 March 2012, Opinion Page. *http://www.nytimes.com/2012/03/18/opinion/ sunday/the-neuroscience-of-your-brain-on-fiction.html?_r=3*.

Sutton, Amy. "School STD Programs Have Limited Influence on Teens' Sexual Behaviors." *Health Behavior News Service*. February 23, 2010. *http://www.cfah.org/hbns/archives/getDocument. cfm?documentID=22229*.

"Understanding Teen Dating Violence: Fact Sheet 2012." PDF Centers for Disease Control and Prevention National Center for Injury Prevention and Control. *http://www.cdc.gov/violenceprevention*.

Junior's diary and cartoons chronicle his simultaneously tragic and outrageously fun attempt to escape from life on the Spokane Indian Reservation.

Although not strictly autobiographical, the book depicts compassionately and accurately the culture of Alexie's childhood on the "rez."

Sex in the Classroom

Fiction books from the SITL list can add a variety of valuable perspectives to health class discussions about the physical, emotional, and ethical aspects of sex, relationships, and sexual decision-making. Students read nonfiction to access direct information and absorb content. They read fiction to understand that content and information.

Rather than focus on one genre or the other, teachers and students find that more learning can occur when fiction books are used to complement nonfiction reading. For example, when the class is required to read and understand teen dating violence by the U.S. Institute of Justice (*http://www.nij.gov/journals/261/teen-dating-violence.htm*), a savvy teacher might also distribute copies of *Breathing Underwater* by Alex Flinn:

Sent to counseling for hitting his girlfriend, sixteen-year-old Nick recounts his relationships with Caitlin and his controlling, abusive father.

The nonfiction text focuses on statistics and pure data, while the fiction text focuses on how Nick feels about hurting Caitlin, and Caitlin's conflicting emotions that allow this abuse to continue.

Dating Violence

- Dating violence is a serious problem in the United States. Many teens do not report it, because they are afraid to tell friends and family.

- Among adult victims of rape, physical violence, and/or stalking by an intimate partner, 22.4 percent of women and 15 percent of men first experienced some form of partner violence between 11 and 17 years of age.

- About 10 percent of students nationwide report being physically hurt by a boyfriend or girlfriend in the past 12 months.

"Understanding Teen Dating Violence Fact Sheet 2012." Centers for Disease Control and Prevention National Center for Injury Prevention and Control. *http://www.cdc.gov/ViolencePrevention/pdf/TeenDatingViolence 2012-a.pdf*

If the health teacher wants to focus on teen pregnancy and parenthood, you can suggest *The First Part Last* by Angela Johnson,

Bobby loves his baby daughter Feather, but he's only sixteen. When will he be able to hang out with the guys, eat pizza, and catch up on his sleep?

Or *Imani All Mine* by Connie Porter,

The unwed mother of a baby girl narrates her progress on the journey to adulthood in an increasingly violent world.

Or perhaps follow the ideas Gail Herman espouses and use Gaby Rodriguez' memoir *The Pregnancy Project:*

For her senior project, Gaby fakes her own pregnancy to learn more about the experiences of teen mothers.

"Talking to kids about contraception and decision-making doesn't lead to an increase in risky behaviors. You want to keep the lines open and foster communication," Susan Rosenthal says in *Health Technology Assessment*. Fiction can foster communication between students—and also between teens and adults.

Health isn't the only class that deserves to be enhanced by fiction. We encourage you to use your SITL list across the curriculum to broaden the audience for fiction books with some sexual content, because SITL books are *not* just about sex and relationships and pregnancy. For each of the titles suggested in this chapter, sex is merely one element in the lives of complex fictional characters. Offer a variety of titles to instructors, so they can choose material that is appropriate for their classes.

Ava McCall of the University of Wisconsin advocates using literature with social studies students because fiction can,

> *... challenge them to think more deeply about social studies content within texts.*
> *Students can compare different perspectives on the same historical event, such as the encounter between Columbus and the Taino, and reasons for including and omitting important ideas. Students can also note similarities and differences among cultures and current and historical events through literature circle discussions.*

The global world is becoming very small, and social studies and language arts teachers are embracing what fiction can help create in their classroom.

In addition, the Core Standards adopted by forty-five states encourage students in secondary schools to look at authors' insights into history, determining from many authors what that time period might tell us. Titles that might be appropriate for social studies or history classes include:

The Absolutely True Diary of a Part-Time Indian by Sherman Alexie:

> *Junior's diary and cartoons chronicle his simultaneously tragic and outrageously funny attempt to escape from life on the Spokane Indian Reservation.*

Does My Head Look Big in This? by Randa Abdel-Fattah:

> *Australian teen Amal has decided to wear the hijab, the Muslim headscarf, full-time.*

Bloody Jack (the series) by L.A. Meyer:

> *Disguised as a boy, Mary "Jackie" Faber hires onto the HMS Dolphin for adventures on the high seas. Pirates, shipwrecks, and tattoos in a foreign port are only part of the adventure.*

A Northern Light by Jennifer Donnelly:

> *In 1906, sixteen-year-old Mattie works at a summer resort, where she learns the truth about the death of a guest. Based on a true story.*

Sold by Patricia McCormick:

> *Lakshmi is thirteen years old when her stepfather sells her into a life of sexual slavery in a brothel in India.*

Current Events classes could consider adding:
Chanda's Secrets by Allan Stratton:

> *Although Chanda lives in a world in which illness and death are common, it is not a place where AIDS can be mentioned.*

Glass by Ellen Hopkins:

> *Kristina is determined to defeat her addiction to crack in order to keep her newborn child.*

Snitch by Allison van Diepen:

> *Julia DiVino and her best friend have vowed to never get involved with the various gangs at their high school. But when Eric Valiente shows up on the scene, everything changes for Julia.*

or even *For the Win* by Cory Doctorow:

> *All over the world, kids play video games ...for money.*

Obviously, these titles might be controversial in a classroom—perhaps too controversial for many schools. Encourage teachers to explore a variety of fiction titles in order to find the book that will fit best into their classroom and their curriculum plan. Also encourage those teachers not to avoid using SITL books for the same reason. Literature circles often include a variety of possibilities, and when any book is a group's choice, that selection is placed squarely into the hands of the student and parent, both of whom know their interests and maturity level.

Many middle school and high school teachers use science fiction literature as a way of increasing students' interest in science. There are many ethical and social ideas that can be explored in a classroom setting that reach deeper into emotions and values by focusing on a character who is facing a dilemma that could affect all of humankind. Science teachers are excited when students bring them books containing factual science mixed in with the fictional story. Readers appreciate when authors use actual science in books, such as Scott Westerfeld's *Peeps*:

> *When Cal arrived at college, he planned to lose his virginity. He didn't plan to contract vampirism.*

Considering vampirism as a parasitic affliction, Westerfeld salts his tale with scientific interludes about real (and disgusting) parasites! Read the section on nematodes during a booktalk. You will make a science teacher's day and create an extremely long hold list for the book—with science teachers at the top!
And *Life as We Knew It* by Susan Beth Pfeffer:

An asteroid has collided with the moon, and now everything has changed.

and *Half Brother* by Kenneth Oppel:

> *Ben gets involved with his parents' research project: teaching sign language to a baby chim-panzee. Then, funding for the project fails.*

These books offer teachers a chance to partner with the librarian on serious science. The Core Standards are adamant that texts, including fiction books, be evidence and research based. Classroom discussions of these books focus on the ethical and scientific dilemmas of fictional characters. Students who become immersed in a time period or geographic setting or character dilemma through a fictional story will be eager to research the concepts they encounter, while teachers will enjoy the unusual perspective provided by fiction. If a list of titles includes both school and public library books, all parties enjoy a wider choice.

Science fiction titles often especially appeal to boys. Science teachers surrounded by reluctant male readers may welcome the discussions sparked by books like *Be More Chill* by Ned Vizzini:

> *Jeremy swallows a pill-sized computer that supposedly will help him get whatever he wants.*

or *Girl Parts* by John M. Cusick:

> *David's parents decide to socialize their son through the use of a perfect robot girl—*
> *a companion with built-in timing for appropriate levels and times for kissing, touching, etc.*
> *If he goes too fast, he receives an electric shock!*

Both of these futuristic novels propose that technology has the potential to improve the social lives of boys, a concept welcomed by awkward young men.

For a more female-centric science reading experience, the class might read *The Espressologist* by Kristina Springer:

> *Jane invents a new "science" (which also happens to be a terrific marketing tool for the coffee shop where she works).*

In this book, Jane proposes the theory that a coffee drink preference can indicate romantic compatibility. She tests the theory by matching up customers at the espresso stand based on their coffee preferences. She further validates the theory when she tries to skew her data in order to match herself with Will, although their coffee orders obviously clash. Jane's is a large, iced, nonfat mocha, no whip. What drink will match to reveal her true love? The book is fluffy

Neuroscience

Neuroscience suggests that reading fiction improves your social skills. "... individuals who frequently read fiction seem to be better able to understand other people, empathize with them and see the world from their perspective ... as we identify with characters' longings and frustrations, guess at their hidden motives and track their encounters with friends and enemies, neighbors and lovers. It is an exercise that hones our real-life social skills ..."

Paul, Annie Murphy. "Your Brain on Fiction." *New York Times Review.* 17 March 2012. *http://www.nytimes.com/2012/03/18/opinion/sunday/the-neuroscience-of-your-brain-on-fiction.html.*

Science Fiction in the Engineering Classroom

"Although science fiction has appeared in science and physics education for many years, the genre has not been widely used to augment engineering education. … the genre can … be used to illustrate the implications of technology and society, along with the many ethical considerations of engineering."

Segall, A. E. "Science fiction in the engineering classroom to help teach basic concepts and promote the profession." *Journal of Engineering Education*, 91(4), 419-419. 29 January 2012. *http://ezproxy.kcls.org/docview/217946043?accountid=46.*

chick-lit and not intended to instruct readers in the use of scientific method, and yet it works for that purpose.

Tough Stuff

Today's teens sometimes face issues outside of the classroom that are tough to understand and even harder to bear. They live in an increasingly complex and increasingly dangerous world. Sharing fiction that contains accurate information about complex subjects can make those tough topics easier to grasp …and possibly, make tough situations easier to survive.

Teens (and adults) can seek the answers they need in fiction as well as nonfiction. Teens read far more fiction outside the classroom than assignments might indicate. Novels allow readers to become emotionally involved with the characters and their decisions about situations, morals, and values. The focus in fiction on "what ifs" and "if I were" draws the reader into the setting. Great fiction puts the reader *there*—making the decision and witnessing the situations created by those decisions. As in real life, at times, this turns out poorly.

In *Before I Fall* by Lauren Oliver:

> *In seven "Groundhog Day do-overs" of the day she dies, Sam learns more about her friends, her boyfriend, her teachers, her family, and herself.*

Sam must repeatedly live over a single day, making different decisions about how each day (and her life) will change. Each time, the reader makes judgments about her decision and relives the day with Sam, hoping the decision she made is the correct one this time. Even the ending of the book asks readers to decide if the last decision she made was really the best one.

A choice that seems "good enough" at first might, in books as in real life, lead to disaster. For example, *You against Me* by Jenny Downham:

> *Things fall apart when fifteen-year-old Karyn says she has been raped at a party. She refuses to leave the house or even participate in life.*

We find the situation in Downham's book reflected in the Center for Disease Control statistics: In 2012, about 10 percent of students nationwide report being physically hurt by a boyfriend or girlfriend in the past twelve months. Karyn alleges she was raped at a party. The fact that she was both drunk and made advances toward Tom complicates the fact of the rape. Was this why she didn't report it until later?

You Against Me allows readers to examine Karyn's brother's changeable motives, as well as Tom's motives, and to ask the hard questions: Is rape ever justified? What responsibility did Karyn have? This is an intricate novel about a complex situation, with an ending that begs for discussion. The topic is tough and the writing is not simple; it is not a book for every teen.

A less edgy—though still controversial—book on the same topic is *Speak* by Laurie Halse Anderson:

> *A traumatic event near the end of the summer has a devastating effect of Melinda's freshman year in high school.*

We consistently recommend *Speak* to eighth graders at the school library and the public library. Melinda is a just-graduated eighth grade girl who is so impressed when a senior boy pays attention to her that she drinks alcohol at a party to impress him, and then cannot escape the rape that ensues. The rape is offstage and handled very tactfully. Melinda finds both her voice and her courage by the end of the book. In school, we refer to this as a "cautionary" tale, both because the eighth grade girls graduating will be invited to parties where there is drinking, and because they are so similarly vulnerable. This YA novel has been regularly recommended by many English teachers, librarians, and parents, and if this highly-popular book helps only one girl, it will be worth it.

It's important to note that, although originally published in 1999, *Speak* is still frequently challenged by individuals who want the book removed from library shelves. In 2010 a challenge by Wesley Scroggins in Missouri led to a vitriolic exchange of web postings between attackers and supporters of the book.

Both *Speak* and *You against Me* raise questions about personal responsibility. The authors portray flawed characters who are very much like the normal teens we talk with every day. Not every teen reader is ready for either book, and neither book is recommended for a recent rape victim! Instead, the books can be helpful, insightful reads for teens who may face a rape situation in the future, as a victim or as the friend or family of a rape victim. Learning tough stuff from fiction makes learning tough stuff from real life a little bit easier.

Original (now reposted from original) citation from the *News Leader, Springfield, MO*:

Scroggins, Wesley, "Opinion: Filthy Books Demeaning to Republic Education," *News-Leader*, 17 September, 2010. *http://www.news-leader.com/article/20100918/OPINIONS02/112020001/Filthy-books-demeaning-Republic-education*

Laurie Halse Anderson's reply with additional resources:

Anderson, Laurie Halse, "This guy thinks *Speak* is pornography," *Mad Woman in the Forest.* 19 September 2010. *http://madwomanintheforest.com/this-guy-thinks-speak-is-pornography/*.

SITL Books Serve More Than One Purpose for Readers

Sometimes, when a teen picks up a copy of *Witch Eyes* by Scott Tracey,

> *Braden has "witch eyes" that give him a unique power, but also make him a pawn in the feuding witch dynasty between his father and his new-found love, Trey.*

s/he is simply looking for a good supernatural story. But students might also read this book to learn more about gay teens—for themselves or for a friend. They may be looking for a book that explores the energy that comes with the frustrations of being a teen, upset because they are not being treated as an adult. Teen angst will always be popular in teen novels, because it will always exist. Teens are *always* sure they are the *only* ones who are this fat, this smelly, this unable to talk with the opposite sex. Vampire and werewolf characters are popular, because they are examples of outcasts who sometimes still get to be heroes.

Of course, reading about angst can sometimes exacerbate the readers' feelings of angst, so teachers and librarians should endeavor to be sensitive about the books they recommend to fragile students. Some teens are ready to understand and discuss the idea of teen suicide. This topic is covered in eighth grade Health Education; however, statistics and facts may be easier for an eighth grader to handle than the emotions that surround the topic in a work of fiction. When a teen asks for a novel about teen suicide, adult alarm bells should sound. We should proceed cautiously and with great care. Only when we are satisfied that a *book* is what the teen actually needs should we hand over a powerful novel on the topic written for teens, such as *Thirteen Reasons Why* by Jay Asher:

> *After the death of his crush, Hannah Baker, Clay Jensen receives a recording from Hannah. She chronicles the circumstances that led to her suicide and the thirteen people who played a role in the terrible choice she made.*

or *Crash into Me,* by Albert Borris:

> *Four teenagers make a pact to road-trip across the country, visiting the sites of celebrity suicides until they get to Death Valley, where they will take their own lives. But, as the trip progresses, they must ultimately decide if life is worth living despite the pain.*

Requests for books about abuse should sound similar adult alarm bells. This subject, like the topic of teen suicide, should be carefully considered in the library collection. Is that student looking for the book because he or she is abused? Because a friend is abused? Because they simply like gritty novels?

We understand that asking for a book on a topic like rape, suicide, or abuse may be a disguised request for help, and we want to be alert for this. That doesn't mean those books don't belong in our collections, because they do. Abuse, particularly sexual abuse within the family, is so hard to talk about. For example, the book *Identical* by Ellen Hopkins

> *In her mother's absence, Kaeleigh becomes the object of her father's sexual attention. Her identical twin Raeanne begins to abuse drugs and alcohol and laments that her father doesn't love her, because she gets none of his attention.*

goes beyond gritty, and it asks questions that many adults have problems answering. Raeanne looks forward to the abuse because, in her mind, it means her father loves her. That is a concept so foreign to the values held by many adults that we have difficulty even talking about it. Yet, it is important that teens have access to this powerful book. This is even one of the teen books we suggest to the PTA, because, while it elicits discomfort when we discuss it, we also see understanding glances.

School librarians have ready access to help in the form of school counselors, who are can be better equipped to talk with teens. Public librarians have access to immediate service providers, such as a local HopeLink office and other crisis care providers.

We know that many adults have "discovered" teen lit in recent years, and that they often recognize the high quality of the writing found in many books written for young adults. We also recognize that the central issues of teen novels—issues of identity, of frustration and fear, and of familial and social discord—are central to the lives of adults as well as those of teens. We encourage parents and teachers to read teen literature on tough topics and to talk about what they read with other adults and with teens. It is one of the reasons we send our book reviews to our local newspapers and places adults would more easily access them.

Minority Groups and the Library

In recent years, "gay literature" has finally found its way into mainstream teen literature. Homophobia exists in the classroom, in the teachers' lounge, in the public library staff rooms, on the streets, and in many homes. Good books about LGBTQ (lesbian, gay, bisexual, transgender, and questioning) teens are becoming more widely available. No matter what we or you or anyone thinks in regard to students' self-identified

---

Don't Let Me Go

Nick came "out" last year, and this year, he wants to make an attempt to stand up for himself at the very beginning of his senior year. He also wants to make other students aware that being a gay teen does not affect straight students. He wears a gay-themed T-shirt to school that gets him sent to the vice-principal, Mr. Wolf.

On Wednesday I found a brown lunch bag secured to my locker with a piece of masking tape. I peeled it off.

"What's that?" Juliet asked.

I shrugged, stuck my hand in, and pulled out a soft, gray T-shirt. I shook out the shirt to read the slogan. I grinned as I turned it around for Juliet to see.

"'I can't even think straight,'" she read. She looked up at me, her mouth agape. "Who put that there?"

I looked inside the bag and all around it for some clue, but there was none. "I have no idea."

I handed Juliet the shirt and let my backpack slip to the floor.

"Nooo." She laughed as I tugged my T-shirt over my head to a few wolf whistles and shoved it in my locker. Juliet stared. "Damn, Nate. That's better than a triple-shot latte for getting the old heart started in the morning."

I grinned and pulled the gray T-shirt over my head.

"You are a troublemaker, Nate Schaper."

By lunch I was back to wearing my shirt inside out. After that, more T-shirts started showing up anonymously on my doorstep, in the mail, again on my locker, under the wiper on my windshield. They said things like Your gaydar should be going off right about now *and* Yes, I am *and* Ask. Tell. *One of my favorites was* I see gay people. *I wore a different shirt to school each day, except for the one that read* The rumor's right. But unless I'm fucking you, it's none of your business. *I thought that might be pushing Mr. Wolf too far.*

Trumble, J.H. *Don't Let Me Go.* Kensington Books, 2012. p112. Reprinted with permission, Kensington Books.

sexual identity, all adults need to be a part of the safety net. All teenagers deserve to be safe. In Dr. Ann Curry's study of Canadian Public Libraries, "If I Ask, Will They Answer?" (*Reference & User Services Quarterly*, 45(1), 2005, p 65-75), one adult posing as a teen was sent to different public libraries in Vancouver, British Columbia. She asked questions about fiction and nonfiction materials the library might have on LGBTQ topics, fiction as well as nonfiction. How would your library respond to this student? What materials does your library offer?

In this book, we have not devoted a chapter to the LGBTQ group, nor to Black teens, or to Asian teens, or any other group separately. Instead we have incorporated the books that focus on these teens in the appropriate places for the plot or theme. As with all the books we highlight, it is the theme, the choices, or the decisions that receive the emphasis on inclusion in our list. We are always seeking more diversity on our list, but dislike those lists that segregate books for ethnic and other minorities.

Yes, there is sex and sexual decision-making in all the books on our list. This should not come as a shock by now; however, the focus of any YA novel is the fusion of choices, story, and themes. A teenager's need for acceptance is a crucial theme in nearly every YA novel. We cannot ignore any teens in our population, and we must be very careful what literature we hand them. LGBTQ books are not solely for LGBTQ teens. Books featuring Black teens are not limited to that reading population. The fact that Micah in *Liar by* Justine Larbalestier:

> *Compulsive liar Micah promises to tell the truth after revealing that her boyfriend has been murdered.*

is a Black teen is obvious, then ignored. We hope that motifs such as gender, race, and ethnic background become moot points in our time. We know they are not. However, even if universal acceptance by other teens is not possible, we hope that eliminating harassment is.

Resources

Anderson, Laurie Halse, "This Guy Thinks *SPEAK* Is Pornography," *Mad Woman in the Forest.* 19 September 2010. Available: *http://madwomanintheforest.com/this-guy-thinks-speak-is-pornography.*

Boyd, Josh. 2004. "A Different Kind of [Text]Book: Using Fiction in the Classroom." *Communication Education* 53, (4): 340-347.

Curry, Ann. "If I Ask, Will They Answer?" *Reference & User Services Quarterly.* (Fall 2005): 65-75.

Herman, Gail N. 1999. "Using Multiethnic Literature in the K-8 Classroom." *Roeper Review* 22, (1): 67-67.

Hopelink. Available: *http://www.hope-link.org.*

McCall, Ava L. "Teaching Powerful Social Studies Ideas through Literature Circles." *Social Studies*, 101(4), 2010. p152-159.

Paul, Annie Murphy. "Your Brain on Fiction." *New York Times.* (17 March 2012): SR6. http://www.nytimes.com/2012/03/18/opinion/sunday/the-neuroscience-of-your-brain-on-fiction.html?pagewanted=all&_r=0.

Rosenthal, Susan, "School STD Programs Have Limited Influence on Teens' Sexual Behaviors." Health Technology Assessment in *Education Research Report*. 25 February 2010. Available: *http://educationresearchreport.blogspot.ca/2010/02/school-std-programs-have-limited.html*.

Scroggins, Wesley. "Opinion: Filthy Books Demeaning to Republic Education," *News-Leader,* 17 September 2010. Available: *http://www.newsleader.com/article/20100918/OPINIONS02/112020001/Filthy-books-demeaning-Republic-education*.

Segall, A. E. "Science Fiction in the Engineering Classroom to Help Teach Basic Concepts and Promote the Profession." *Journal of Engineering Education,* 91(4), 419-419. Available: *http://ezproxy.kcls.org/docview/217946043?accountid=46*

Sutton, Amy. "School STD Programs Have Limited Influence on Teens' Sexual Behaviors." *Health Behavior News Service*, February 23, 2010.

CHAPTER 10

Writing It on the Wall:
Reviewing Steamy Books

This is the homework chapter. You knew there would be work involved—whether you are a librarian, teacher, student, or parent. Even if you are not part of the aging process, our little brains can only hold so much without starting to push through some stuff that we just don't often use. Translation: You do need to write it down. Reviews will jog your memory when your brain is tired, whether you are prepping for a booktalk, or whether you just want to remember a plot or the names of characters. This is not a "Do as I say, not as I do" sort of chapter. It is a memo to write, because you will remember it better (according to your third grade teacher), and also because you need the PR. It's just the *write* thing to do! (groans accepted)

Writing a Book Review, What to Do with It

To optimize our always-scarce time as librarians, whenever we read and review a new book for the SITL list, we make a practice of "three-cycling" the book review, using each book review in at least three different ways. Here's our starter list of places to use and re-use book reviews:

- We post reviews on the SITL blogspot, so that readers all over the world can access them.

- We send the reviews to our colleagues, friends, and family via email and Facebook. Our co-workers enjoy reading teen literature, and they are just as time-crunched as us. They don't necessarily make the time to cruise our blog, but a review delivered to their in-box can help them choose a teen book they will enjoy. In smaller libraries staffed by "non-librarians" or in larger libraries staffed by "non-teen-specialists," it is empowering for staff to have some familiarity with teen literature, so they will feel they can talk knowledgeably with teens about books. Sharing reviews of great books connects these adults with books *and* teens. With few exceptions, we make it a practice never to "friend" someone under eighteen on Facebook, but we always answer emails from students who request books.

- We send the reviews to the PTA newsletter and the local small-town newspaper. Book reviews make excellent space-fillers, which is something that editors love to have on-hand. Sometimes our reviews will be printed in these publications months or even years after we write them, depending on the space available.

- We print out copies of the reviews for our booktalking notebook. If our brains go empty when we are trying to remember which books we want to recommend, the notebook serves as a useful memory tool.

- We post the book reviews in the library, adjacent to the shelf where the book normally "lives." This technique, borrowed from big-box stores, really boosts circulation of spotlighted items.

- We print selected book reviews on bookmarks and leave the bookmarks stuck in "read-alike" books. For example, a bookmark review of a the dystopic world of *Ready Player One* by Ernest Cline,

> *Wade Watts lives mostly online.*

A Sample Book Review

TITLE/AUTHOR: *All These Things I've Done* by Gabrielle Zevin

HOOK: Sixteen-year-old Anya is the heir to to the "family business": chocolate.

PLOT DESCRIPTION: In the year 2083, chocolate is a controlled substance, and Anya's family is a modern mafia, importing chocolate and other prohibited luxuries to New York. Her parents were both killed in mob hits, leaving Anya in charge of a younger sister, a brain-injured older brother, and a dying grandmother. Anya considers herself the least romantic girl in the world ... until she falls in love with Win Delacroix, the son of New York's new assistant DA.

Then Anya's ex-boyfriend nearly dies from eating a poisoned bar of Balanchine Chocolate, and the story begins to twist and turn and twist again. Sex: 3; Cussing: 0; Violence: 2 *alcohol, bullying, death, drinking, drugs, dystopia, grieving, kissing, nudity, sexual situations*, Star Trek *sex*, and *violence*.

READER REACTION: Crime, drama, chocolate, forbidden romance ... and this is only the first book! At least two more in the *Birthright* series are already in the works.

ALERTS: This book contains some sexual situations (including a steamy "near miss" scene in a hotel room) with no actual body parts on the page. There is no cussing, some not-very-bloody mob violence, and several scenes of alcohol consumption by teens; in 2083, alcohol is legal for all ages, but coffee is not.

RECOMMENDED AUDIENCE: Recommended for readers age twelve to adult.

might be placed in a copy of *For the Win* by Cory Doctorow:

All over the world, kids play video game ... for money.

We share our book reviews with regional review groups such as WASHYARG (the Washington Young Adult Review Group) at the quarterly meetings and in the printed material (affectionately known as "The WashRag") distributed to members.

And, of course, we include tiny bits of the book review on some of our booktalking lists for Sex in the Library!

Structure for a Book Review

After years of reading books and writing reviews, we've streamlined our book review process. We always try to include a book cover illustration, and we put that at the top. We also fully admit to students that WE judge a book by the cover, even though they told us not to do that in library school. The book cover is followed by the following:

- *Title and other important information.* Depending on where you are using the book review, you will sometimes provide only the title and author, but you may want to keep publisher, ISBN, and retail price in your original review notes, in case you need to retrieve that information easily.

- *A "hook" sentence or two.* This can be the first sentence of the in-person booktalk, an excerpt from the book, or an extremely brief summary of the plot. The hook should be short and catchy. Depending on the audience for this review, you may want to just note the page number of the excerpt you like, so that you can find it again on the day of your booktalk.

- *Plot description.* The age(s) and gender(s) of the protagonist, the setting, and the conflicts encountered. No spoilers! As a general rule, we don't talk about the last half of the book. As we tell the students, "This is a booktalk, not a book report." It's honestly no fun to read halfway into the book and find no surprises. A longer excerpt can also be placed here, if a short excerpt wasn't used as a hook.

- *Reader reaction.* This is the place where we talk about what we *personally* enjoyed (or did not enjoy) about a book: the writing style, the characters, the illustrations, etc. If the author gives accurate descriptions of an activity, a process, or an object, it gets mention here. If the book is scary, gross, or tear-jerking, this is the place to talk about those aspects. In a booktalk or in a personal conversation, an astute or lively student remark could be put here too—for you to use with other booktalks, the PTA, or with teachers. In fact, solicit personal comments that could be used in a variety of ways in your reviews or booktalks. You don't have to name names, so be sure to protect the innocent.

- *Alerts.* Because many of our book reviews are read by adults who may want to share the book with teens, we include a list of potential pitfalls at the end of our book reviews. Teen readers tell us that they appreciate the alerts also—nobody likes being ambushed by bad language if they were expecting a "no cussing" book. In addition to sexual content, it also seems that most people appreciate a heads-up about violence and gore. We avoid "rating" the books in the same way that movies are rated, because we find that some people don't mind cussing but don't want books with demons, or they seek out books with realistic street-lingo but prefer to avoid on-page sexual situations. The movie-rating system is too general, and we like to provide very specific alerts for each book. Our alert labels include (but are not limited to): abstinence, alcohol, bullying, child abuse, cussing, death, drinking, drugs, dystopia, gay friends, grieving, homosexuality, incest, kissing, magic, masturbation, nudity, paranormal, pregnancy, prejudice, prostitution, rape, religious beliefs, safe sex, sexual questioning, sexual situations, "*Star Trek* Sex," STDs, straight friends, suicide, and violence. We know many parents, teachers, and even students who skip the review and go straight to the labels. It is not our recommended approach of looking at a review, but may give a quick idea of the content, if not the crux of the book. Remember that we also review books we dislike, so if you are a die-hard label-reader-review-skipper, be warned!

- *Recommended audience.* This can be an age- or grade-related recommendation or it can be more detailed. If a book will mostly appeal to girls, we say so. If it works well with historical fiction assignments, we mention that. If it is a good book for group discussions, we include that recommendation in this part of the review.

Reviewing "Bad" Books

When writing reviews, our goal is to accurately describe the book, so the reader can make informed choices about whether or not to buy, borrow, read, and recommend the book. This goal sometimes conflicts with the traditional advice, "If you can't say something nice, don't say anything at all." Talking about the strengths *and* the weaknesses of a book is essential to provide good information to the reader. We do know that you have so much more to say during a bad review and could even wax poetic about the points or devices you didn't like, but that wouldn't accomplish much here, would it? Save that for the staff room/water cooler/librarian meetings.

Book reviews published in *VOYA* magazine address the gap between quality and popularity directly by scoring separately the quality of writing and popularity with teen readers of each title. Remember that a book doesn't have to be *good* to be *enjoyable*.

In fact, a book that an adult reader thinks is cliché, predictable, shallow, sappy, or didactic may be exactly the kind of story that appeals to certain teen readers. A teen who feels overwhelmed with life changes might be comforted by books with predictable characters, clichéd writing, and a plot that is described in full by the cover illustration. Readers who want a book to provide escape from their lives might be comforted by unrealistic fiction. A youth facing tough choices is sometimes thrilled to find a book that hammers home a didactic message to support the decision-making process, even in a heavy-handed manner. Sappy romances and tear-jerking teen tragedies appeal to readers for a variety of reasons. For these reasons, we try very hard to be sparing with the label "not recommended."

Instead, we like to use the "read-alike" strategy: recommending *good* (or *better*) books to readers without disrespecting the books they already enjoy. For example, teens who enjoy smart-talking male narrators like Leon in *How to Get Suspended and Influence People* by Adam Selzer:

> *Leon sarcastically narrates the events that result when he decides to make an avant-garde sex education movie as an assignment for his "gifted and talented" class.*

might also enjoy the troubled-but-smart narrator in *King of the Screwups* by K.L. Going:

> *After getting in trouble yet again, popular high school senior Liam, who never seems to live up to his wealthy father's expectations, is sent to live in a trailer park with his gay "glam-rocker" uncle.*

We didn't love *How to Get Suspended*; however, we recognize that teen readers *do* enjoy it. And that's okay: Our review includes notes about the predictability, along with the comedic strength, of the characters and situations in the book.

We are honest (though sometimes tactful, in a nod towards that motherly advice about saying something nice) in our reviews: If the story is poorly-written, we'll put a note about that in the review. Being poorly-written, predictable, and clichéd is *not* necessarily reason to avoid purchasing a book, especially in public libraries charged with providing popular titles. The steady demand for books in the Gossip Girl series overrides our knowledge that the books are exceptionally flawed. When we talk to students who love Gossip Girl, we try to point them towards other books like *The Luxe* by Anna Godbersen:

> *In Manhattan in 1899, five teens of different social classes lead dangerously scandalous lives, despite the strict rules of society and the best-laid plans of parents and others.*

The Luxe series appeals to the same audience as Gossip Girl, but is slightly redeemed from the "trashy fiction" pile by the historical setting.

We are very careful when reviewing books that contain inaccurate information. If there is a single factual mistake, we will cite that mistake specifically in the review, as we did in the review of *Jumping Off Swings* by Jo Knowles:

> *Every time Ellie hooks up with a new guy, she's sure that there will be more to the encounter than sex, and that she will finally feel loved. But the "one-time thing" with eager virgin Josh gets much more complicated when Ellie gets pregnant.*

"The condom slipped off" is an unlikely plot-point, and we noted this in our review of the book, along with some criticism of less-than-terrific writing style. Teens could research the idea of a condom "slipping," themselves, but it may be easier to point them to a reference like *Go Ask Alice* (not connected to the book by the same title), a Columbia University website, that states a condom, correctly used, is 98 percent effective. That two percent includes ripping and slipping; as part of that two percent, "slippage" is very minor. We don't like teens gathering inaccurate information from a fiction book. The story still has redeeming qualities, however, including some excellent-but-flawed adult characters.

There are, of course, some books that we don't recommend to be purchased by any library for any readers. The books we find unredeemable are those filled with sexist or racist characters, inaccurate information, heavy moral messages, poor writing, and a completely unbelievable plot.

In the uncomfortable cases where a book is highly-sought-after by teen readers but also highly inaccurate, we find that talking to students one-on-one is a good strategy. Many teens want to read popular faux memoirs like *A Child Called It* and *Go Ask Alice* without understanding that the narratives are mostly, if not entirely, fictional. As adults charged with educating teens, we want to give them access to the material and also make sure that they are aware of the untrustworthy nature of information presented in these books.

In some cases, new information about purported "nonfiction" accounts demonstrates that the information in the book is untrue or plagiarized. These controversies make great conversation during booktalks. Teachers and students appreciate the librarian's awareness of up-to-date information about books and authors.

Whom Do You Trust?

This is your best time to shine. Your students trust you. Their parents want to know you better *and* to trust you. Your teachers need to know about the books they don't have time to read themselves. They all want to know what you think about a book. They may not agree with you, and that's okay, too. Adults often don't agree with each other. You want to encourage discussion. As they read your reviews and listen to your booktalks, students understand your point of view and even your quirky style. Getting to know you helps build their trust.

Your goal is to put the right book into the hands of each student, and it is your intention to understand that student. One way to accomplish this goal is to have students write reviews. Does your school or public library have a website or blog where reviews could be posted? Some students are posting good book ideas for their friends already on Facebook, Twitter, and other social media outlets. Capitalize on that! When a fellow student recommends a book to a friend, that book often begins to circulate heavily. Peer recommendations are often more important to teens.

Reviews from PTA members can also be effective. While you are talking with them about SITL, be sure to ask them for *their* reviews—and share these reviews through local and social media! Any time you enlist the aid of the parents, your program becomes stronger. Parents want to know different aspects of a book than students want to know. Whether students want to admit it or not, they also trust what parents say, although again, they may not agree. What would inspire the student who sees reviews of the same book by the librarian, the student, the teacher, and the parent? How different would they be? How great a display would that make?

Hey! I'm Talkin' to YOU

Of course, you are whining by now that you don't have time to do all of this! Remember, there are two of you working on this project. The partnership you created in Chapter 1 still exists! Talk to each other, so the two of you are not necessarily reviewing the same books. Of course, once you read each other's terrific reviews, you will want to read all the books. Forward each other's reviews to all your groups. Your administrators will be impressed with your collaboration. The teachers will realize they have double the number of great books to recommend, and the students will be excited to cross library lines, so they can grab the books they want more quickly. When *School Library Journal* published their plea for public and school librarians to work together, they asked the librarians what the "best investment" that their (public) library has made. Among the top three answers was "savvy staffers." That's YOU!

Re-use Your Reviews

If you find yourself writing book reviews for your own use, we encourage you to follow the "three-cycling" model described at the beginning of this chapter. Share your reviews with other people. Perhaps you can arrange a "review swap" with other librarians in your institution, allowing all of you to learn more about the books in your collections. Your local newspaper may be able to use the reviews as filler material, and teachers are always looking for new title ideas for their students—not to mention their own reading fun. If your institution has a regular internal newsletter or daily bulletin, consider periodically contributing a book review. Be creative, and be generous.

Resources

"Common Reasons for Condom Failure." *Go Ask Alice: Columbia Health.* Columbia University. 9 July 2012. *http://goaskalice.columbia.edu/common-reasons-condom-failure.*

CHAPTER 11

Afterglow

What We've Learned

We learn something new every time we present a SITL booktalk. Sometimes the new information is shocking, or at least amazing. We were shocked ten years ago when students informed us that graphically-depicted violence in teen literature is perfectly acceptable, because "It's on the news every night." The same group of students amazed us by asserting that on-page sexual situations were unacceptable in a middle-school library, because movies about that sort of stuff weren't rated for them.

We've learned that most people don't know that the school library and the public library are not just different locations. Parents and students—and even teachers—have told us that the differences between the mission of the school library and the mission of the public library surprised them. They had no idea that these two institutions, which look so similar, actually serve dramatically different functions in the community. Armed with their new knowledge, they've told us that they plan to visit both places a little more often.

We've learned that the audience for teen books is broader than we ever knew. When presenting SITL to PTA groups, we learn that parents are interested in reading teen literature—not just to keep in touch with the reading habits of their offspring, but also because an increasing number of adults are recognizing that books written for teens are actually *good*.

We know that the library is a haven for some teens. Some students initially come to the library for homework help, but they come back because they feel welcomed by the staff (and the collection).

We know that not all books circulate "legally." Sometimes SITL books wander around the library unattended, visiting the poetry collection or the books about Ancient Egypt. Sometimes books go AWOL for months at a time and return to the library with scars, tattoos, and hickeys that they cannot explain. We are proud that our libraries are places that teens want to return books, even if they need to take them anonymously.

What Has Changed

Often, what we learn from teens makes us proud to be part of the educational team that is guiding them towards adulthood. They don't just *know* stuff, they *think* about stuff, and they aren't too proud to change their opinions when they get new information.

When we started these booktalks almost ten years ago, students were uncomfortable hearing the word "homosexual" spoken aloud in school. The majority of students at that time told us in clear terms that they were not comfortable with the concept of same-sex relationships, that they didn't know any homosexual people, and that they didn't want to read about the topic. We couldn't help noticing the tiny, nearly-silent minority of students who did not speak up to contradict these outspoken classmates, but more than one made silent eye contact with us, begging us non-verbally to pay attention to *their* needs as well as those of the outspoken majority.

In recent years, thanks in part to a very assertive "welcoming and affirming" curriculum in the local school district, as well as some legal changes in the status of homosexual couples in our home state, this attitude among teens has changed dramatically. We recognize that this situation is not the same in every location or every school district. However, we do want to emphasize that changes like this are happening in the attitudes of younger generations. We'd like to think that teachers and books have had some positive influences on those changes. These days, when we booktalk locally, books about homosexuality, bisexuality, transgendered characters, and other sexual questioners are accepted as routine: Our audience generally recognizes that these fictional characters need to be represented in school and public library collections for teens—just as "mainstream" characters have been represented for many years.

As our own population becomes more diverse, librarians are constantly seeking diversity in teen novels. More than twenty-six heritage languages are spoken in homes within our service district. Families now also include single parents, married single-sex parents, grandparents raising children, foster parents raising children, and teen parents raising children. The diversity in our population *must* be reflected in our library collection, and this diversity must include non-stereotypic characters from a wide variety of cultural, racial, and ethnic backgrounds. The publishing industry is still not diverse enough, but publishers are, finally, now beginning to pay attention to the needs of modern readers.

We've also seen a huge (and very welcome) increase in SITL books written for boys. Authors like Sherman Alexie, Don Calame, Cory Doctorow, Rebecca Serle, and J.H. Trumble are writing books about the male experience that boys actually want to read!

Alas, we have *not* seen nearly enough books that portray realistic use of contraception. Although contraception is sometimes discussed among fictional teen characters, its occurrence as a "plot point" is almost always based on contraception failure. We challenge authors to incorporate and discuss the practice more in teen lives—after all, real teens do, increasingly, use contraception. Why don't fictional teens use it, too?

You never thought you'd hear us say this, but it's true: We want more books about abstinence. We want characters (especially girls) to make decisions responsibly and to stick by their decisions for more than a few chapters. Too many "abstinence" books are preachy, didactic, and driven by a single issue. We know that the lives of teens are complex, and we want literature that reflects this.

What to Do Now

We hope that after reading this book, our readers will want to do some SITL booktalking of their own in order to engage teens and adults in conversations. We've had fun, engaged with students in a whole new way, and met some fascinating people as a result of our SITL presentations. You will be surprised, perhaps, that your skills are equal to the challenge of talking about sexual situations in books written for teens.

Remember that nobody wants to talk about mission statements and acquisition policies, but almost everybody has an opinion about books. Use those opinions, harness that energy, and get people talking and thinking about books and libraries. Some people may get mad, but by providing good information about teen books to them, we know that even more people will get informed. We think that's a good thing.

If you have questions, comments, thoughts or suggestions about SITL booktalks, or if you'd like to invite Mary Jo and Aarene to visit your library, conference, or high-class penthouse dinner party, please contact us via the blog website: *http://www.sexinthelibrary.blogspot.com.*

PART II

The Good Stuff: Book Reviews

When we write book reviews for other people to read, we follow the more formal structure outlined in Chapter 10. Depending on the audience, we edit the format, include relevant information, and leave out extraneous details that are not of interest to that specific group of readers.

For this chapter, we shortened the reviews to allow room for many titles. While we recommend that you include book cover illustrations when booktalking or writing reviews, space limitations required that they be excluded here. The information in this chapter is tailored to the reading audience of this book: librarians, teachers, and parents. Each entry provides a basic plot summary, age recommendations, quick descriptor words, reader reactions (including our own), and alerts. For a more complete book review, visit the SITL website: *http://www.sexinthelibrary.blogspot.com* or find Sexinthelibrary's book reviews on *Goodreads*.com.

Many books belong in several categories. *Beauty Queens*, for example, could easily go in the categories of *Girl Power, Rainbow Connection*, and *First Times*, but we think the book is hilarious, so we put it in the *Laughter* category.

Alert Words

We include a list of alert words, or topics, for each title. This is intended to help you select titles for specific audiences and booktalking situations, as well as to help familiarize you with each book's content.

> *abortion, abstinence, alcohol, bullying, child abuse, cussing, death, drinking, drugs, dystopia, gay friends, grieving, gore, homosexuality, incest, kissing, magic, masturbation, nudity, paranormal, pregnancy, prejudice, prostitution, rape, religious beliefs, safe sex, sexual questioning, sexual situations, "Star Trek Sex," STDs, straight friends, suicide, and violence*

Some are self-explanatory. The others are described below:

- *Abstinence* doesn't always last for an entire book. Just as in real life, the choice to say "no" might be a long-term decision or a temporary one. It's an uncommon choice in teen literature at the moment, though, and we want to recognize it where it does exist.

- *Alcohol* is cited if it appears in the story. The characters might not be drinking; a minor character might have an alcohol problem. This contrasts with *drinking*, which is used as a descriptor when a main character is actually imbibing on the page.

- *Bullying* can include many aspects of the action. Though we usually think of bullying as happening between age-mates, in SITL literature, an adult might bully a teen or another adult. We consider any physical, verbal, and emotional abuse of a young person to be *child abuse*. We wish the justice system agreed with us.

- *Cussing* usually involves taboo words; in some futuristic novels or stories that take place outside of the United States, the words may be different, but the intent is the same. We are aware that made-up cuss words don't offend readers as quickly as the wash-your-mouth-out classics.

- *Grieving* might include grieving over death or grieving over another type of loss.

- *Prejudice* is multi-dimensional. One character might be prejudiced against the Islamic religion or prejudiced in thinking all vampires are bad. Prejudice might, or might not, be related to *religious beliefs,* which might also include a religious sentiment as it applies to any spiritual belief system, including that of traditional religions, as well as that of Martians or mer-people.

Rating System

Sex: Rated 0 through 5
> 0. None at all
> 1. Thoughts about the opposite sex
> 2. Kissing, touching, sexual thoughts, and questioning
> 3. On-page descriptions of kissing, touching, or masturbation; more detailed sexual thoughts and/or questions; *Star Trek* sex
> 4. On-page sexual situations
> 5. Detailed, on-page sexual situations and naked bodies

Cussing: Rated 0 through 5
> 0. None at all
> 1. No taboo words; some uncharacteristic words used as cuss words
> 2. Minor cuss words used infrequently
> 3. Cuss words used more frequently
> 4. Cuss words used often; major cuss words used
> 5. Frequent cussing; major cuss words

Violence: Rated 0 through 5

    0. None at all

    1. No intended violence

    2. Minor violence: unplanned hitting without bloodshed, "fighting words"

    3. Hitting or kicking—with or without blood; no weapons

    4. Pre-meditated hitting, kicking, or possible use of weapons; bloodshed and/or injury

    5. Pre-meditated intent to cause serious injury or death; weapons used

Reader reactions are drawn from our own experiences and comments from teen readers, online and in-person.

Alerts

We want our readers to be aware of potentially controversial material without making them paranoid. Not all readers are alike, and not all will agree that "alert" topics are "controversial."

Brave New Worlds: Futuristic and Dystopic Novels

- *All These Things I've Done* (Zevin)

- *Divergent* (Roth)

- *For the Win* (Doctorow)

- *How I Live Now* (Rosoff)

- *Life as We Knew It* (Pfeffer)

- *A Long, Long Sleep* (Sheehan)

- *Matched* (Condie)

- *Ready Player One* (Cline)

- *Unwind* (Shusterman)

Cline, Ernest. *Ready Player One*. Crown, 2011. 384p. $24. 978-0-307-88743-6. $14 Trade pb. 978-0-307-88744-3.

HOOK: Play a video game, win a billion bucks. Who's with me?

REVIEW: The year is 2044, and eighteen-year-old Wade, like almost everyone else in the world, regularly escapes from grim reality to spend most of his waking time in OASIS, the online community of video simulation games. Wade is a "gunter," a game player dedicated to locating the elusive Easter Egg prize hidden somewhere in the nearly-infinite OASIS. The creator of OASIS was obsessed with the pop culture of the 1980s and left hundreds of clues for gunters hidden within 1980's movies, books, music, television shows, and even commercials The first to find the Egg will inherit a fortune in cash and controlling interest in the OASIS. Unfortunately, there are some unscrupulous bad guys who don't mind cheating—or even killing—to win the Egg.

Recommended for readers 13 and up.

Sex: 3; Cussing: 3; Violence: 5

bullying, cussing, death, dystopic, gay friends, grieving, magic, masturbation, sexual situations, violence

READER REACTION: Anyone who has ever gotten immersed in a book, a movie, a video game, or a face-to-face session of Dungeons and Dragons will relate to Wade's experience in OASIS. Anyone who can recite the entire script of *Monty Python and the Holy Grail,* knows every line ever spoken on *Star Trek* (original series and/or any of the prequel/sequel/spin-off series), played Pac-Man for uncounted hours, or ever rolled for damage to an imaginary monster will revel in the retro-geekiness of the narrative. A fun, action-filled dystopian adventure.

ALERTS: Comic book violence and some off-stage "real world" violence, cussing, and two paragraphs of non-graphic virtual sex with an unsatisfactory anatomically-correct haptic doll, plus some awesome friendships and a sweet romance. Most (but not all) of the violence happens within the simulated game world.

Condie, Ally. *Matched.* Dutton, 2010. 384p. $17.99. 978-0-525-42364-5. $9.99 Trade pb. 978-0-14-241977-9.

HOOK: The Society that controls every life, every decision, even the food of each citizen, is completely benevolent. Yeah. Right.

REVIEW: Cassia is thrilled to attend her "matched" banquet and discover her life-mate, chosen for her by the Society. She is enthralled that her match is her best friend Zander. When she logs in to view details about Zander, she sees, fleetingly, that her "match" is really Ky, who cannot legally be matched. This begins her obsession over something the Society says she can't have, and gradually Cassia begins to query the difference between safe love and true love. Although the main plot is somewhat predictable, sub-plots and supporting characters are intriguing: Cassia's grandfather's personal resistance; the control of people through drugs; the unexpected importance of poetry and music.

Recommended for readers age 13 and up.

Sex: 1; Cussing: 0; Violence: 1

abstinence, death, drugs, dystopia, grieving, kissing, prejudice, violence

READER REACTION: Students love arguing about the series: Is Cassia in love, or do the secret manipulations of the Society cause her to fall in love with Zander . . . and with Ky? How does a person fall in love? This is a great book for parent/student and book circle discussion groups.

ALERTS: Although there is no sex in the first book, subsequent volumes in the series do employ *Star Trek* sex.

Doctorow, Cory. *For the Win.* Tor, 2010. 475p. $17.99. 978-0-7653-2216-6. $10.99 Trade pb. 978-0-7653-3384-1.

HOOK: All over the world, kids play video games . . . for money. Sounds like a great job? Well, it isn't.

REVIEW: The premise of this book is true: "Farming" video games for virtual treasure is a real and very lucrative industry, especially in third-world countries like India and China. The kids who play the games and win the virtual treasure from them don't make much money, of course. Their bosses make most of the money, selling magic swords, talking mushrooms, and virtual gold for *real* money to rich first-world gamers. Doctorow's fiction-heavily-embedded-with-real-stuff tale reaches critical mass when a mysterious woman called Big Sister Nor starts to organize the sweatshop virtual workers of the world into a world-wide union . . . and meets with real-world resistance.

Recommended for readers age 14 and up.

Sex: 2; Cussing: 3; Violence: 4 (virtual and real)

bullying, child abuse, cussing, death, dystopic, prejudice, sexual situations, violence

READER REACTION: Doctorow's fans press this book onto unsuspecting friends, who often become new fans of the author. Gamers are thrilled with this dystopic window into their world, but the book also appeals to readers who don't love gaming but do love a good story. Wil Wheaton from *Star Trek: The Next Generation* is the ultimate audiobook reader for this project.

ALERTS: Doctorow's book has riveting action and great characterization, and thus captured many adult readers. Embedded in the story of the Webblies are mini-lectures about economics, politics, and massive multiplayer online role-playing games (MMORPGs), which somehow, miraculously, are fascinating rather than boring.

Pfeffer, Susan. *Life as We Knew It.* Harcourt, 2006. 352p. $17. 978-0-15-205826-5. $7.99 Trade pb. 978-0-15-206154-8.

HOOK: An asteroid has smacked into the moon, knocking it ever-so-slightly out of a normal orbit . . . and changes absolutely everything.

REVIEW: The disrupted tides destroy much of the eastern seaboard. The erupting volcanoes fill the atmosphere with grey grit that blocks sunlight. The weather continues to worsen: Temperatures are dropping, and rain and snow continue to fall, even in summer. Crops are failing, livestock are slaughtered for food until very few remain, and survivors of the cataclysm scavenge for necessities from the homes and bodies of the dead.

Recommended for readers age 13 and up.

Sex: 1; Cussing: 1; Violence: 2

bullying, dystopic, grieving, violence

READER REACTION: **This is realistic survival fiction at its best.** An astonishing number of readers mentioned that they *did*, in fact, check the contents of the home pantry while reading this book. The story inspires discussions about survival techniques, the ethics of stealing from the dead, and the politics of starvation. **Science teachers love this book because of the obvious research possibilities.**

ALERTS: This is the first book in the series; later in the series, the natural human reaction to procreate before dying is present. The second and third books in the series also contain more on-page violence than the first title.

Rosoff, Meg. *How I Live Now.* Wendy Lamb Books, 2010, 2004. 124p. $7.99 Trade pb. 978-0-553-37605-0.

HOOK: Aarene liked this book. Mary Jo hated it. Arguing about it may be the best "book hook" we've ever used.

REVIEW: Fifteen-year-old Daisy wants out of New York City and away from her pregnant stepmother. She goes to live with her cousins in rural England. There, isolated by war and unchaperoned by adults,

Daisy and her first cousin Edmond fall into a passionate and (mostly) secret—and extremely forbidden—love affair.

Recommended for readers age 15 and up.

Sex: 3; Cussing: 2; Violence: 3

dystopic, incest, sexual situations, Star Trek *sex, violence*

READER REACTION: The book received the 2005 Michael L. Printz Award. Teen readers seem to be evenly divided in their opinions: Of those who finished reading it, only about half claimed to like it, but several said that it was impossible to put down, even when they *didn't* like the story.

ALERTS: The distaste factor is high, and the rationale for the romance seems pretty random, but what teen romance makes sense? Certainly, most modern adolescents avoid incest while falling in love (or lust), but the lure of the forbidden is believably and consistently strong for Daisy, who is a troubled and distinctly unreliable narrator.

Roth, Virginia. *Divergent*. Katherine Tegen Books, 2011. 496p. $16.99. 978-0-06-202402-2. $9.99 Trade pb. 978-0-06-202403-9.

HOOK: Ten initiates will succeed; the rest will be left "Factionless" and homeless or dead.

REVIEW: Although raised by the Abnegation (self-denying) faction, sixteen-year-old Tris has never felt that serving others is truly the right niche for her. At the Choosing ceremony she selects Dauntless (courage) as her new faction, and immediately, she is required to jump off the side of a building. Tris' suitability for Dauntless is somewhat questionable—her secret aptitude test shows that she is Divergent and not suited for only a single faction. This could be a strength, but Dauntless leaders are convinced that it is a fatal flaw, and Tris must hide her true nature in order to survive.

Recommended for readers age 13 and up.

Sex: 3; Cussing: 0; Violence: 4

bullying, death, drinking, drugs, dystopic, kissing, prejudice, sexual situations, violence

READER REACTION: The narrative is quick-moving, thought-provoking, and at times quite violent. Tris is attracted to one of the Dauntless trainers, but one aspect of her personal "fear landscape" (no spoilers here!) puts this book onto the Sex in the Library list. Great characters, fast plotting, and two more books in the series.

ALERTS: The second book in the series places this series squarely into the SITL list: it has the best example of *Star Trek* sex that we have seen in a long time.

Sheehan, Anna. *A Long, Long Sleep*. Candlewick Press, 2011. 342p. $16.99. 978-0-7636-5260-9. $10.99 Trade pb. 978-1-78062-094-7.

HOOK: This book is the ultimate "fractured fairy tale": a retelling of Sleeping Beauty in the far (and dystopic) future!

REVIEW: Rosalinda is sixteen; however, she was born nearly one hundred years ago. Locked away in a chemically-induced slumber inside a stasis tube, Rose peacefully slept through the Dark Times that killed millions and left her orphaned and heir to the enormous UniCorp fortune. Now that she's been kissed awake by handsome Brendan, Rose must find her place in a world that is completely different from what she knew before falling asleep. This Sleeping Beauty story goes beyond recasting of an old tale into a science fiction framework. Rose is fully-realized, with deep flaws that she desperately tries to hide from the world, including herself. The deeply-buried memories of why she slept is key. The futuristic world, ruled by mega-corporations, is just possible enough to be frightening, as well as fascinating.

Recommended for readers age 13 and up.

Sex: 3; Cussing: 1; Violence: 2

abuse, bullying, death, dystopic, kissing, Star Trek *sex, violence*

READER REACTION: Rose's passivity is frustrating, but as the book develops, readers develop both empathy and sympathy for her. As a survivor of very subtle abuse, Rose responds to her situation as she has been taught. The supporting characters in the story allow her to grow beyond her childhood conditioning and into a fully-realized adult who deserves a happy ending (which she will hopefully earn for herself!).

ALERTS: Cuss words have changed in the future, so they are not offensive to 21st century readers. The *Star Trek* sex is so tactful, we almost missed it!

Shusterman, Neal. *Unwind.* Simon and Schuster, 2007. 352p. $17.99. 978-1-4169-1204-0. $9.99 Trade pb. 978-1-4169-1205-7.

HOOK: What if your parents could decide that you were just not what they wanted? In this story, pre-birth abortion is illegal but getting rid of teenagers isn't.

REVIEW: In the future, things are different. Abortion is forbidden by law; instead, the constitutional amendment called "The Bill of Life" allows parents to choose retroactive elimination for children between the ages of 13 and 18. It's not really murder, insists the law: "Unwound" children aren't dead. They continue to live, but in a divided state. When Connor discovers his unwind order, he runs away. While trying to escape, he joins forces with Risa, an orphan ordered for unwinding due to governmental budget cuts, and Lev, a boy marked from birth as a religious "tithe unwind." What will happen when the harvesters catch up to them?

Recommended for readers age 13 and up.

Sex 1; Cussing 1; Violence 4

bullying, child abuse, cussing, death, dystopia, kissing, religious beliefs, suicide, and *violence*

READER REACTION: We carry this book to the PTA with us, because it's guaranteed to engender lively discussions! Only Neal Shusterman could successfully interweave issues like abortion, terrorism, suicide bombers, and religious obligations with a suspenseful survival story that appeals to teens. The story works powerfully.

ALERTS: The premise of the story may disturb sensitive readers. An excellent choice for book group discussions. The sequel, *UnWholly* (2012), continues the story, adding more characters, more complex situations, and more violence.

Zevin, Gabrielle. *All These Things I've Done.* Farrar Straus Giroux, 2011. 368p. $16.99. 978-0-374-30210-8. $9.99 Trade pb. 978-1-250-01028-5.

HOOK: Throw a few random chocolate kisses to students. Then show the book and tell them, "Sixteen-year-old Anya is the heir to the family business: smuggling chocolate."

REVIEW: In 2083, chocolate is a prohibited substance, and Anya Balanchine's family is modern mafia, importing chocolate and other banned luxuries to New York. Her parents were both killed in mob hits, leaving Anya in charge of a younger sister, a brain-injured older brother, and a dying grandmother. Anya considers herself the least romantic girl in the world, until she falls in love with Win Delacroix, the son of New York City's new assistant district attorney. When Anya's ex-boyfriend nearly dies from eating a poisoned bar of Balanchine Chocolate, the story begins to twist and turn and twist again. Crime, drama, chocolate, and forbidden romance figure in a believable dystopic future where alcohol is permitted, but paper and water are rationed and caffeine and chocolate are outlawed.

Recommended for readers age 12 and up.

Sex: 3; Cussing: 0; Violence: 2

alcohol, bullying, death, drinking, drugs, dystopia, grieving, kissing, nudity, sexual situations, Star Trek *sex, violence*

READER REACTION: Readers hoping for hardcore dystopic or mafia fiction are mostly disappointed with this book, but readers who like star-crossed romances and complex characters enjoy it. The "banned chocolate" theme seems more like an attention-getting device than an actual plot-point, but it does develop further in the second book of the series.

ALERTS: This book contains some sexual situations (including a steamy "near miss" scene in a hotel room) with no actual body parts on the page. There is no cussing, some not-very-bloody mob violence, and several scenes of alcohol consumption by teens. In 2083, alcohol is legal for all ages, but coffee is not.

Can't Feel My Head: Sex and Addiction

- *The Deadly Sister* (Schrefer)
- *Falling* (Wilhelm)
- *Glass* (Hopkins)
- *Stoner & Spaz* (Koertge)
- *Very LeFreak* (Cohn)

Cohn, Rachel. *Very LeFreak.* Knopf, 2010. 320p. $16.99. 978-0-375-85758-4. $9.99 Trade pb. 978-0-375-85096-7.

HOOK: We often read about addictions in teen fiction; seldom do we read about addiction to technology. REVIEW: Veronica (Very) has always been a "love 'em and leave 'em" kind of gal. Very is also techno-obsessed. She is always plotting a playlist based on what is happening to her at any moment. So far, her roommate has not just put up with her, but also helped her out of problematic situations. Very enjoys multiple sexual partners, and she thinks her playlists help her deal with frequent breakups. Her best friend and her roommate stage an intervention, and Very is forced to a twelve-step techno camp. But will Very confront the real problem?

Recommended for readers age 15 and up.

Sex: 5; Cussing: 3; Violence: 1

abstinence, cussing, drinking, drugs, kissing, sexual situations, Star Trek *sex, STDs*

READER REACTION: Sexual situations aside, readers love Very and really enjoy the idea of techno-addiction. We suspect some of our teens border on that obsession.

ALERTS: As with other books by this author, we love the heroine, but will mostly find her only in a public library. The content is generally too explicit for school libraries and conservative communities.

Hopkins, Ellen. *Glass.* Margaret K. McElderry Books, 2009, 2007. 704p. $17.99. 978-1-4169-4090-6. $10.99 Trade pb. 978-1-4169-4091-3.

HOOK: This is a novel-in-verse format, an attraction to many teen readers. The author was "un-invited" to a 2010 teen lit festival in Texas, because her books were considered too controversial.

REVIEW: We first met Kristina in *Crank,* as she traded her great life for a pregnancy and her boyfriend's addiction to meth. This sequel brings Kristina back home, but suffering from post-partum depression. Although she thought she was cured of her addiction, it only takes one misstep to fall down into the long tunnel again. Now, living with her mother, caring for a baby, and working a dead-end menial job, Kristina becomes addicted to speed. Of course she loses everything again, trying to feed her habit while surviving, which includes living with and having sex with her old boyfriend's buddy. This is the middle book of a series, in which Kristina is introduced to a more potent form of meth called *glass.*

Recommended for readers age 14 and up.

Sex 3; Cussing 2; Violence 2

alcohol, child abuse, cussing, drinking, drugs, kissing, pregnancy, sexual situations, Star Trek *sex*

READER REACTION: Teens follow this author. Much can be learned about drug abuse from this book, and students can understand what addicts experience. Health teachers have used excerpts from this book to show addicts' feelings and thoughts.

ALERTS: This book is powerful—and depressingly real. Understand the needs of the reader who wants this book.

Koertge, Ron. *Stoner & Spaz.* Candlewick, 2011, $6.99 Trade pb. 978-0-7636-5757-4.

HOOK: People usually ignore Ben completely, or treat him like a Brave Boy Overcoming Handicap. By contrast: Colleen bosses him around, steals his candy, and makes fun of his disability . . . and Ben loves her.

REVIEW: Ben knows that he's attracted to Colleen because she's pretty and he's weird-looking; because she doesn't care what she wears and he dresses carefully to disguise his cerebral palsy; because he thinks she's brave and he thinks he's not. But he's also attracted to Colleen because she's the first girl he's ever really talked to, the first girl who teases him about his leg braces instead of pretending they don't exist. She challenges him to go out in public, to try drugs, and to direct his own movie instead of hiding in the back rows of the Rialto. Ben accepts her challenges, but when he challenges her to sober up, give up the drugs and straighten out, he discovers that Colleen needs more than courage.

Recommended for readers age 14 and up.

Sex: 3; Cussing: 2; Violence: 2

abuse, bullying, cussing drinking, drugs, kissing

READER REACTION: If this were a TV movie instead of a book, the closing credits would roll over footage of Ben shooting a documentary of Colleen's one-year "sobriety birthday." But author Koertge doesn't give the readers a cheap conclusion, choosing instead a more realistic—and ultimately more satisfying—close to the story. Ben's narrative voice is strong and cynical; Colleen's is earthy and realistic. The story is unexpectedly sweet and gritty in all the right places. The sequel, *Now Playing: Stoner & Spaz II*, is equally wonderful, but contains more obvious sexual situations between Ben and Colleen.

ALERTS: Colleen doesn't do drugs because she's weak or stupid—she has real problems that anyone would prefer to avoid. The situations are strong, and some readers may be bothered.

Schrefer, Eliot. *Deadly Sister.* Scholastic, 2010. 352p. $17.99. 978-0-545-16574-7. $9.99 Trade pb. 978-0-545-16575-4.

HOOK: Picture yourself out jogging. Now picture yourself finding the dead body of the most popular boy in school. As you look closer, what do you see in the mud? Your sister's phone.

REVIEW: Abbey is jogging and finds the body of a popular fellow classmate. She also finds her sister Maya's cell phone next to the body. Maya is a known stoner, school dropout, and unpredictable character. Abbey's only thought is to save Maya and find the real killer. The plot twists and leads us down many paths. This is an interesting study in sisterhood and loyalty.

Recommended for readers age 12 and up.

Sex 1; Cussing 3; Violence 5

alcohol, bullying, cussing, death, drinking, drugs, gay friends, grieving, kissing, prejudice, violence

READER REACTION: There is plenty of suspense to make this a completely satisfying story—one where the suspense lasts all the way to the final word. Eighth graders will love this. The high school crowd will own it completely.

ALERTS: Maya and Abbey's parents are confused and confusing. They are both lawyers, but seem to have many problems dealing with people—and the world in general.

Wilhelm, Doug. *Falling.* Farrar, Straus and Giroux, 2007. 256p. $17. 978-0-374-32251-9.

HOOK: What would you do if your idolized brother became a drug addict?

REVIEW: Matt and his brother Neal were both star basketball players. Neal was not offered the scholarship he wanted, and decided to "take the year off," which meant that he began selling and using drugs. Matt reacts by dropping out of everything, avoiding home, avoiding his basketball friends, and avoiding his life. He invents a pseudo-life online and meets Katie, a girl who goes to the same high school. The story is told alternately by Katie and Matt, so we get their viewpoints as well as that of their friends.

Recommended for readers age 13 and up.

Sex: 1; Cussing: 3; Violence: 1

abstinence, alcohol, bullying, cussing, drinking, drugs, kissing

READER REACTION: The brothers have a stereotypical set of clueless parents, caring friends, and problems finding the right path. The story, however, is satisfying with a problem-solving, suspenseful plot.

ALERTS: This book makes the rounds in parent/student book groups who love to debate the situation: What could you have done that would help a friend? A classmate? A son or daughter?

Fangs and Fur: Supernatural Sex

- *After the Golden Age* (Vaughn)

- *Boys that Bite* (Mancusi)

- *Daughter of Smoke and Bone* (Taylor)

- *Lies Beneath* (Brown)

- *Lips Touch Three Times* (Taylor)

- *Peeps* (Westerfeld)

- *Pretty Dead* (Block)

- *Rampant* (Peterfreund)

- *Shiver* (Stiefvater)

- *Sweet Evil* (Higgins)

- *Tantalize* (Smith)

- *Twilight* (Meyer)

- *Witch Eyes* (Tracey)

Block, Francesca Lia. *Pretty Dead.* Harper Teen, 2009. 195p. $16.99. 978-0-06-154785-0. $8.99 Trade pb. 978-0-06-154787-4.

HOOK: When is a vampire book *not* a vampire book?

REVIEW: Charlotte is a stereotypical, tormented vampire: eternally young, gorgeous, brilliant, wealthy, and lonely. When her young vampire-wannabe companion Emily commits suicide, Charlotte is drawn to Emily's boyfriend Jared. In a stereotypical vampire book, Jared would become a vampire, so that he could "live" forever with Charlotte. But that isn't how this story transpires. Instead, Charlotte slowly reverses herself and begins showing symptoms of becoming human again. William arrives to remind Charlotte of their long shared history of death and destruction. Francesca Lia Block upholds her reputation for gorgeous, lush writing and deep acknowledgement of the literary traditions that she dumps end-over-end. The story is hypnotic and impossible to put down.

Recommended for readers age 15 and up.

Sex: 5; Cussing: 2; Violence: 4

death, drinking, grieving, kissing, magic, nudity, paranormal, sexual situations, suicide, violence

READER REACTION: Teens who love vampire stories love this. Teens who are tired of vampire stories like it, too.

ALERTS: With Block's signature magical-realism prose and sexual symbolism everywhere, this book appeals to mature teens who savor Charlotte's unusual transformation and delayed coming-of-age.

Brown, Anne. *Lies Beneath*. Delacorte, 2012. 320p. $17.99. 978-0-385-74201-6. $8.99 Trade pb. 978-0-385-74202-3.

HOOK: "I hadn't killed anyone all winter, and I have to say I felt pretty good about that."

REVIEW: Calder is a merman, with three mermaid sisters/monsters who feed on the human "aura of happiness." Unfortunately, the humans die afterwards. The mer-family needs to avenge their mother's death. In the mer-world, a promise is sacrosanct. With many plot twists and turns, Calder and his sisters pursue the man responsible. However, Calder falls in love with Lily, the man's sixteen-year-old daughter. Calder keeps telling Lily, "This is not Disney's Ariel." These mer-folk are killers who pull readers under in a trance that turns into terror.

Recommended for readers age 13 and up.

Sex: 2; Cussing: 2; Violence: 5

abstinence, alcohol, bullying, child abuse, cussing, death, kissing, magic, nudity, paranormal, prejudice, violence

READER REACTION: This is a mer-MAN book! While dark, the character really works for guys. These mer-folk are strongly reminiscent of vampires, and their tale will entrance readers . . . right before it terrifies them.

ALERTS: Revenge is a strong motive, perhaps overly prominent in this story. The anatomy questions of how mermaids have sex, or why humans give up their children remain unanswered and troubling. There are holes in this story.

Higgins, Wendy. *Sweet Evil*. Harper Teen, 2012. 464p. $8.99 Trade pb. 978-0-06-208561-0.

HOOK: How well do you know early biblical creatures? Sure, you know angels and archangels, and the story of the Satan downfall, but do you know nephilim?

REVIEW: Good-girl Anna knows she is different—she can see auras; she can smell odors literally a mile away. When she goes to a band opening with her best friend Jay, Anna cannot read the aura of the drummer, although he appears to have a red "badge" flaring from his chest. It is no surprise that Anna and (bad boy) Kaiden are drawn to each other, first because Kaiden seems to know Anna's true nature, and later because the sexual tension is just too irresistible. This is no ordinary romance. Anna and Kaiden are both nephilim, the children of demons. On Anna's sixteenth birthday, her adoptive mother reveals her other secret.

Recommended for readers age 15 and up.

Sex: 2; Cussing: 2; Violence: 2

abstinence, alcohol, child abuse, cussing, death, drinking, drugs, kissing, magic, nudity, paranormal, prostitution, rape, religious beliefs, sexual situations, violence

READER REACTION: Angels seem to be popular with girls, while demons appeal to boys. This book catches the attention of both. "Hot and steamy" doesn't begin to express the episodes that bring the two teens together, making this book for mature teens.

ALERTS: Although incidents do not happen on-page, characters recount past rape events. Kaiden is a demon; it is unrealistic to expect him to defer sex. While the book is based on biblical legends of demons, the author takes great liberties. There are many plot holes, which may be filled in later books.

Mancusi, Mari. *Boys That Bite.* (series) Berkley, 2006. 262p. $10.99 Trade pb. 978-0-425-20942-4.

HOOK: Mancusi is a TV producer and writer. Readers can see the screenplay style in this series. It is easily compared to the *Buffy* series.

REVIEW: Identical twins Rayne and Sunshine are heading to a rave. Sunshine is bitten by vampire Magnus, which is a real coup— except that the bite had been intended for Rayne, who had pre-arranged to become a vampire. Sunny now has three weeks to stop the vampire change. S*poiler alert!* While Rayne still wants to become a vampire, she is told at the end of book one that she is the new vampire hunter!

Recommended for readers age 13 and up.

Sex: 2; Cussing: 2; Violence: 2

abstinence, cussing, kissing, magic, paranormal, vampires

READER REACTION: Great summer reads; fans of *Buffy* love this series. Fans of serious vampire fiction turn up their noses. The banter between the three main characters is perfect for middle school readers.

ALERTS: This reads like a TV script; situations and characters are fun, but stereotypical.

Meyer, Stephenie. *Twilight.* Little, Brown, 2008, 2005. 544p. $10.99 Trade pb. 978-0-316-03838-6.

HOOK: *Twilight* and its sequels need no hook; teens either love or hate them—but including *Twilight* in a booktalk will ensure that teens will speak up with their opinions!

REVIEW: Seventeen-year-old Bella chooses to move to her dad's house in the rainy town of Forks, Washington, rather than go with her mom to Florida. Bella describes herself as pale, average, and awkward, but that is clearly not how she is viewed by her new classmatesespecially Edward Cullen, a gorgeously graceful and handsome senior who seems oddly fascinated by Bella and her tendency towards clumsiness. Then Bella discovers that Edward and his family are vampires—members of a clan which has chosen to hunt only wildlife instead of humans. But just because Edward doesn't want to feed upon humans doesn't mean that Bella is completely safe with him.

Recommended for readers age 13 and up.

Sex: 2; Cussing: 1; Violence: 1

abstinence, death, kissing, magic, paranormal, prejudice, religious beliefs, vampires, violence

READER REACTION: This book has transcended generations and genders. "Going all *Twilight*" has become synonymous for teen longing.

ALERTS: While there is no cussing, and the violence is mostly implied, the sexual tension runs high between the girl and her vampiric boyfriend. Their relationship is necessarily cautious, especially in book 3.

Peterfreund, Diana. *Rampant*. Harper Teen, 2009. 416p. $17.99. 978-0-06-149000-2. $8.99 Trade pb. 978-0-06-149004-0.

HOOK: Purple sparkles? Rainbow poop? Astrid knows that unicorns aren't like that. They are actually bloodthirsty monsters.

REVIEW: Sixteen-year-old Astrid's mother always told her daughter that *real* unicorns are not flying, sparkling fairy-tale beasts, but rather murderous, poisonous monsters (now extinct) that can only be killed by virgin girls like Astrid. Of course, Astrid's mom is a complete kook. That's what Astrid thought, anyhow, until the night when her boyfriend got himself gored by a murderous, poisonous monster with a single horn growing out of its head. The likable narrator explores the boundaries of knowledge and beliefs without lecturing the reader.

Recommended for readers age 14 and up.

Sex: 4; Cussing: 1; Violence: 4

death, magic, paranormal, religious beliefs, rape, sexual questioning, sexual situations, Star Trek *sex, violence*

READER REACTION: The strong female voice and anti-glitter unicorn lore in this novel easily grab the interest of girls who are moving away from fairy tale-like stories.

ALERTS: Some excellent butt-kicking battle scenes are interspersed with scenes of sexual questioning, including the role of virginity, the definition of rape, and the power of love.

Smith, Cynthia. *Tantalize*. Candlewick, 2007. 310p. $17.99. 978-0-7636-2791-1. $8.99 Trade pb. 978-0-7636-4059-0.

HOOK: Print out "Prey" and "Predator" menus ahead of time. Help students visualize the choices on the menus. Wear red cowboy boots!

REVIEW: Quincie Morris has grown up in the family restaurant business. At age seventeen, she is the driving force behind opening a new restaurant with a unique image: Sanguini's, the first restaurant in Austin with a vampire theme. The food will be exquisite and the staff will be thematically costumed. But then the chef is murdered, and Quincie's best friend—a hybrid werewolf—is the prime suspect. Werewolves and vampires are just the beginning in this suspenseful and tangled plot. There are also were-alligators. And were-armadillos. And even were-vampires! Alternately creepy and fun, with lovely (and later, horrible) descriptions of menu items from both the Prey Menu and the accompanying Predator Menu.

Recommended for readers age 13 and up.

Sex: 3; Cussing: 0; Violence: 3

abstinence, alcohol, bullying, cussing, death, kissing, grieving, magic, nudity, paranormal, prejudice, rape, religious beliefs, sexual situations, Star Trek *sex, vampires, violence*

READER REACTION: This is a natural for junior high teen fans of vampire stories. The combination of dark fantasy and just plain silly (*were-alligators?*) works.

ALERTS: The audiobook seems more explicit than the print version. *Tantalize* has a dark ending that modulates towards optimism in the sequels. The first and third books in the series really play to the titillation aspect of vampires; while sex is an obvious theme, the aspect of waiting until the right time is also present.

Stiefvater, Stephanie. *Shiver.* Scholastic, 2009. 392p. $17.99. 978-0-545-12326-6. $9.99 Trade pb. 978-0-545-12327-3.

HOOK: Each of these books is written in a different color. Talk about the high quality writing in these books compared to other werewolf books. Students appreciate well-written stories.

REVIEW: Seventeen-year-old Grace has been fascinated with the wolves that live in the woods near her Minnesota town ever since she was attacked by the pack as a child and then rescued by a single wolf. Eighteen-year-old Sam has been fascinated by Grace since the day of her attack—the day that he, in the form of a wolf, rescued her. The interconnected vulnerability of all of the characters is beautifully written.

Recommended for readers age 13 and up.

Sex: 3; Cussing: 2; Violence: 2

alcohol, bullying, cussing, death, drugs, kissing, grieving, magic, nudity (in in book two), paranormal, prejudice, Star Trek *sex, violence*

READER REACTION: While the main attraction is the swoon-worthy romance, friendship is the overriding theme that gets teens talking. The series is good for discussion.

ALERTS: Adults in this series appear in an adverse light. While drugs are a problem for one character, he matures during the series, leaving readers more optimistic.

Taylor, Laine. *Daughter of Smoke and Bone.* Little, Brown, 2011. 418p. $18.99. 978-0-316-13402-6. $9.99 Trade pb. 978-0-316-13399-9.

HOOK: "Once upon a time, an angel and a devil fell in love. It did not end well."

REVIEW: Historic Prague is perfect. We love Karou, with her blue hair and artistic gifts. We love her spunk and her obvious love for the monsters who are her family. We worry when the black handprints appear on doorways that Karou uses to do errands for her foster father, Wishbone. We want to dismiss the awful feeling of dread we have about Wishbone and his work. We love Akiva, with his perfect angel face and body, and we cheer as he and Karou discover each other. Then we are blind-sided and we bleed as we watch, helpless, but understanding when the book "does not end well."

Recommended for readers age 13 and up.

Sex: 4; Cussing: 2; Violence: 4.5

death, drinking, grieving, kissing, magic, paranormal, sexual situations, Star Trek *sex, violence.*

READER REACTION: Readers who liked this author's earlier book *Lips Touch Three Times;* hand-sell the title to other readers.

ALERTS: The intensity of the writing provokes strong feelings about this book and the story. This would be an excellent choice for mature book discussion groups.

Taylor, Laini. *Lips Touch Three Times.* Levine, 2012. 288p. $17.99. 978-0-545-05585-7. $14.99 Trade pb. 978-0-545-05586-4. ‹G›

HOOK: This book is part wordless graphic novel, making it perfect for "show and tell." Be sure to use the hardcover in which the illustrations are much more dramatic.

REVIEW: Three stories pivoting around a single kiss:

- A dead grandmother might be the only one who can save Kizzy from the seductive promises of the goblins.

- An old woman makes a demonic deal to save the lives of children, and agrees to allow a newborn baby to take on a curse to bind the deal—a curse that holds until the baby grows up and falls in love.

- A tale of mothers, children, a fey, and magical race called the Druj.

The tales are dark, enticing, and entrancing, with hints of longing and a hope (but not a promise) of salvation that will draw readers into each story, beautifully illustrated in shades of red and grey.

Recommended for readers age 14 and up.

Sex: 3; Cussing: 0; Violence: 4

child abuse, death, drugs, grieving, kissing, magic, paranormal, prejudice, rape, religious belief, sexual situations, violence

READER REACTION: Readers rush to share this book with each other.

ALERTS: This book is for mature girl readers who have a knowledge and interest in mythology/faerie (not *fairy* tales). It is deceptively gruesome.

Tracey, Scott. *Witch Eyes.* Flux, 2011. 336p. $10.99 Trade pb. 978-0-7387-2595-6.

HOOK: This is a Romeo and Juliet story with a huge twist.

REVIEW: Braden has "witch eyes," always shifting and changing. His eyes allow him to see everything that has happened in a specific location: the truth, emotions, and the deaths. To prevent migraines that accompany his visions, he wears sunglasses, even indoors, and must learn to control this gift. Unaware of the rivalry between his family and a competing dynasty, he is totally unprepared for falling in love with their son and heir, Trey. Braden only wants to be independent from both factions of lies, misleading statements, and deceptions that involve the entire town. Trey has a unique pull on Braden, however, especially after their first kiss. There is a prequel, *Homecoming*, and a sequel, *Demon Eyes*.

Recommended for readers age 12 and up.

Sex: 2; Cussing: 2; Violence: 3

bullying, cussing, death, drinking, gay friends, homosexuality, kissing, magic, paranormal, prejudice, religious beliefs, sexual questioning, straight friends, violence

READER REACTION: Teen readers like the way Braden's sexuality is handled matter-of-factly. The idea of a boy "witch" has become mainstreamed, thanks to Harry Potter. Braden's unique powers are a powerful draw to a very likeable character.

ALERTS: Violence is really demon-slaying, bad-guy violence—not terribly graphic, but intense.

Westerfeld, Scott. *Peeps.* Razorbill, 2005. 312p. $8.99 Trade pb. 978-1-59514-083-8.

HOOK: Read any one of the science chapters and you will grab your audience by the throat (descriptions of nematodes, screwworms, and lice are riveting!).

REVIEW: When Cal arrived in New York City to attend college, he promptly went out to lose his virginity. Unfortunately in the process, Cal also picked up an unusual sexually transmitted disease: a parasite that causes all the symptoms (and strengths) of vampirism. Fortunately, he is partially resistant to the disease—although he is strong, pale, light-sensitive, and hungry for meat, he doesn't (immediately) go crazy and start eating people. Alternating with chapters of Cal's story are scientific chapters: graphic and tremendously icky information about real parasites, including *toxoplasma gondii*, pigeon mites, and other really yucky bugs that have literally plagued humans and animals throughout history.

Recommended for readers age 12 and up (with a strong stomach).

Sex: 3; Cussing: 2; Violence: 4

cussing, death, drinking, kissing, paranormal, Star Trek *sex, violence*

READER REACTION: This twist on "vampirism" as a disease, alongside very scientific research chapters, grabs teens and makes the rounds easily. Science teachers love this. We did not love the sequel.

ALERTS: The "eewwww" factor is high—and it's absolutely fascinating. The hunting of the vampire disease originators rates a four for violence, but much of the violence is off-page.

Vaughn, Carrie. *After the Golden Age.* Tor, 2011. 304p. $24.99. 978-0-7653-2555-6.

HOOK: Wouldn't it be great to have superheroes for parents? Though wouldn't it suck if your parents were superheroes, and you don't have any super powers at all?

REVIEW: Forensic accountant Celia West is the daughter of superheroes Captain Olympus and Spark, but her only "talent" seems to be a gift for getting kidnapped and held for ransom. When the insane super-villain Simon Sito (aka The Destructor) is captured and prosecuted for tax evasion, Celia finds her chance to help bring evil to justice. Her investigation uncovers a conspiracy that might be the key to the origin of Commerce City's superheroes—and more.

Recommended for readers age 14 and up.

Sex: 3; Cussing: 1; Violence: 5 (off-page, comic book violence)

kissing, paranormal, Star Trek *sex, violence*

READER REACTION: This book is not a parody of superhero comic book stories—rather, it is a re-casting of the story-type. The plot twists keep pages turning with fast action, excellent writing, great characters, a unique setting, a little romance, and some tactful off-page sexual situations. The prose reads just like a comic book, but without the pictures. The author clearly knows her superhero literature and uses all the customary themes and conventions to enhance the story.

ALERTS: This book is written and published for adult audiences, but it will be welcomed by teens.

First Time for Everything:
First Kisses, First Relationships, First Sexual Experiences

- *Alice* series (Naylor)

- *Color of Earth* (Hwa)

- *Derby Girl* (aka Whip It) (Cross)

- *Forever* (Blume)

- *Girl Parts* (Cusick)

- *Lost It* (Tracy)

- *Purity* (Pearce)

- *When It Happens* (Colasani)

Blume, Judy. *Forever.* Atheneum, 2002, 1975. 216p. $18.99. 978-0-689-84973-2. Simon Pulse, 2007. $8.99 Trade pb. 978-1-4169-3400-4. $7.99 Trade pb. 978-1-4169-4738-7.

HOOK: Catherine and Michael are sure that their love will last forever.

REVIEW: Catherine and Michael meet and fall in love. After much discussion, they decide to have sex. Catherine visits Planned Parenthood and receives birth control pills, which she uses faithfully to avoid pregnancy. This book was the first antidote to puritanical teen lit that insisted that "bad girls" got pregnant and lived horrible lives thereafter. Although Michael and Catherine's relationship does not survive to the end of the book, readers will always remember them fondly. In her introduction to the reissue of her classic "first time" book, Judy Blume reminds readers that when she wrote *Forever*, "safe sex" meant "don't get pregnant." Decades later, safe sex is more complicated, but the feelings surrounding first love are universal.

Recommended for readers age 13 and up.

Sex 4; Cussing 1; Violence 0

abstinence, drinking, drugs, kissing, nudity, pregnancy, sexual situations, Star Trek *sex*

READER REACTION: For more than thirty years, teens have appreciated the viewpoint that sex is a normal part of life.

ALERTS: After all these years, concerned adults are still concerned about this novel.

Colesani, Susane. *When It Happens. Viking,* 2006. 336p. $17.99. 978-0-670-06029-0. $8.99 Trade pb. 978-0-14-241155-1.

HOOK: Tell me if you've heard this one: Girl wants love, girl finds love with the stud of the senior class, girl finds he only wants one thing, girl sees male best friend as only best friend, best friend wants more. But really, this book is NOT that simple. Want more?

REVIEW: Girl finds love with the wrong boy who is, of course, with the "in" crowd. True love waits for her in the form of the boy she sees as a friend. This is the all-too-familiar story of teen romances, and one that still sells. Told in alternating chapters by Sara and Tobey, they eventually find each other, as we knew they would. But wait—there's more! Sara and Tobey are honest with themselves and with the reader. They want romance, and yes, more than that—they *are* teens—but there is more to romance than just sex. And there is more to life than just romance. The situations are plausible; the decisions deceptively simple.

Recommended for readers age 15 and up.

Sex: 3; Cussing: 1; Violence: 1

abstinence, kissing, sexual situations, Star Trek *sex*

READER REACTION: This simple story still grabs teens, because it is, ultimately, about decision-making. No drugs, no alcohol, just "simple" teens. Both boys and girls love this story, because it sheds light on the opposite sex and highlights teen brains.

ALERTS: Ultimately, the teens make decisions about *when* to have sex, not *if* to have it. Little consideration is given to safe sex.

Cross, Shauna. *Derby Girl. (Whip It)* Henry Holt, 2007. 240p. $17.99. 978-0-8050-8023-0. As *Whip It.* Square Fish, 2009. $8.99 Trade pb. 978-0-312-53599-5.

HOOK: Quick movie segments or roller derby Youtube clips will have teens clamoring for this book, but talk about the book, too!

REVIEW: Unhappy Bliss doesn't live with hip parents in a socially-savvy city on the coast. Instead, she lives in a backwater Texas town where the music is "all country, all the time," and top social honors are reserved for beauty queens with gigantic hair. Then Bliss discovers roller derby. She lies about her age, gives herself a "derby name," and joins the team. Her life as a derby girl, complete with fishnet stockings, wild makeup, wild parties, and a brand-new boyfriend with great taste in music brings Bliss more happiness than she ever envisioned . . . until her parents find out. And her best friend gets mad. And Bliss gets busted for being under-age. But there's still that great boyfriend . . . right?

Recommended for readers age 14 and up.

Sex: 4; Cussing: 3; Violence: 3

alcohol, bullying, cussing, drinking, drugs, kissing, sexual situations, violence

READER REACTION: It has all the leaping, diving, blocking, spinning, blood, and orneriness you expect from a sassy girl with pent-up energy to burn. Teens love the book, and the movie was great, too.

ALERTS: The movie follows the book closely, but glosses over the sex scene in the swimming pool, which the book shows explicitly.

Cusick, John M. *Girl Parts.* Candlewick, 2010. 240p. $16.99. 978-0-7636-4930-2. $7.99 Trade pb. 978-0-7636-5644-7.

HOOK: As a commercial: Do you find it hard to talk to girls? Want an easier way? How about Girlfriend 2.0?

REVIEW: After David and his friends watch with laughter at a classmate who commits suicide online, his parents decide that he needs socialization—NOW. They obtain a "socialization robot girl" for him. Rose is designed as a companion with built-in timing and responses for appropriate intimacy. When David discovers that Japanese robots are not *really* anatomically correct, he loses interest in her, especially when she becomes capable of making her own decisions. Charlie can't afford a robot but appropriates Rose after she leaves David. Because she is a robot, he feels he can talk to her—after all, she is programmed to listen. He finds someone to make her a "real girl." But will the robot corporation allow their expensive robot to roam free?

Recommended for readers age 14 and up.

Sex: 3; Cussing: 2; Violence: 2

abstinence, alcohol, bullying, cussing, drinking, kissing, nudity, sexual situations, Star Trek *sex, suicide*

READER REACTION: Fun and quirky, this story lacks character development. The appeal of this book is to reluctant male readers, and while the "robot with a heart" is appealing, the inventive idea just barely saves the book from earning a shrug.

ALERTS: The serious beginning may put some readers off; the serious subject of true friendship is treated lightly—maybe too lightly.

Hwa, Kim Dong. *The Color of Earth.* First Second, 2009. 320p. $16.95 Trade pb. 978-1-59643-458-5.

HOOK: This is a graphic novel. The illustrations are wonderful. Use them.

REVIEW: This Korean graphic novel relates the story of Ehwa who helps her mother with their tavern/restaurant. Her mother has chosen to remain single after the death of her husband. This choice is considered unusual and inappropriate in rural Korea in the early 20th century. Ehwa and her mother are very close, but their closeness does not stop Ehwa from wondering about love. She and a close friend share moments of wondering and sexual questioning that are more explicit, because of the Korean *manhwa* illustration style. Ehwa develops love interests with a boy who is studying to be a monk and has taken a vow of celibacy, and with a local rich boy. These too, are colored by the cultural mores of the rural Korean setting.

Recommended for readers age 15 and up.

Sex: 4; Cussing: 3; Violence: 1

kissing, masturbation, nudity, sexual situations, Star Trek *sex*

READER REACTION: Girls love this "coming of age" story. The book uses beautiful metaphors with flowers and landscape; indeed, the entire book is beautifully done. However, it is also outside the background and sophistication of suburban American teens. Elwa's mother must tolerate the offensive and crude remarks of the male tavern customers because of the cultural setting, and this is difficult for modern students to understand. This is first in a trilogy.

ALERTS: Although a visually stunning book, this could easily reach the distasteful button in conservative communities and should be placed in the hands of more mature readers.

Naylor, Phyllis Reynolds. *Alice on Board. Alice* series. Atheneum, 2012. 288p. $16.99. 978-1-4424-4588-8.

HOOK: Using the twenty plus books in the series, you need only introduce the latest if you have fans; if you do not, it may not be worth introducing.

REVIEW: The chronicles of Alice are legion, beginning with middle school. We have watched her friends, loves, and decisions on very important issues. Her dad is one of the best parent role models in teen literature. The process of Alice finding her way through puberty and love, with all its embarrassing moments, has been a focus of the series. This latest installment finds Alice working on a cruise ship in the Chesapeake Bay before starting college. While there is nothing new in the latest book, the entire series should be taken as a whole. Alice is frank, honest, and inquiring into every aspect of teen life, and this is what makes the series popular.

Recommended for readers age 13 and up.

Sex: 3; Cussing: 2; Violence: 2 (note: these ratings apply to the entire series)

abstinence, bullying, cussing, death, drinking, drugs, gay friends, grieving, homosexuality, kissing, nudity, pregnancy, prejudice, religious beliefs, safe sex, sexual questioning, sexual situations, Star Trek *sex, STDs*

READER REACTION: Although the series is popular with teens, not all books in the series are recommended for younger teen readers. Those who have been following Alice's adventures do so with soap-opera-like devotion. Although some teens have wearied of the story, some still have a crush on Patrick.

ALERTS: Due to the stories' frank and honest narrative, *Alice* is a series that is continually questioned for appropriateness by many parents.

Pearce, Jackson. *Purity.* Little, Brown, 2012. 224p. $17.99. 978-0-316-18246-1.

HOOK: How important is a promise, really?

REVIEW: Just before Shelby's mom died, she made Shelby promise three things: to listen to her father, to love as much as possible, and to live without restraint. Now Shelby is sixteen, and her father has asked Shelby to attend the Princess Ball, an annual father-daughter event that culminates with girls taking a vow of purity. Shelby panics at the thought of a conflict between Promise One and Promise Three: How can she live an unrestrained life if she vows to live a pure life? Aided by her friends, Shelby tries to exploit a loophole in the process by losing her virginity before taking the purity vow . . . but she has mixed feelings.

Recommended for readers age 14 and up.

Sex: 4; Cussing: 1; Violence: 0

abstinence, alcohol, death, grieving, kissing, nudity, safe sex, sexual situations, Star Trek *sex*

READER REACTION: Although the plot sounds fluffy, this story is filled with great characters. Teen readers laughed frequently and needed a hanky for the final chapter.

ALERTS: On-page sex with a sympathetic near-stranger boosts the "sex-rating," but the sweetness of the characters, especially Shelby's well-intentioned father, redeems much of the book.

Tracy, Kristin. *Lost It.* Simon and Schuster, 2007. 288p. LB $15.99. 978-1-4352-0458-4. $8.99 Trade pb. 978-1-4169-3475-2.

HOOK: Tess didn't start her junior year of high school planning to lose her virginity under an upside-down canoe.

REVIEW: At the beginning of the novel, Tess tells readers that she lost her virginity. Tess is very honest about the relationship that led to sex (in the outdoors, which she hates). Yet, there are many other "losses" in the novel, and these are the real focus. Some of the side moments are the best: a friend who needs to blow up a poodle; parents "trying to find themselves;" Tess's grandmother—not a cookie-baking little old lady! And there are many "laugh out loud" moments that make this a quick, fun read.

Recommended for readers age 14 and up.

Sex: 4; Cussing: 1; Violence: 1

kissing, sexual situations, Star Trek *sex*

READER REACTION: Teens love Tess and her quirky sense of humor. Quickly they realize that this book is much more than they expected.

ALERTS: The book is honest about a first sexual experience. It is not graphic or gratuitous, but it is in the first section of the novel for an important reason.

Girl Power: Strong Young Women

- *Big Fat Manifesto* (Vaught)
- *Forever in Blue* (Brashares)
- *Graceling* (Cashore)
- *The Hunger Games* (Collins)
- *Liar* (Larbalestier)
- *The Luxe* (Godbersen)
- *A Northern Light* (Donnelly)
- Touch (Accardo)
- *The True Meaning of Cleavage* (Fredericks)
- *Until I Die* (Plum)

Accardo, Jus. *Touch.* Entangled Press, 2011. 400p. $9.99 Trade pb. 978-1-62061-013-8.

HOOK: Extreme skateboarding girl meets hot guy who kills with just a touch. What's not to like?

REVIEW: After drinking too much and riding a skateboard along the roof of a barn, seventeen-year-old Deznee stumbles into Kaleas, who is being chased by guys in blue bodysuits brandishing Tazers. Dez helps Kale, who is a total hottie, despite looking like he'd "gone ten rounds with a weed-whacker," and brings him to her house to shower off the blood and mud. He is terrified to see a photo of her father and petrified when dad arrives home. Dez lives to piss off her father, so she helps Kale escape from her house, thus beginning the first part of a series about creatures like Kale, who are genetically altered beings called Sixes. Each creature has a different power. Kale can kill people with just a touch, but why doesn't it work on Dez?

Recommended for readers age 13 and up.

Sex: 3; Cussing: 4; Violence: 5

abstinence, alcohol, bullying, child abuse, cussing, drinking, drugs, kissing, nudity, paranormal, sexual situations, violence

READER REACTION: This book appeals to both boys and girls. Dez is a wise-cracking, gutsy heroine, but Kale is an engaging character as well, especially in the fight scenes. There are several holes: With all this advanced technology, why weren't Sixes implanted with a chip in case they escaped? Why didn't Dez's father have someone watching her? Sixes with "just the needed power" keep cropping up conveniently at the last minute.

ALERTS: Even as a "bad guy," Dez's father is too stereotypical.

Brashares, Ann. *Forever in Blue.* Delacorte Press, 2007. 416p. $18.99. 978-0-385-72936-9. $9.99 Trade pb. 978-0-385-73401-1.

HOOK: Fans of *The Sisterhood of the Traveling Pants* will love the fourth and final installment.

REVIEW: The Sisterhood (Carmen, Lena, Bridget and Tibby) are separated once again by geography, but united in their common memories and fondness for each other. They are now eighteen and just out of their first year of college. Their strong friendship, symbolized by the pants, binds them together and anchors each in time of distress. This idealized friendship is a graceful, comforting read as the characters leave adolescence and begin making steps towards adulthood.

Recommended for readers age 12 and up.

Sex: 3; Cussing: 2; Violence: 1

alcohol, cussing, drinking, grieving, kissing, lots of giggles, nudity, Star Trek *sex*

READER REACTION: Fans of this chick-lit series are legion, and it has aged relatively gracefully since the first book was published in 2003. Readers unfamiliar with the series will be unable to follow the action—this book does not stand alone.

ALERTS: There really is sex in the fourth book! Unlike the other titles in the series, where sexual situations were taken off page, this book includes on-the-page canoodling.

Cashore, Kristin. *Graceling.* Houghton MIfflin, 2008. 480p. $17.00. 978-0-15-206396-2. $9.99 Trade pb. 978-0-547-25830-0.

HOOK: Some people in Katsa's world are "graced" with special talents. Katsa seems to have a strong talent for killing.

REVIEW: Katsa's grace for killing was discovered at the age of eight, when she smashed the nose bone of an inappropriate older relative, killing him. Since then, her uncle the King has honed Katsa's talent and exploited her ability to bully and punish his adversaries. Katsa understands her loyalties to the King, and has been (outwardly) following orders, but she also has found a way to undermine his influence within the kingdom. When she meets Prince Po, he nearly kills her in a sword fight—and Katsa has met her match.

Recommended for readers age 13 and up.

Sex: 2; Cussing: 1; Violence: 3 (one scene is a 5)

abuse, gay friends, grieving, kissing, magic, prejudice, straight friends, Star Trek *sex, violence*

READER REACTION: This book transcends gender among readers—boys read it even though the main character is a girl. We like the strong female character, we like the relationships between Katsa and her friends, as well as the romantic relationships, and we love the action.

ALERTS: Some readers are distressed at the thought of a female "hit man."

Collins, Suzanne. *The Hunger Games*. Scholastic Press, 2010. 384p. $10.99 Trade pb. 978-0-439-02352-8.

HOOK: Allusions to the movie will hook any teen. Ask students to imagine taking a sibling's place in a gladiator-style duel to the death.

REVIEW: The most horrible day of the year in District Twelve is "Reaping Day," when two young people are randomly chosen to participate as Tributes in the brutal Hunger Games. When sixteen-year-old Katniss Everdeen's younger sister is chosen, Katniss doesn't hesitate: She volunteer's to take Prim's place. In order to survive, she must win the game. In order to win, she will have to kill the other Tributes, even those who have become her friends and allies. With themes of oppression and rebellion intricately woven with a tale of survival and abiding love, the quick-paced action sequences are interspersed with nail-biting suspense.

Recommended for readers age 13 and up.

Sex: 1; Cussing: 1; Violence: 5

abuse, bullying, death, drinking, dystopic, grieving, violence

READER REACTION: Teens and pre-teens, as well as adults, have loved this series, and the movie perpetuates the fascination. Although the central character is female, this is not a "girls-only" book.

ALERTS: Parent reaction is strong to the violence in the series. There is plenty of material for discussions of literary themes within the book, such as the environment and man's inhumanity to man. While some adults are disturbed by the brutal storyline, other adults and most teen readers are captivated by this tale of heroics, violence, loyalty, and love.

Donnelly, Jennifer. *A Northern Light*. Harcourt, 2003. 400p. $17. 978-0-15-216705-9. $9.99 Trade pb. 978-0-15-205310-9.

HOOK: The central murder in the book is based on a real case that can be researched; teens often gravitate to books that are based on actual events.

REVIEW: In 1906, Grace Brown was murdered. Fictional-character Mattie is placed within this historical situation as a worker at the hotel where Grace was murdered, and is one of the last people to see Grace alive. Grace gave Mattie letters which she asked her to burn. This is also the story of Mattie and her small town, where education is not important, especially for girls. The writing deals gracefully and unflinchingly with racial injustice, subjugation of women, poverty, and family loyalty. Life for women was especially hard, and girls were treated as objects and property. The chapters gradually reveal Mattie's life and the mystery of Grace's death.

Recommended for readers age 13 and up.

Sex: 3; Cussing: 2; Violence: 4

abstinence, bullying, cussing, death, drinking, kissing, pregnancy, Star Trek *sex*

READER REACTION: The length, the murder, and the sexual references all place this book in the hands of a more mature reader. The book is successful for mother/daughter reading groups.

ALERTS: Sexual references are harsh because of the time and place. In one potentially problematic scene, Mattie encounters a landlord exacting sex for rent; the scene is tactful but distressing.

Fredericks, Mariah. *The True Meaning of Cleavage.* Simon Pulse, 2004. 240p. $9.99 Trade pb. 978-0-689-86958-7.

HOOK: The cover and title lend themselves to pre-conceived notions. Could there be different definitions of "cleavage?"

REVIEW: Sari and Jess have been good friends forever. Now, entering high school, Sari, pretty and developed, enjoys the attention that popular senior, David, suddenly shows her. Jess is concerned that this is causing Sari to diminish their friendship, and is even more concerned that David wants to keep the relationship secret until he can break up with his popular girlfriend. As Jess expresses these concerns to Sari, their friendship suffers even more. Sari and David's relationship becomes sexual and "secret with promises." This is a story about Jess as well, as she enters high school and observes the cliques, politics, and confusion, and the loss of her best friend.

Recommended for readers age 12 and up.

Sex: 3; Cussing: 2; Violence: 1

abstinence, bullying, kissing, Star Trek *sex*

READER REACTION: This is an age-old theme, but well done, which speaks to young teens. Readers relate to and bond with both characters; they care about the outcome.

ALERTS: The sexual encounters between Sari and David are muted and off-page.

Godbersen, Anna. *The Luxe.* HarperCollins, 2008. 464p. $9.99 Trade pb. 978-0-06-134568-5.

HOOK: Allow the girls to drool over the dresses in the cover illustrations for the series.

REVIEW: The year is 1899, and amid decadent parties of the very rich, New York's high society is talking about the astonishing betrothal of the prim-and-proper Elizabeth Holland to the well-born, but badly-behaved, Henry Schoonmaker. On the day of the wedding, Elizabeth is indeed the center of attention . . . at her funeral. Five teens lend themselves to five books in the series, each cover featuring a different fabulous dress. This is a steamy and suspenseful historical tale of scandalous affairs, clandestine trysts, and backstabbing "friends." The clothing is gorgeous, the food is sumptuous, and the love interests are tangled.

Recommended for readers age 12 and up.

Sex: 3; Cussing: 1; Violence: 1

alcohol, death, drinking, grieving, homosexuality, kissing, Star Trek *sex*

READER REACTION: The book is light, but thoroughly enjoyable. It has been compared to *Gossip Girls* for good reason, and that same group of readers will love this! Tired of the normal "historical fiction" book reports? Look no further.

ALERTS: There are several tactful, off-page, but clearly sexual, situations.

Larbalestier, Justine. *Liar.* Bloomsbury, 2009. 384p. $9.99 Trade pb. 978-1-59990-519-8.

HOOK: Talk like Micah. Tell your audience that you are a liar, but wouldn't lie to them; then tell them you just lied, but are telling the truth now; then tell them that was all a lie . . . and that if they read this book, they will be discussing it with their friends for weeks. Talking about the controversy surrounding the cover grabs students as well.

REVIEW: Micah begins by telling us that she is a liar, has always been, but is not lying to us now. Her boyfriend, Zach, has been brutally murdered. Well, he was only her boyfriend in secret. Actually he was dating Sarah, the most popular girl in class. Micah, by contrast, is an outcast with a very odd family. Slowly she tells us she is Black . . . and white. Micah tells us she did see Zach that night, but she didn't kill him. In the next chapter, she tells us she was lying about some things. The story takes a paranormal turn. Or is she lying about that, too? The twists and turns of the story keep you reeling. And, of course, Micah might be lying about the whole thing.

Recommended for readers age 14 and up.

Sex: 3; Cussing: 3; Violence: 4

abuse, alcohol, bullying, death, drinking, kissing, paranormal, sexual situations, StarTrek *sex, violence*

READER REACTION: Teens (and adults) either love or hate this book; some are still wondering about it; but everyone is talking about it, and everybody has an opinion. It takes the concept of "unreliable narrator" to new heights.

ALERTS: This is a tough book to place in any category, and some readers may object to the on-page sexual situations, although they are modestly handled.

Plum, Amy. *Until I Die.* Harper Teen, 2012. 368p. $17.69 Trade pb. 978-0-06-200405-5.

HOOK: If you love someone, would you die for them? If it is your job to save people but not the person you love, could you still die for them?

REVIEW: Vincent and Kate have fallen in love in Paris, the city of love. Vincent is a Revenant, a sort of guardian angel/ancient human mix. The mission of his kind is to save the lives of humans. However, each time they do, they "die," falling into a deep sleep for three days while they are guarded by another Revenant. The bond between Kate and Vincent is so strong that even when Vincent is "dead," he and Kate communicate telepathically. The Revenants need a new champion and all eyes turn to Vincent. There are also double crosses, spies, and twists. Kate and Vincent keep their secrets from each other.

Recommended for readers age 13 and up.

Sex: 2; Cussing: 1; Violence: 5

abstinence, death, drinking, kissing, magic, paranormal, violence

READER REACTION: Kate is a strong leader on her own; she doesn't wait around for Vincent, and she doesn't do foolish things so he can rescue her. There is much that is predictable in the plot. But the biggest prediction will have to wait for the last book! *Until I Die* is #2 in the series. We didn't like the first book (*Die for Me*). We look forward to the third book, *If I Should Die.*

ALERTS: The final fight scene raises the violence rating; otherwise the level would be lower.

Vaught, Susan R. *Big Fat Manifesto*. Bloomsbury, 2008. 336p. $8.99 Trade pb. 978-1-59990-362-0.

HOOK: She's not plus-sized, or large, or overweight, or obese. She's *fat*.

REVIEW: Jamie needs scholarship money for college, so she decides to write a weekly school newspaper column about being fat. With her friends, she investigates injustices at clothing shops, restaurants, and doctor's offices, "outing" those who would dare to oppress her or chastise her for being fat. Then her boyfriend announces his intention to have bariatric surgery. Jamie is a strong-voiced female character with a lot of self-esteem and a bunch of anger. She is not interested in slimming down—she wants to be accepted the way she is. And don't assume that the fat girl doesn't have a sex life, either. It's tactful, but it's there.

Recommended for readers age 12 and up.

Sex: 2; Cussing: 2; Violence: 2

bullying, cussing, grieving, kissing, prejudice, prostitution, sexual situations

READER REACTION: Even readers who don't want to read about a fat girl get drawn into the story by Jamie's strong, engaging, sassy-and-sarcastic voice.

ALERTS: Don't give this just to large teens, but to anyone who will agree to read the first two pages.

Havin' My Baby: Pregnancy and Other Side Effects of Sex

- *After* (Efaw)
- *Bumped* (McCafferty)
- *Every Little Thing in the World* (de Gramont)
- *First Part Last* (Johnson)
- *Imani All Mine* (Porter)
- *Jumping off Swings* (Knowles)
- *November Blues* (Draper)

de Gramont, Nina. *Every Little Thing in the World*. Atheneum, 2010. 288p. $16.99. 978-1-4169-8013-1. $8.99 Trade pb. 978-1-4169-8015-5.

HOOK: Sometimes smart people do dumb things. Sometimes bad choices count more than good education.

REVIEW: In spite of comprehensive sex education classes at the private school she has attended since kindergarten, sixteen-year-old Syd is unintentionally pregnant. When she and her best friend Natalia are caught by the police for "borrowing" Natalia's parents' car, the girls are shipped off to a wilderness canoe camp in Canada. Syd wrestles with the ethics of her situation, which is complicated by Natalia's recent discovery that she is adopted, and by both girls' attraction to boys at the camp. This is a story with plenty of questions and no easy answers. Syd's narrative voice is strong, and her changing relationship with her parents is deftly depicted.

Recommended for readers age 14 and up.

Sex: 3; Cussing: 2; Violence: 0

abortion, alcohol, cussing, grieving, homosexuality, incest, kissing, nudity, pregnancy, safe sex, sexual situations

READER REACTION: Readers recognize that sometimes smart people do dumb things in real life, but many of them are amazed to see this concept as part of a book! Most agree that making mistakes is universal, and that the main character's journey to take responsibility for her choices is worthwhile. The multiple plot-lines make this book seem more like real life than an "afterschool special."

ALERTS: Minimal cussing, some underage drinking, some nudity (including skinny dipping in the lake), and some pre-sexual intimacy, but no on-page intercourse.

Draper, Sharon. *November Blues.* Atheneum, 2007. 320p. $17.99. 978-1-4169-0698-8. $7.99 pb. 978-1-4169-0699-5.

HOOK: November is pregnant, her boyfriend is dead. Her boyfriend's parents want the baby. Now what?

REVIEW: After the death of her boyfriend, Josh, sixteen-year-old November realizes that she is pregnant. Jericho, Josh's cousin, grieves the loss of a best friend. November must deal with all the stresses of a teenage mother, from school issues to morning sickness. November is supported by her mom, although the pregnancy causes an obvious strain on their relationship. November must also deal with Josh's wealthy parents. They want this baby, their last link to their only son. They have the resources November and her mother could never have. *Battle for Jericho* begins and *Just Another Hero* finishes this trilogy with a multitude of characters and problems—most important, school violence.

Recommended for readers age 13 and up.

Sex: 2; Cussing: 1; Violence: 1

death, drinking, drugs, grieving, kissing, pregnancy, prejudice, religious beliefs

READER REACTION: This story is about relationships—between mother and daughter, with friends who help, with friends who disappear, and between grandparents and daughters-in-law. Teens observe every aspect of a pregnancy through November's trips to the doctor's office and her conversations with her girlfriends and mother. They see this also from the emotional side. Health teachers like this book for that reason.

ALERTS: The romance side of the pregnancy happened in the first book in the trilogy, leaving the pregnancy-related facts for this book.

Efaw, Amy. *After.* Viking, 2009. 350p. $17.99. 978-0-670-01183-4. $8.99 Trade pb. 978-0-14-241590-0.

HOOK: Devon is sitting at home pretending to be sick when her mother returns from work. The policeman who is going door-to-door looking for clues about the baby in the dumpster notices the blood on Devon.

REVIEW: Straight-A student Devon, exceptional soccer team member, and good girl, has given birth. Devon says she didn't even know she was pregnant. When she is taken to court for abandoning her baby in a trash can, she still claims that she was unaware of even giving birth. Bits and pieces of the story are told in flashbacks, and we learn of the unprotected sex that resulted in Devon's pregnancy. Will Devon be tried as an adult or juvenile for the murder of the baby? Does she really remember nothing? Will she spend her life in prison?

Recommended for readers age 13 and up.

Sex: 3; Cussing: 2; Violence: 4

abstinence, child abuse, cussing, death, kissing, nudity, pregnancy, sexual situations, Star Trek *sex, violence*

READER REACTION: Students are mesmerized by the idea behind the book; some find it hard to believe, but all have an opinion on whether Devon knowingly killed her baby or was psychologically unable to understand. Efaw leaves that decision up to the reader. Give this one to teachers who love to see students conduct research.

ALERTS: The scene in the bathroom where Devon gives birth is a horrific scene, not for the less mature student.

Johnson, Angela. *The First Part Last.* Simon & Schuster, 2010, 2004. $7.99 Trade pb. 978-1-4424-0343-7. $6.99 pb. 978-0-689-84923-7.

HOOK: Share the cover. This is a book from a teen *father's* viewpoint.

REVIEW: Bobby wanted to be an artist. Instead he's a single dad struggling to raise his baby daughter, Feather. He knows nothing about babies. He is scared and exhausted. At sixteen, he just wants to hang out with the guys and have pizza, but his parents refuse to babysit, forcing him to take full responsibility.

Recommended for readers age 13 and up.

Sex 2; Cussing 2; Violence 0

kissing, pregnancy, prejudice, religious beliefs, Star Trek *sex, sexual situations.*

READER REACTION: Teens love this compassionate view of teen fatherhood. The back-and-forth timeline in different chapters is somewhat jarring. The shortness of the story and the unusual perspective is attractive to reluctant readers. Khalipa Oldjohn narrates the audio version and really makes the story come alive.

ALERTS: At times, this feels like a cautionary tale, but is saved by Bobby's poetic voice. It is an interesting side note that Bobby and Nia are both middle class kids, when many readers might expect the stereotype of poor Black families.

Knowles, Jo. *Jumping off Swings.* Candlewick, 2009. 240p. $16.99. 978-0-7636-3949-5. $7.99 Trade pb. 978-0-7636-5296-8.

HOOK: Every time Ellie hooks up with a new guy, she's sure that there will be more to the encounter than sex, and that she will finally feel loved. But the "one-time thing" with eager virgin Josh gets much more complicated when Ellie gets pregnant.

REVIEW: The events of nine months after a fateful night in Josh's van are told by four narrators: Ellie and Josh, plus their friends Corinne and Caleb, who live complicated lives of their own. Their voices are mostly realistic, although the situations often seem straight out of an "afterschool special." The "condom slipped off" situation that causes the pregnancy seems somewhat plausible. Sexual situations are described in flashback sequences, without graphic details, and childbirth is treated with similar distance: Ellie repeats the phrase "it hurts so much" frequently, until she is sedated for the caesarean-section birth. Adult characters are flawed, but the reader understands that most of the parents really do love their teen offspring, even if they lack the ability to express their love openly.

Recommended for readers age 13 and up.

Sex: 3; Cussing: 2; Violence: 1

Abuse, bullying, cussing, drinking, kissing, nudity, pregnancy, safe sex, sexual situations

READER REACTION: Teens looking for an emotional problem-novel with minimal cussing find this book engaging enough. The writing is repetitive (we got tired of the word "empty") and the characters are mostly predictable, but the situation speaks to teens from a place of fear: "What if nobody loved me?"

ALERTS: The issues associated with sexual situations, underage drinking, and partying are good for discussion when paired with concepts like relationships and self-confidence.

McCafferty, Anne. *Bumped.* Balzer and Bray, 2011. 336p. $16.99. 978-0-06-196274-5. $8.99 Trade pb. 978-0-06-196275-2.

HOOK: In this up-tempo dystopian novel, teen pregnancies are not only normal, they are vital.

REVIEW: A virus renders everyone over the age of eighteen infertile, making teen pregnancy essential for the survival of humanity. Pregnant teens are considered the apex of beauty and the center of importance, and sixteen-year-old twins Melody and Harmony have only two years remaining until obsolescence. Melody is a contracted pro-pregger, who has signed with an agent to produce a very expensive delivery that will pay for a top-notch college, as well as her adoptive parents' debts. Harmony, raised in a conservative Amish-esque community, has run away from her adoptive family to bring her newly-found twin into a state of grace with God. Absolutely nothing goes as planned.

Recommended for readers age 14 and up.

Sex: 3; Cussing: 1; Violence: 1

abstinence, alcohol, bullying, cussing, drugs, dystopia, gay friends, grieving, kissing, pregnancy, prostitution, religious beliefs, sexual situations, Star Trek *sex*

READER REVIEW: The narration-swapping is confusing to some, and annoying to a few. Some readers don't get the satire; others get it, but think that religion is unfairly "dissed." Is an "up-tempo dystopia" really a "dystopia"? Some readers are skeptical; others just laugh and enjoy the silliness of the futuristic lingo. Fun slang and the twist on cultural values almost mask important messages about teen sexuality, sibling rivalry, religious tolerance, and the difficulty of living a life different from the one that parents and society expect. The sequel, *Thumped,* continues the story with more social commentary and twin identity swapping.

ALERTS: Lots of talk about sex and sexual situations, plus one instance of steamy *Star Trek* sex, but nothing happens on the page. This book would be interesting to discuss and contrast to Libba Bray's *Beauty Queens.*

Porter, Connie. *Imani All Mine.* Mariner Books, 2000, 1999. 224p. $13.95 Trade pb. 978-0-618-05678-1.

HOOK: Try to find the attractive cover; several editions exist, but only one is pretty.

REVIEW: Tasha is African-American, fifteen, fat, and alone. When she is approached by a boy whose only interest is sex, she is understandably easily seduced. Baby girl Imani is the result, and for the first time, Tasha has something that is "all mine." This story of inner city life is harsh, real, and tragic. The unsentimental story of an already-pregnant teen who tries to understand sex and love itself is beautifully written. Faith plays an important role in Tasha's life, and ultimately, in her decisions.

Recommended for readers age 14 and up.

Sex: 5; Cussing: 4; Violence: 4

abstinence, bullying, child abuse, cussing, death, drinking, drugs, grieving, kissing, pregnancy, prejudice, rape, religious beliefs, Star Trek *sex, violence*

READER REACTION: Is this a book of hope or despair? Teens who read the story have opposite feelings about it. A great book for discussion groups.

ALERTS: The text uses Ebonics and no punctuation for conversations. The themes in this book are mature and sometimes graphic. The tendency to see Tasha as a stereotypical Black girl is one that needs caution, because she isn't.

Hit Me Baby, One More Time:
Violence and Dysfunctional Relationships

- *A Bad Boy Can Be Good for a Girl* (Stone)
- *Because I Am Furniture* (Chaltas)
- *Boys Lie* (Neufeld)
- *Breathing Underwater* (Flinn)
- *Identical* (Hopkins)
- *Living Dead Girl* (Scott)
- *Sold* (McCormick)
- *Speak* (Anderson)
- *You against Me* (Downham)

Anderson, Laurie Halse. *Speak.* Farrar, Straus and Giroux, 1999. 224p. $17.99 Trade pb. 978-0-374-37152-4. $9.99 pb. 978-0-312-67439-7.

HOOK: The summer before high school, Melinda went to a party, drank more than she should, and agreed to go "out back" with a handsome senior boy . . . who raped her. But when she tried to call 911, Melinda was unable to say anything. The cops busted the party—and now everybody is mad at Melinda.

REVIEW: Melinda's inability to vocalize the cause of her distress at the party gets much worse before it gets better. On the first day of school, she realizes that nobody in school will talk to her, because they think she ratted out the party. So she stops talking—literally. It is only through an art class that Melinda finally learns to express herself through an assignment. Her communication is non-verbal at first, but gradually, Melinda gathers words to protect herself, and *finally* words (and actions) to accuse her assailant.

Recommended for readers age 13 and up.

Sex: 3; Cussing: 2; Violence: 4

alcohol, bullying, cussing, drinking, kissing, prejudice, rape, violence

READER REACTION: Many students are familiar with the 2004 film made from this book, but other students are always quick to say that the book was much better than the movie. We recommend *Speak* to every eighth grade girl. Melinda's triumph at the end of the book speaks volumes to young girls. *Speak* is one of the few books in Aarene's public library teen collection that needs to be replaced frequently, as it literally gets read to pieces each year.

ALERTS: *Speak* has garnered more than its share of censors. Volumes have been written about this book. It is a story to be talked about in PTA groups, teacher meetings, and book groups. Although frequently censored because of the scary nature of the sexual assault, *Speak* is a powerful and popular book among middle school readers, and we encourage this. The fictional scenario is completely plausible, the traumatized heroine is precisely the age of our eighth grade students, and the ferocity of peer pressure in middle school is only exceeded by the amount of peer pressure in high school.

Chaltas, Thalia. *Because I Am Furniture.* Viking, 2009. 369p. $8.99 Trade pb. 978-0-14-241510-8.

HOOK: The book is written in blank-verse poem format, so choose a page and read it aloud when your booktalk needs to be slowed down and made serious. Have counseling pamphlets available because of the serious nature of this topic.

REVIEW: Anke's father beats up her brother and sexually assaults her sister, but he ignores Anke. She must be the lucky one, to escape his rage, but sometimes Anke feels that he must love the others much more than he loves her. Against her father's wishes, Anke joins the school volleyball team, and it is there that she finds the strength and the voice to speak up and defend her family. Written in sparse verse form, Anke's inner turmoil finally boils over. Will speaking up destroy her family?

Recommended for readers age 14 and up.

Sex: 3; Cussing: 3; Violence: 5

Bullying, child abuse, cussing, drinking, incest, kissing, nudity, rape, sexual situations, violence

READER REACTION: This is a moving, disturbing story. It will stay with the reader long after they finish it. Violent and sexual situations are indirectly referenced, as Anke and her family deny that they occur. The "distancing feeling" given by the novel-in-poetry form helps readers choke down horrible situations. It is a novel that lends itself to research on child abuse through health or social studies classes, but should be assigned carefully, with alternate books available to readers.

ALERTS: This book can be distressing for fragile readers. The subject is very difficult to understand from the outside. Parents may object to the content; alternately, they may encourage discussion of the topic. Bring it to the attention of your PTA—it is guaranteed to get people talking.

Downham, Jenny. *You against Me.* David Fickling Books, 2011. 416p. $16.99. 978-0-385-75160-5. $9.99 pb 978-0-385-75266-4.

HOOK: Is it still rape if you said you wanted to have sex, then drank too much and decided at the last minute you didn't want sex?

REVIEW: Mikey and his sister Karyn are trying to hold their lives together in a poor section of a seaside British town. Things fall apart when fifteen-year-old Karyn says she has been raped at a party and refuses to leave her house. Vowing revenge, Mikey crashes a party at the home of the accused rapist, and ends up falling in love with the boy's sister, Ellie. The situation is messy. The novel is given depth by Ellie's relationships with her parents, her adored brother, and now Mikey. Is Ellie reacting to her parents? To Mikey? She is unsure. She gave a statement to the police, but what did she actually see the night of the incident?

Recommended for readers age 14 and up.

Sex: 3; Cussing: 2; Violence: 5

abstinence, alcohol, bullying, cussing, drinking, grieving, kissing, nudity, prejudice, rape, sexual situations, Star Trek *sex, violence*

READER REACTION: This is a complicated, interesting look at what rape is and how differently each of the characters react. All the characters are very believable.

ALERTS: The too positive ending is flawed and leaves readers with too many questions.

Flinn, Alex. *Breathing Underwater.* HarperTeen, 2002. 272p. $9.99 Trade pb. 978-0-06-447257-9.

HOOK: Nick doesn't understand Caitlin's treachery. He only slapped her to keep her in line, because he loves her so much.

REVIEW: On page one, readers learn that Caitlin and her family have been granted a restraining order against Caitlin's former boyfriend Nick, and Nick has been assigned to anger management training. Nothing has ever made Nick so angry. Nick is smart, charming, and athletic. He also has a secret that he can't tell anybody, not even Caitlin, who seems to understand everything else about him. He's so desperate to keep her love all to himself that he starts to control her behavior: first verbally, and then physically. Through Nick's journal, the reader comes to understand that Nick didn't spontaneously start abusing Caitlin. Abuse is something that Nick learned about at home.

Recommended for readers age 14 and up.

Sex: 3; Cussing: 3; Violence: 3

abuse, bullying, cussing, drinking, grieving, kissing, sexual situations, suicide, violence.

Reader Reaction: This book offers the unique perspective of being told from the point of view of a teen abuser. The situation is tough and sympathetically told, without making excuses for classic abusive behavior. We recommend the book to boys, but also to girls because of Caitlin's frightening but typical response to abuse.

ALERTS: The topic is strong, and the story is powerfully told. Fragile readers may wish to avoid it.

Hopkins, Ellen. *Identical.* Margaret K. McElderry Books, 2010. 592p. $17.99. 978-1-4169-5005-9. $10.99 Trade pb. 978-1-4169-5006-6.

HOOK: Some books should not be used to "hook" a student into reading. This is one of those books that should be talked about gently, but with feeling. Someone in your audience may need it.

REVIEW: Raeanne and Kaeleigh are the identical twin daughters of a Superior Court judge and his wife. When a horrible accident nearly kills the entire family, the wife runs for Congress, creating an empty spot in the family—both in their home and in their hearts. With her mother away, Kaeleigh becomes the object of her father's sexual attention. Lamenting that her father doesn't love her because she gets none of his attention, Raeanne begins abusing drugs and alcohol. Kaeleigh begins to cut herself and becomes bulimic. This is a pit so deep it seems impossible to find a way out.

Recommended for readers age 15 and up.

Sex: 5; Cussing: 3; Violence: 5

alcohol, bullying, child abuse, cussing, drinking, drugs, grieving, incest, nudity, sexual situations, violence.

READER REACTION: This novel is so agonizing that readers are almost soothed by the fact that it is told in blank verse. Anything more would be too hard to read. While it is a dark novel, it speaks volumes to readers about the psychology of abuse.

ALERTS: Because of the incest, the drugs, and the sheer horror of the novel, it is best placed in the hands of mature students. As with this author's other books, talking about *Identical* guarantees interesting discussions in PTA programs.

McCormick, Patricia. *Sold.* Hyperion, 2008. 263p. $8.99 Trade pb. 978-0-7868-5172-0.

HOOK: Lakshmi owes Mumtaz 20,000 rupees. This is how she does the math:

- If six men come to her room every night, and each pays Mumtaz 30 rupees, then Lakshmi can subtract 180 rupees each day from her debt.
- If she does this for 100 more days, her debt will be almost paid.

But then Shahanna teaches Mumtaz about "city subtraction":
- Half of the money the men pay goes to the debt.
- Mumtaz charges 80 rupees each day for food.
- Mumtaz charges 100 rupees per week for a bed and pillow.
- The doctor charges 500 rupees each month for a shot, so the girls won't become pregnant.

That's when Lakshmi knows that math will not save her, and she will never escape.

REVIEW: Lakshmi is thirteen years old when her stepfather sells her to an "auntie" traveling to the big city. The auntie has promised Lakshmi's mother that the girl will go to work as a maid in the city. However, the fictional Lakshmi—like up to 12,000 real Nepali girls each year—is sold into a life of sexual slavery in an Indian brothel. Gradually, Lakshmi forms friendships that help her survive. Still, her life is mostly without hope. The girls fear Mumtaz, the corrupt police, and the Americans who might take them from the brothel only to shame them and abandon them on the streets.

Recommended for readers age 13 and up.

Sex: 3; Cussing: 3; Violence: 3

alcohol, bullying, child abuse, cussing, death, drinking, drugs, prostitution, rape, religious beliefs, sexual situations, Star Trek *sex, violence*

READER REACTION: There are Youtube videos available to offer students when they ask for the facts behind this novel. No one reads this book without being shaken.

ALERTS: The author's research for this novel included visits to shelters in Kathmandu, the Himalayas, and Calcutta, where she interviewed women and girls rescued from the sex trade. The sexual situations are tactfully described; they are, nonetheless, appropriately horrible.

Neufeld, John. *Boys Lie.* D.K. Children, 1999. 176p. O.P. 978-0-7894-2624-6.

HOOK: Imagine that a friend has just been assaulted. What do you do?

REVIEW: When Gina is assaulted in the swimming pool, neither she nor her mother know how to deal with the situation. They move to a new town, hoping to leave the issue behind them. Her new friend's sister splashing in the ocean brings back the horrible memories, and Gina's screaming fit alerts every-one to her problem. She receives comfort and understanding from *most*, but three boys in her new eighth grade class decide that what Gina needs is a "good" sexual experience. One of them attacks her, thinking that because of the prior attack, she will never tell.

Recommended for readers age 13 and up.

Sex: 3; Cussing: 1; Violence: 3

bullying, drinking, kissing, nudity, sexual situations, violence

READER REACTION: This book is great to use during "Bullying Week." Teens have embraced it, because it shows an understanding of their feelings and an understanding of bullying that can lead to abuse.

ALERTS: This book is out of print, but available from used booksellers. It has been such a popular and defining book for so many teens, we had to include it here. Parents have embraced this book as a con-versation starter with daughters.

Scott, Elizabeth. *Living Dead Girl.* Simon Pulse, 2008. 176p. $16.99. 978-1-4169-6059-1. $8.99 Trade pb. 978-1-4169-6060-7.

HOOK: How would you react if a man in a uniform told you to follow him? You were loitering, after all. Your group moved on. What if you were ten years old?

REVIEW: While separated from her group on a museum field trip, Alice is approached by a uniformed guard, who offers to take her back to her class. Of course, Alice believed this authority figure, just as, at ten, she also believed that if she didn't do what he said, he would kill her family and burn down their house. But her name isn't Alice. He changed that when he changed her into his sex slave.

Recommended for readers age 13 and up.

Sex: 3; Cussing: 3; Violence: 5

bullying, child abuse, cussing, death, grieving, nudity, rape, sexual situations, violence

READER REACTION: This book is not for all readers and not for the faint of heart. It is a short story that will haunt you for a long time.

ALERTS: This horror story of a sexual perversion reaches the "eewwww" factor in a hurry. Never graphic, the obvious sex is both beyond horrible and very believable. Yet, we feel this is an important enough book that we present it to eighth graders to allow us to talk about abductions and fighting back. This is another great book to discuss with the PTA.

Stone, Tanya Lee. *A Bad Boy Can Be Good for a Girl.* Wendy Lamb, 2006. 228p. $7.99 Trade pb. 978-0-553-49509-6.

HOOK: This is about the guy who "only wants one thing," and the girls who date him.

REVIEW: Josie is a strong, opinionated, self-assured freshman when the popular senior jock asks her out. She falls for his charm, and is amazed at her own hormonal response. Then the guy dumps her, because she won't "put out." Furious and hurt, Josie writes a warning to other girls about him in the blank endpapers of the school library's copy of Judy Blume's book *Forever*. Nicolette and Aviva have different but equally unhappy relationships with the same boy, and they ultimately join the ranks of girls who find solidarity in the scribbled margins of *Forever*.

Recommended for readers age 14 and up.

Sex: 4; Cussing: 3; Violence: 1

abstinence, abuse, bullying, cussing, drinking, kissing, nudity, sexual situations

READER REACTION: Written in verse form, this hot, topical novel is a quick, vital, and sometimes painful book to read. Josie is the most eloquent of the girls—and her desire to take action in response to a horrible experience is laudable. If only more library books had similar annotations—think how many mistakes we all might avoid! The edgy nature of the topic and the sexual content attracts some readers and repels others. As always, controversy makes for a great discussion.

ALERTS: Sexual situations late in the book are explicit.

Laughing My Butt Off: Sex and Humor

- *Angus, Thongs and Full-Frontal Snogging* (Rennison)
- *Beauty Queens* (Bray)
- *Carter's Unfocused One-Track Mind* (Crawford)
- *How to Get Suspended* (Selzer)
- *Swim the Fly* (Calame)

Bray, Libba. *Beauty Queens.* Scholastic Press, 2011. 396p. $18.99. 978-0-439-89597-2. $9.99 Trade pb. 978-0-439-89598-9.

HOOK: A planeload of teen beauty pageant contestants crash-lands on a (supposedly) deserted island. Will they turn all *Lord of the Flies*? Will the Sparkle Ponies prevail?

REVIEW: The survivors face bigger challenges than pageant judges: finding food, water, and shelter. Led by Miss Texas, the girls continue to work on their pageant prep. Unbeknownst to the beauty queens, the Corporation (a sponsor of the Teen Dream contest and purveyor of beauty supplies to the unbeautiful) also has a presence on the island. And apparently, the tragic, "accidental" demise of plucky beauty queens would send ratings—and sales of feminine depilatory cream—way, way up. At first, the girls seem homogenous: mostly white, mostly blonde, mostly dumb. As the story delves deeper into the back-story of each main character, readers discover that there is substance within even the whitest, blondest, and dumbest beauty queen in the group.

Recommended for readers age 14 and up.

Sex: 5; Cussing: 3; Violence: 3

abstinence, alcohol, bullying, cussing, death, gay friends, grieving, homosexuality, kissing, nudity, preju-dice, safe sex, sexual questioning, sexual situations, Star Trek *sex, straight friends, violence*

READER REACTION: Teens totally get the satire. They love the pokes at modern consumer culture; they enjoy the empowerment message, too. Frequent "commercial interruptions" (footnoted commentary boosting Corporation products, television shows, and opinions) break an already-funny story into smaller, hilarious sound-bites. Those who listened to the audiobook (read by the author) recommend it to their friends—including their adult friends.

ALERTS: This book contains sexual situations, LGBTQ characters, feminists, corporation stooges, an insane dictator of a tiny country called ChaCha, and some really good tips on alternative uses for feminine depilatory cream.

Calame, Don. *Swim the Fly.* Candlewick Press, 2009. 345p. $7.99 Trade pb. 978-0-7636-4776-6.

HOOK: The goal for the summer is to see a real, live girl naked.

REVIEW: Matt, Sean, and Coop, best friends since grade school, always set a goal for themselves for the summer. This summer, the goal is to see a real, live girl naked. While working towards the goal, Matt also decides that he will impress Kelly, a new girl on his swim team, by swimming the grueling 100-yard fly. This is a laugh-out-loud, read-the-funny-bits-to-your-friends book. The author has a strong background in writing situational comedy for television, which translates clearly into this story. The book is full of slapstick scenes featuring absurd plans of three teen boys.

Recommended for readers age 13 and up.

Sex: 2; Cussing: 3; Violence: 2

bullying, cussing, drinking, kissing, masturbation, nudity, sexual situations

READER REACTION: This is definitely a "boy book," featuring plenty of farts jokes, poop jokes, vomit jokes, poop jokes, catchy dialogue, and more poop jokes. What junior-high guy wouldn't love this book? And what adult guy wouldn't love this book? Or is that redundant? Teachers, as well as students, enjoy it—even those who aren't guys.

ALERTS: Locker room language and raunchy (but silly) situations may not be appropriate for all readers.

Crawford, Brent. *Carter's Unfocused One-Track Mind.* Hyperion, 2012. 304p. $16.99. 978-1-4231-4445-8. $8.99 Trade pb. 978-1-4231-4450-2.

HOOK: Although not so hilariously comical as others in this section, the conversation where Carter apologizes to Amber for sophomore boys being *sophomoric.* is very sweet and amusing. It gives the novel a tinge of being serious, as well as laugh-out-loud funny (p30-31). Otherwise, just read the bathroom scene where he slips in feces and gets vomit in his ear.

REVIEW: Will Carter, now a sophomore, is building up through football, thinking about a theater school in New York City, and still hoping for sex with Abby. He and his friends join what seems like an unsupervised party every weekend, create a "fight club" with one pair of gloves and one pair of ski gloves, go camping and start a major fire, and generally have a bunch of cool adventures. Realistic? Not a chance. Laugh-out-loud funny? You will need to wipe away the tears. Even after you put the book down, you will still have visions of the bathroom floor full of pee, feces, vomit, and Will slipping across the bathroom floor, and getting puke in his ear.

Recommended for readers age 14 and up.

Sex: 3; Cussing: 3; Violence: 2

abstinence, alcohol, bullying, cussing, drugs, kissing, nudity, paranormal, pregnancy, safe sex, sexual situations, Star Trek *sex*

READER REACTION: Set up for junior high humor, this is the third and predicted final in the series. Crawford writes plays, and this book reads as though it were a movie script. Students have chosen this (and his other books) to do reader's theater and book report scripting.

ALERTS: The overall tone is one of kids getting away with some very stupid stunts—with a "not to be tried at home without supervision" warning. Carter's parents and sister are concerned and intelligent, but Carter and his buddies are not.

Rennison, Louise. *Angus, Thongs, and Full-Frontal Snogging.* Harper Collins, 2006, 2000. 247p. $9.99 Trade pb. 978-0-06-447227-2.

HOOK: Read the first page of the "kissing" lesson out loud. Students will be clamoring for the rest of the book once they've heard it!

REVIEW: Georgia Nicholson reveals all the details of her tragic life: her gigantic nose, her bizarre cat, and her fascination with Robbie the sex god. Written in diary form brimming with extreme British slang, the outrageous humor is irresistible. Over-the-top melodramatic? Yes. And what teen doesn't have at least a smidgeon of melodrama lurking millimeters beneath the skin? The humor is non-stop, the slang is bizarre and amusing, and the situations are fun and mostly-harmless (although Georgia would hardly agree!)

Recommended for readers age 12 and up.

Sex: 2; Cussing: 3 (British cuss words only); Violence: 0

Cussing, kissing

READER REACTION: Teen girls love the humor, although some think that Georgia is shallow and self-absorbed (and they are correct). Most of them agree that reading this book in a quiet place like a classroom or public transit is a bad idea, because it's impossible not to laugh out loud.

ALERTS: The slapstick fun of weird slang words continues for ten books, but the main joke is always the same: Georgia does impulsive stuff to impress guys and she talks funny.

Selzer, Adam. *How to Get Suspended and Influence People.* Laurel Leaf, 2008. 192p. O.P. pb. 978-0440-42160-3.

HOOK: Leon thinks sex education class is boring. He's got a plan to fix that.

REVIEW: Fourteen-year-old Leon sarcastically narrates the events that result when he decides to make an avant-garde sex education movie as an assignment for his "gifted and talented" class. Leon's video is weird but comforting, irrational but informative—and very quickly banned at school. Leon and his classmates address some common contradictions found in public school, where masturbation is often called normal but more often considered vulgar; where nudity may be classical but still censored; and where kids and adults will never see eye-to-eye. Although the story is relatively predictable, the writing is quirky, engaging, and funny.

Recommended for readers age 13 and up.

Sex: 2; Cussing: 2; Violence: 1 (the garage blows up as result of an experiment, not terrorism)

cussing, kissing

READER REACTION: This fast-paced novel appeals to middle school readers who wonder what "normal" is and if they will ever get there. It's fun, funny, and contains more than a little bit of social commentary, too.

ALERTS: Everyone recognizes the hypocrisy of public schools and polite society, where teens are told that the changes of puberty are normal and not to be ashamed of, but where talking about sexual topics like masturbation is strictly forbidden. This book takes that concept and runs wild with it.

Mostly Harmless: Great Books with a *Little* Bit of Sex, Drugs, Violence, or Rock-and-Roll

- *The ABC's of Kissing Boys* (Ferraro)
- *Along for the Ride* (Dessen)
- *Americus* (Reed)
- *Bloody Jack* series (Meyer)
- *Confessions of a Serial Kisser* (Van Draanan)
- *Crazy in Love* (Mackall)
- *Games* (Gorman)
- *Marcelo in the Real World* (Stork)
- *Sex Kittens and Horn Dogs* (Wood)

Dessen, Sarah. *Along for the Ride.* Viking, 2009. 416p. $19.99. 978-0-670-01194-0. $9.99 Trade pb. 978-0-14-241556-6.

HOOK: Auden thinks her life is perfectly normal. Nobody else seems to agree.

REVIEW: Auden has always worked hard to be the "perfect daughter." In the summer after high school, Auden decides to spend some quality time with her dad, his new wife, and their new daughter. In her new town, Auden makes friends of her own age for the first time. She takes a job in a clothing boutique staffed by girls who try to make her welcome. Then, while wandering the streets of town at night she meets up with Eli, another teen with time on his hands. Together, they do the things that Auden never did as a kid: bowling, food fights, and delivering newspapers. But just because she learns to ride a bike doesn't mean Auden has really changed, does it?

Recommended for readers age 13 and up.

Sex: 2; Cussing: 0; Violence: 0

death, drinking, grieving, kissing, sexual situations

READER REACTION: A sweet story of friendship, families, and growing up. Fans of the author will enjoy the cameo appearances of characters from earlier books, as well as the comfortable quality of the narrative.

ALERTS: The book contains some kissing and a tactfully vague "hooking-up" scene on the beach, but no cussing or violence.

Ferraro, Tina. *The ABC's of Kissing Boys.* Delacorte, 2009. 224p. LB $11.99. 978-0-385-90569-5. $8.99 Trade pb. 978-0-385-73582-7.

HOOK: Do you know how to kiss? Want lessons? Each chapter starts with a different type of kiss, A to Z!

REVIEW: Parker doesn't make the varsity soccer team, but she has a plan: Her brother's best friend, a handsome college guy, agrees to kiss Parker, passionately and in public. The problem? Parker is worried that she will look silly because she has never kissed anyone before. The solution: The handsome best friend/next door neighbor boy will give kissing lessons. Can you predict what happens next?

Recommended for readers age 12 and up.

Sex: 2; Cussing: 1; Violence: 1

Kissing

READER REACTION: This is a silly book. But there is something in the interplay between Parker and Tristan that is just so much fun, and girls love the story. The side plots involving the workings of soccer, building a leader, and the coach, and the sub-plot between the two fathers keep the book from being a single silly story.

ALERTS: This is a fun, fast read, with a predictable plot and enjoyable characters. If you can find something objectionable here, we will be amazed.

Gorman, Carol. *Games.* Harper Collins, 2007. 288p. $17.99. 978-0-06-057027-9.

HOOK: "I wonder if Tabitha is used to boy-girl relationships. She must have kissed other boys before yesterday. She sure is good at it. I'm a strong believer in education, so if she wants to teach me the nuances of great kissing, I wouldn't try to stop her." (p116)

REVIEW: Mick and Bret (Boot) are in eighth grade, and what started off as name calling and yelled insults has escalated. Both have been suspended for fighting each other. Both boys are bullies. Both have fathers with larger problems.Enter the new principal, who decides that after the latest fight, the boys' sentence is to play games in the room next to his office every day. Now, enter Tabitha, the cute girl at school, who seems to like both of them, seeking any information about their fights. With this crazy cast of characters, how could anything be what it seems?

Recommended for readers age 12 and up.

Sex: 2; Cussing: 2; Violence: 4

bullying, child abuse, cussing, kissing, violence

READER REACTION: Just looking at the plot line, these boys would not seem like likeable protagonists. However, their feelings and the double-crossing Tabitha make this a sought-after read for both boys and girls.

ALERT: Give this book to school principals—they will love it!

Mackall, Dandi Daley. *Crazy in Love.* Dutton, 2007. 192p. $6.99 Trade pb. 978-0-14-241157-5.

HOOK: Do you hear voices in your head? Do you listen to them? Do you argue with them?

REVIEW: High school senior Mary Jane flirted with Jackson, who reciprocated, even though he was already dating the popular and gorgeous Star. The entire girl posse breaks into two factions: those who support Mary Jane, and those who are upset at the breach. Mary Jane hears two very distinct voices in her head giving contrary advice: Plain Jane, who wants her to be the "good girl" and M.J., the sexy alternative. Mary Jane and her two best friends took a vow of chastity before marriage, but her best friend Alicia is now having sex with her college boyfriend; Red is not, because her boyfriend believes in God.

Recommended for readers age 13 and up.

Sex: 2; Cussing: 1; Violence:

abstinence, kissing, religious beliefs, Star Trek *sex*

READER REACTION: The banter between the voices is funny and witty. The obvious, hit-you-over-the-head moral is not: "All girls who have sex before marriage will live in utter disappointment; all girls who abstain will be happy."

ALERTS: While we listed *Star Trek* sex, it is off-stage concerning a friend, not Mary Jane.

Meyer, L. A. *Bloody Jack.* Graphia, 2010, 2002. 320p. $8.99 Trade pb. 978-0-15-205085-6.

HOOK: (Slash the book through the air like a sword) Swashbuckling adventures, knife fights, cannons, pirates, hidden identity, and first love. What more do you want?

REVIEW: Gone are the days of scrounging for food as an orphan in eighteenth-century London! Mary "Jacky" Faber hires onto the *HMS Dolphin* disguised as a boy, travels the world, and has countless adventures. While *Bloody Jack* stands alone nicely, it is the first volume of a long series of action-adventure stories. Most stories take place on the high seas, where Jacky meets numerous historical figures, as well as literary characters like Captain Ahab and Mike Fink. The books are fast-moving historical adventures, narrated by a cocky girl who has plenty of courage and ingenuity.

Recommended for readers age 12 and up.

Sex: 2; Cussing: 2; Violence: 3

abstinence, bullying, cussing, death, drinking, sexual situations, violence

READER REACTION: Fast-moving action scenes are interspersed with fascinating details of life onboard a 1797 sailing vessel, along with the protagonist's musings about observations of her shipmates and experiences in foreign ports.

ALERTS: Later volumes in the series feature some "near-miss" sexual situations, (mostly *Star Trek* sex), more cussing, and more violence, as the characters participate in battles at sea and on land.

Reed, M.K. and Hill, Jonathan. *Americus*. First Second, 2011. 224p. $18.99. 978-1-59643-768-5. $14.99 Trade pb. 978-1-59643-601-5. ⬤

HOOK: What's more interesting to you: a bunch of gossipy neighbors or a really great book?

REVIEW: Eighth graders Neil and Daniel would rather read books in their favorite fantasy series *The Chronicles of Apathea Ravenchilde* than pay attention to their gossipy classmates or the adults in their small town of Americus. However, Daniel's mom is convinced that Apathea is the work of the devil and sends her son away to military school, leaving Neil alone to defend his favorite book. Fortunately, Neil isn't alone in loving the book. Following the example of the main character in *Apathea*, Neil learns to stand up to bullies on behalf of other book-lovers, gains the confidence of classmates and the local library staff, and even starts a new romance with a fellow-bookworm. Three cheers!

Recommended for readers age 12 and up.

Sex: 2; Cussing: 1; Violence: 1

kissing

READER REACTION: This is a great graphic novel depicting terrific friendships inspired by books. Teens enjoy this book. Librarians love it.

ALERTS: There are depictions of bullying and some badly behaved adults. Conservative Christian parents are not portrayed kindly, but librarians are!

Stork, Francisco X. *Marcelo in the Real World*. Arthur A. Levine, 2009. 320p. $17.99. 978-0-545-05474-4. $8.99 Trade pb. 978-0-545-05690-8.

HOOK: Marcelo doesn't understand people, and now he has to work with them.

REVIEW: Marcelo is at the high-functioning end of the autism spectrum, and his classes at Paterson have taught him many skills for living in the "real world." However, his high-powered lawyer dad isn't satisfied with Marcelo's progress and insists that the boy take a summer job at the law firm, rather than working with the ponies in the therapeutic riding center at Paterson. While there, Marcelo meets people from all ends of the "real world" spectrum, including musically-talented Jasmine in the mailroom, snobbish personal secretaries, and the lecherous son of one of the lawyers. Marcelo also becomes personally involved in the law firm's biggest case when he discovers the photograph of a victim in the trash and decides that he must take action.

Recommended for readers age 13 and up.

Sex: 1; Cussing: 1; Violence: 1

abstinence, bullying, sexual situations

READER REACTION: Marcelo's strong, distinctive voice tells the unusual story of a self-possessed teen eager to fit in without sacrificing his own values and interests. Those who enjoyed the voice of Christopher in *The Curious Incident of the Dog in the Night-Time* by mark Haddon will also love reading about Marcelo.

ALERTS: While there is no cussing or kissing, there is much thought and discussion about sex and sexual attraction (the whole concept baffles Marcelo), but no action on-page.

Van Draanen, Wendelin. *Confessions of a Serial Kisser.* Knopf, 2009, 2008. $9.99 Trade pb. 978-0-375-84249-8.

HOOK: Evangeline wants one fabulous, passionate kiss.

REVIEW: Evangeline has been keeping her head down since her parents separated. She didn't try out for the volleyball team,she refuses to talk to her dad, and she spends most of her time concentrating on homework and trying to keep the condo tidy so her mom can relax. While sorting through laundry, Evangeline discovers her mom's secret stash of bodice-ripper romance novels. Intrigued, Evangeline reads one and decides that what she needs most is a fabulous, passionate kiss like the ones between Delilah and Grayson in *The Crimson Kiss.* Evangeline's search for the perfect kiss quickly gets out of hand, and soon she has a reputation as a "serial kisser." Will she ever find passion and happiness?

Recommended for readers age 12 and up.

Sex: 2; Cussing: 1; Violence: 1

kissing

READER REACTION: The pink cover art (on the hardcover edition) and chick-lit plot are misleading. This is actually a carefully-crafted, well-told story about a teen's search for identity and love. The unexpected ending was a delight, and characters of the parents are well-rounded.

ALERTS: The title is more problematic for parents than the actual story. For that reason, this is a great book to hand parents.

Wood, Maryrose. *Sex Kittens and Horn Dawgs Fall in Love.* Delacorte, 2006. 256p $8.99 Trade pb. 978-0-385-73277-2.

HOOK: Use the title. Wait for the tittering to stop. Then explain the tame plot line.

REVIEW: Felicia and pals call themselves the Kittens—supposedly the "Sex Kittens," although they admit that they aren't very experienced in the "sex" part yet. Felicia and the other Kittens attend the Manhattan Free Children's School and spend much of their school day skipping class, while (supposedly) working on independent and original learning projects. For example, Felicia writes poetry: endless reams of haiku poems mostly focused on the "Horn Dawg" (boy) of her desires, Matthew. Matthew doesn't dream of poetry OR Felicia . . . he dreams of science. By making her science fair project a study of the "thing that makes the one you love love you back," Felicia hopes to finally capture the scientific heart of the Dawg of her dreams.

Recommended for readers age 12 and up.

Sex: 2; Cussing: 1; Violence: 1

kissing

READER REACTION: Light, fluffy, and fun. There are no scenes of violence, no drugs, and no sexual situations—but there are many giggle-ful moments and a few sweet, but unexpected kisses in the lives of the Kittens.

ALERT: The only problem with this book is the racy title. Parents react to the title even after they know the plot of the book.

"N-O" Spells No: Abstinence and Refusals

- *Between* (Warman)
- *Does My Head Look Big in This?* (Abdel-Fattah)
- *Memoirs of a Teenage Amnesiac* (Zevin)
- *Pushing the Limits* (McGarry)
- *Ready or Not* (Cabot)
- *Running Loose* (Crutcher)
- *Sister Wife* (Hrdlitschka)

Abdel-Fattah, Randa. *Does My Head Look Big in This?* Scholastic, 2005. $16.99. 978-0-439-91947-0. $9.99 Trade pb. 978-0-439-92233-3.

HOOK: How many teen girls do you know—personally—who wear a hijab, the Muslim headscarf? Whether the answer is "many" or "none," you will want to meet Amal and read about the first year she decided to wear the hijab.

REVIEW: Against the advice of her parents and some of her friends, Australian teen Amal has decided to wear the *hijab*, the Muslim headscarf, full-time. The story of her eleventh grade year chronicles her experiences with family, friends, classmates, neighbors, and total strangers, as she comes to terms with her religious beliefs. Amal's life isn't always focused on religion. On the contrary, her life is a lot like the lives of other girls her age: She worries about grades, zits, and peer pressure. She wonders about boys and friends, and she anticipates the future with curiosity.

Recommended for readers age 12 and up.

Sex: 1; Cussing: 1; Violence: 1

abstinence, alcohol, bullying, drinking, prejudice, and *religious beliefs.*

READER REACTION: This book gives the "post 9-11 Muslim experience" not only a human face, but a set of diverse human faces. Amal's best friends are also Muslim, but they and other supporting characters choose to express their religious beliefs in a wide variety of ways, adding depth to the story. The audio-book read by Rebecca Macauley provides an auditory "Aussie immersion" experience for the listener.

ALERTS: Although it's a little preachy at times, this is still a nice view into a world often disparaged by the media.

Cabot, Meg. *Ready or Not.* HarperTeen, 2008. 256p. $8.99 Trade pb. 978-0-06-147996-0.

HOOK: What do you do after you've saved the president of the United States?

REVIEW: In this sequel to *American Girl,* Samantha is still dating the president's son, David. However, she has fallen into a "truth trap:" She implies that they have been sleeping together. This makes life complicated because of the president's "Return to Family" program. Sam, David, and students at school engage in the social politics of premarital sex.

Recommended for readers age 13 and up.

Sex: 2; Cussing: 2; Violence: 0

abstinence, cussing, kissing, STDs

READER REACTION: Readers either love or hate this book. Some feel betrayed that the "sugar and fluff" they expect from this author is anchored by real life decision-making and scenes ripped from a sex education classroom. Others are thrilled that Samantha and David's relationship matures in a realistic (if not idealistic) way.

ALERTS: The themes of premarital sex, birth control, and abortion in this book are more complex than themes in the *Princess Diaries* series. We agree with many readers, however, that after all the growth we see in Sam throughout the book, the ending is just silly.

Crutcher, Chris. *Running Loose.* Greenwillow, 2003. 216p. $8.99 Trade pb. 978-0-06-009491-1.

HOOK: Louie has everything a small-town high school guy is supposed to want: a secure place on the football team, a gorgeous girlfriend, a good family. So, what's the problem?

REVIEW: While Louie has some irritating enemies at school and the coach is obviously a jerk, his best friend is still the quarterback, and life seems pretty good. But when he witnesses a teammate throwing a play to intentionally hurt the opposing team's best guy—with the coach's blessing—Louie quits the team in protest and becomes an outcast. He still has his friends, his family, and Becky. Until, tragically, he doesn't. Louie and Becky have one of the nicest teen relationships in literature: They grow gradually towards intimacy, but in a surprising twist, it is Louie who decides that he isn't ready to take the Next Step. The author creates realistic, flawed characters who grow through tough situations, and tells a sports-saturated story that even non-sports fans will enjoy.

Recommended for readers age 13 and up.

Sex: 2; Cussing: 2; Violence: 3

abstinence, alcohol, bullying, child abuse, cussing, death, drining, grieving, kissing, nudity, prejudice, sexual situations, violence.

READER REACTION: Crutcher's books appeal both to guys who want to read about sports and to girls who want to read about relationships. He expertly balances the two, while bringing up important social issues that matter to teen readers.

ALERTS: *Running Loose* is one of this author's earliest books, and one of the most socially "tame." Still, there is cussing, racial slurring, and some sexual situations that will be objectionable to some readers.

Hrdlitschka, Shelley. *Sister Wife.* Orca Books, 2008. 269p. LB $21.95. 978-1-4420-0076-6. $12.95 Trade pb. 978-1-55143-927-3.

HOOK: Here's a question for the girls: Have you ever thought about getting married some day? How about getting married at age fifteen? How about getting married at age fifteen to a much older man who is already married to five other women?

REVIEW: Fifteen-year-old Celeste has always questioned her faith, but she knows little of life outside of her small, old-fashioned, polygamous faith-based town of Unity. Although she is intrigued by stories told by a girl from outside the community, Celeste was raised in a family with multiple mothers and many children, and has always assumed that she would live in a similar family when she reached the age of marriage. She is attracted to a young man of her faith, but he wants to leave Unity and wants her to leave with him, rather than marry the much older man chosen for her by the Prophet. Celeste wants more than the community can give her, but how can she shame her family and leave them behind?

Recommended for readers age 13 and up.

Sex: 2; Cussing: 1; Violence: 1

abstinence, bullying, pregnancy, prejudice, religious beliefs, sexual situations.

READER REACTION: The multiple-narration strategy works well for this story, allowing the continually questioning perspective of Celeste to be balanced by that of her younger sister Nanette, who is happy within her community.

ALERTS: It's interesting to note that Celeste finally rejects her family and religious community *after* giving birth to her first child within the plural marriage.

McGarry, Katie. *Pushing the Limits.* Harlequin Teen, 2012. 403p. $17.99. 978-0-373-21049-7. $9.99 Trade pb. 978-0-373-21086-2.

HOOK: Both Echo and Noah want to be normal. Defining "normal" is the problem.

REVIEW: Echo appears in the school office, returning after a long absence. She is waiting for her counselor. Noah, incredibly hot, all-around bad boy, is waiting for the same counselor. Both are hiding secrets. Echo wears long sleeves that cover the wrist-to-elbow scars that are healing on both arms; Noah has been expelled from several group homes for fighting. Echo must date the insipid Luke in order to be re-admitted to the "in" crowd. Echo and Noah both want to be normal. Just what is normal, really? This book is told in alternating voices as the two career toward each other and toward exposing their desperately hidden secrets. Minor characters are caricatures: Echo's parents, their friends, and even the counselor are stereotyped.

Recommended for readers age 13 and up.

Sex: 2; Cussing: 5; Violence: 5

abstinence, alcohol, bullying, cussing, death, drinking, drugs, gay friends, grieving, kissing, nudity, prejudice, safe sex, sexual situations, and *violence*

READER REACTION: Teens race through this book, barely slowing for the smoking hot romance to learn all the answers. The many subplots slow the reading down for those looking for either romance or answers to Echo's mystery. More discriminating readers will want more from the author. While we enjoy a happy ending, this one is just too saccharine!

ALERTS: Having a boy refuse even when girl wants sex is an unusual plot point, but author Chris Crutcher's characters in *Running Loose* made it much more believable.

Warman, Jessica. *Between.* Walker, 2011. 480p. $17.99. 978-0-8027-2182-2. $9.99 Trade pb. 978-0-8027-3386-3.

HOOK: When pretty, popular, wealthy Elizabeth Valchar wakes up on the morning of her eighteenth birthday, she's dead.

REVIEW: Nobody knows exactly what happened, including Liz, who is stuck "between" life and death, seeking answers and haunting her hometown, her friends, and her family. The only person who can see Liz is Alex . . . and he's dead, too. The narrative gradually unwinds clue after tiny clue, drawing the reader deeper into the complex life of a pretty girl who seemed to have it all, but perhaps really didn't. Liz is not a sympathetic character, especially at first: She is shallow, petty, and mean. Yet, as the story delves deeper into the past, Liz remembers (and readers learn) that her life was not as perfect as it appeared . . . and that the accidental death on the family yacht might not have been an accident.

Recommended for readers age 13 and up.

Sex: 2; Cussing: 1; Violence: 2

abstinence, alcohol, bullying, child abuse, death, drinking, drugs, grieving, kissing, nudity, religious beliefs, sexual situations, violence

READER REACTION: The mystery is not perfect—astute readers will figure out the connection between Liz and Alex long before Liz understands it—and there are a few plot holes. However, the storytelling is riveting. The characters draw readers into the story, and the "real feeling" of high school life, as well as the complexities of imperfect adult relationships, rings absolutely true.

ALERTS: The "issues" of this book (anorexia, peer pressure, drunk driving, and more) are buried deeply. It's almost *not* an "issue book," except, of course, that it totally *is* an issue book. The issues are part of the characters, rather than part of the plot, which makes for a much better story.

Zevin, Gabrielle. *Memoirs of a Teenage Amnesiac.* Farrar, Straus and Giroux, 2007. 288p. $17. 978-0-374-34946-2. $8.99 Trade pb. 978-0-312-56128-4.

HOOK: Think for a moment about all the things you have done, and seen, and thought about in the last four years. Now, think about what your life would be like if you couldn't remember anything that had happened to you in that time. How would your life be different?

REVIEW: Naomi loses a coin toss and is obligated to run back to put away the yearbook camera. On her way, she slips, falls, and bangs her head—and wakes up with no memory whatsoever of the last four years. As she explores the artifacts of her life, trying to remember who she was, Naomi asks many questions about the kind of person she remembers being four years ago, and compares her memory with what she sees in her life now. Does she obsess over her weight? Is she really upset with her mother over the divorce and a new sister? Is she the kind of girl who would have sex with her boyfriend? And . . . just who are her *real* friends?

Recommended for readers age 13 and up.

Sex: 2; Cussing: 2; Violence: 1

abstinence, alcohol, kissing

READER REACTION: The medical angle of the book is intriguing to students and has even been used by teachers who want to combine scientific research with literature. Students relate to Naomi and the high school scene in general. The idea of having to learn who you are by looking at clues in the environment is one that intrigues both students and teachers.

ALERTS: The parents suffer from lack of development. Dad is a fleshed-out character, and has a good relationship with Naomi, but other relationships are not as expanded. The romance (which readers will spot long before Naomi figures it out) is sweet and lovely.

Not Dead ... Yet: Death and Dying and Sex

- *A Monster Calls* (Ness)
- *Before I Die* (Downham)
- *Before I Fall* (Oliver)
- *Chanda's Secrets* (Stratton)
- *Crash into Me* (Borris)
- *Deadline* (Crutcher)
- *The Fault in Our Stars* (Green)
- *Thirteen Reasons Why* (Asher)
- *Tomorrow When the War Began* (Marsden)

Asher, Jay. *Thirteen Reasons Why.* Razorbill, 2011, 2007. 336p. $10.99 pb 978-1-59514-188-0.

HOOK: "You don't know what goes on in anyone's life but your own. And when you mess with one part of a person's life, you're not messing with just that part. Unfortunately, you can't be that precise and selective. When you mess with one part of a person's life, you're messing with their entire life. Everything ... affects everything." (p.201, trade edition)

REVIEW: When Clay Jensen receives a shoebox in the mail filled with cassette tapes, he doesn't know what to think. He finds a tape player (who has a tape player anymore?) and starts to listen. The voice he hears on the tape is Hannah Baker . . . who killed herself. Using the cassettes, Hannah tells the stories—thirteen of them—to explain the reasons why she committed suicide. Clay feels guilty and confused. He knows how he feels about Hannah, but he never knew how she felt about him—or anybody else—until now.

Recommended for readers age 13 and up.

Sex: 3; Cussing: 2; Violence: 2

alcohol, abuse, bullying, cussing, death, drinking, drugs, grieving, rape, sexual situations, suicide

READER REACTION: Although the issue of suicide is central to the story, this is not an issue-only book. It is, instead, a character-driven book: Even stereotypical characters like "the popular girl" have depth and detail. Hannah might be dead, but her perspective lives on as she tells the story of the events leading to her suicide. The book is compelling, powerful, deeply affecting, and highly recommended.

ALERTS: Suicide is a sensitive topic, especially in middle school.

Borris, Albert. *Crash into Me.* Simon Pulse, 2010. 272p. $9.99 Trade pb. 978-1-4169-9827-3.

HOOK: The characters continually make Top 10 lists, all related to suicides (top ten celebrity suicides, etc.). Any of these could be read aloud.

REVIEW: Four teens meet through an online suicide blog. They decide to each choose the gravesite of a famous suicide, and these sites become the journey on the "Celebrity Suicide Road Trip" they will take from New York to Death Valley, where they have agreed upon a group suicide pact. The story is told through the eyes of Owen, who is the master of suicide statistics. He has attempted suicide many times. There are some pretty funny times and simple teen moments. There are disclosures and even romance. The focus, however, is on the growth of the teens toward understanding their problems, backgrounds, faults, and emotions.

Recommended for readers age 13 and up.

Sex: 3; Cussing: 2; Violence: 2

abstinence, alcohol, bullying, child abuse, cussing, death, drinking, drugs, homosexuality, kissing, sexual questioning, Star Trek *sex, suicide*

READER REACTION: Suicide is a topic of high interest to teens. While the theme is handled with compassion, it is also conveyed realistically. This could be problematic for immature readers. Borris does not flinch from the very authentic emotions and does not preach.

ALERTS: Any time teens talk about "how to . . .," adults talk about keeping them away from books that encourage them to make attempts. These are great opportunities for conversations with well-meaning adults. Checking out this book is *not* necessarily a "suicide warning sign," but as always, when dealing with this topic, be alert.

Crutcher, Chris, *Deadline.* Greenwillow, 2009. 336p. $9.99 Trade pb. 978-0-06-085091-3.

HOOK: Ben Wolf is eighteen years old . . . and he's dying.

REVIEW: Eighteen-year-old Ben Wolf gets the news right before he starts his senior year in high school: He's dying of a rare and aggressive blood disease. Against the advice of his doctor, Ben decides to forego treatment entirely, and he also decides to keep his illness secret from everyone. Ben's last year is full of courage. Though scrawny, Ben makes the football team at his tiny Idaho high school and plays a successful season alongside his athletically gifted brother Cody. He gathers the nerve to talk to his secret love, super-hottie-athlete-girl Dallas Suzuki. He is so affected by Alex Haley's biography of Malcolm X that he challenges his classmates and his town to overcome their prejudices. And just when Ben is really enjoying his life, his illness starts to intrude.

Recommended for readers age 13 and up.

Sex: 3; Cussing: 2; Violence: 3 (domestic violence)

abstinence, alcohol, cussing, death, drinking, grieving, kissing, nudity, religious beliefs, safe sex, sexual situations, Star Trek *sex, violence*

READER REACTION: Highly recommended for sports fans (Crutcher makes football sound soooo cool, even to non-sport fans) and readers looking for a well-written, substantial book about one kid's attempt to make the world a better place.

ALERTS: If you're seeking a light and fluffy tearjerker, avoid this book. In fact, avoid everything ever written by this author. Crutcher is well-known as the author of thought-provoking, award-winning stories of substance abuse, bigotry, child molestation, and neglect, and this book is no exception. Despite the heavy subject matter, one message shines through: "Life is short. Whatever you really want to do, do it now."

Downham, Jenny, *Before I Die.* Ember, 2009. 336p. $20.95. LB 978-0-606-10646-7. $9.99 Trade pb. 978-0-385-75183-4.

HOOK: On page one of this book, Tessa is puking her guts out and facing her own imminent death. She's been through treatment, remission, recurrence, and more treatment, and the docs say they can't help her anymore. Grabbing a Sharpie marker, Tessa scrawls her bucket list on the wall beside her bed.

REVIEW: British teen Tessa is dying of leukemia. She's been through four years of treatments, remissions, and recurrence, and at the beginning of the book, she faces reality: She is dying, fast. But she's not ready yet. Tessa makes a list of things she wants to do before she dies. Some are sweet, others are dangerous. She has nothing to lose, and she doesn't have much time. *Sex* tops the list. *Drugs* are number two. *Travel the World* is number seven, but she's willing to swap that for *Get Parents Back Together. Fall in Love* isn't on the list at all, but it happens anyhow.

Recommended for readers age 16 and up.

Sex: 4; Cussing: 2; Violence: 1

cussing, death, drinking, drugs, grieving, kissing, sexual situations

READER REACTION: Read this with a box of tissues handy. Although readers know from page one that Tessa is dying, they become involved with the characters, and the final thirty pages of the book are very powerful. One reader told me, "This is the book that Lurlene McDaniel *wished* she could write." Some adults question the parental permission granted to Tessa to explore her bucket list, but in the context of the story, it makes sense.

ALERTS: Ths is not a book to read while using public transit, sitting in a classroom, or in another public space. Readers should give themselves permission to experience the loss of a fictional friend without fear of embarrassment. We don't recommend this book for young or fragile readers, because some of Tessa's "bucket list" choices are pretty ill-advised, although they are perfectly understandable, given the circumstances.

Green, John. The Fault in Our Stars. Dutton, 2012. 336p. $17.99.978-0525478812.

HOOK: Cancer books suck. This book doesn't suck.

REVIEW: Seventeen-year-old Hazel has been surviving terminal cancer for four years when she meets Augustus Waters, who lost a leg to the osteosarcoma. Hazel and Gus are smart, they are witty, they read, they discuss, they are both very ill. Do you think you know how this story ends?

Here's a word rarely used to describe a cancer book: sexy. This book is funny, it's goofy, it's sad, it's appalling, and it's sexy.

Highly recommended for readers age 13 and up.

Sex: 3 (Star Trek Sex); Cussing: 2; Violence: 0

death, drinking, grieving, kissing, sexual situations, "Star Trek Sex"

READER REACTION: The world is a better place because this book has been published ... and that's not a small thing. Readers value the realistic, ugly depiction of cancer, as well as the articulate characters who are not defined by their disease. This is a great book for parent/student and book circle discussion groups.

ALERTS: Have a hankie or two (or three or four) ready. Although the author avoids cheap "cancer book" stereotypes, these are not characters that readers willingly release gently into that good night.

Marsden, John. *Tomorrow When the War Began.* Scholastic, 2006. 304p. $8.99 Trade pb. 978-0-439-82910-6.

HOOK: They could run away. They could surrender. They choose to fight back.

REVIEW: During Australian summer (Christmas break), a group of rural teens go camping in the outback. When they tire of eating junk food and long for some real chow, they go home to get better food and discover their farms and town deserted, with livestock and pets left dead and dying. Their town has been captured in a brief war, and survivors are being held captive in the fairgrounds. The teens now find themselves in a guerrilla war. Emotions run the range from appropriate strategy to inappropriate thoughts. Told from Ellie's viewpoint, death, fear, destruction, romance, heroism, and even religion play a role in very real and definable teen emotions. First in a worthwhile series.

Recommended for readers age 13 and up.

Sex: 1; Cussing: 1; Violence: 5

death, dystopia, grieving, kissing, suicide, violence

READER REACTION: While often compared to the movie *Red Dawn,* most readers agree that *Tomorrow When the War Began* is the better story: better plot, better characters, better setting, better action.

ALERTS: This book is *violent*. The characters are at war—and although they do feel remorse for actions that cause the death of enemy soldiers, the remorse doesn't slow them down when it's time to take action again. As the series continues, there is even more violence, as well as some undisguised sexual content. Managers of libraries in conservative communities will want to discuss where the final books in the series are housed.

Ness, Patrick. *A Monster Calls*. Candlewick Press, 2011. 216p. $16.99. 978-0-7636-5559-4.

HOOK: Thirteen-year-old Conor is surprised by the monster at his window, because it's not the nightmare he has been expecting. (Be sure to use the hardcover when showing the book; the paperback cover is awful!)

REVIEW: The monster who visits Conor takes the shape of a walking, talking, terrible yew tree that tells awful stories and demands the worst possible thing from Conor: the truth. It sounds scary, but the book isn't actually scary. It sounds crazy, but the story ultimately makes sense. The monster (cancer) that haunts Conor is one that affects many teens and their families. Make this book available *before* the monster comes calling, and keep a hanky ready for the final chapters.

Recommended for readers age for readers 12 and up.

Sex: 2; Cussing: 1; Violence: 2

bullying, death, grieving, magic, Star Trek *sex*

READER REACTION: The problem with this book is that the plot sounds completely stupid. Ignore the plot description and just read a page or two. Allow yourself to be sucked into Conor's darkness, his fear, and his dread, and learn why the monster is called to walk.

ALERTS: We wouldn't have thought enough of the sex in this book to include it on the SITL list, but the children's librarian who questioned the book was clearly freaked out by the implication of very-far-off-page *Star Trek*-esque intimacy. Clearly, she doesn't spend much time with teen literature (or teens, either!), but if a very tactful passing reference to intimate married adults bothers you, then avoid this book. Otherwise, go find it and read it and share it with other readers.

Oliver, Lauren. *Before I Fall.* Harper Collins, 2011. 496p. $17.99. 978-0-06-172680-4. $9.99 Trade pb. 978-0-06-172681-1.

HOOK: Use a reference to the movie *Groundhog Day*; almost all students have seen it.

REVIEW: Samantha has always been part of the popular crowd. Her perfect life is up-ended when Sam is killed in a car accident. However, the next morning, Sam wakes to the prior day, and begins a cycle of reliving that final day over and over. She understands that the day is repeating, and alludes to the movie *Groundhog Day*, but doesn't understand *why*. Sam assumes that she is immune to repercussions and begins experimenting with wild variations on her behavior, even seducing her math teacher. Gradually, Sam understands that she has the opportunity to change her behavior and attitudes, and that she will be caught in the endless loop until she figures out what needs to change.

Recommended for readers age 16 and up.

Sex: 2; Cussing: 2; Violence: 2

abuse, alcohol, bullying, death, drinking, kissing

READER REACTION: Teens love the change from the prissy, stuck up girl to the understanding, caring teen. Despite the fantastic premise, the evolution of the character is very realistic. This book begs to be discussed, especially the ending.

ALERTS: While over-indulgent Sam is involved in sex, drugs, stealing, and drinking, these are only mentioned. One major issue addressed by the story is that all of the characters assume that these elements are an essential part of being in the "in-crowd."

Stratton, Allan, *Chanda's Secrets.* Annick Press, 2004. 200p. $11.95 Trade pb. 978-1-55037-834-4.

HOOK: Movie tie-ins sell books. This was made into a movie called *Life, Above All.*

REVIEW: At sixteen, Chanda faces more in life than anyone at any age should. She has moved from her rural home in sub-Saharan Africa to a large city. After her father dies in the diamond mines, Chanda survives a series of horrible step-fathers, only to have the latest "dad" dumped in front of their house, dying. What nobody will say is that he is dying of AIDS, that Chanda's mother is dying of AIDS, and that Chanda and her brothers are possibly infected as well. The disease cannot be mentioned in the villages at all. Chanda is powerful in her awareness and convincing in her constant questioning. Stark, real, forceful.

Recommended for readers age 13 and up.

Sex: 4; Cussing: 2; Violence: 4

alcohol, bullying, child abuse, death, grieving, nudity, pregnancy, prejudice, prostitution, rape, religious beliefs,, sexual situations, Star Trek sex, STDs, suicide, violence

READER REACTION: *Chanda's Secrets* has won many awards internationally. Because of the research behind the book, it has been used in health, social studies, and science classes. There is also a sequel (*Chanda's Wars*) and a movie.

ALERTS: Since this book first appeared, many other books, fiction and nonfiction, have appeared on the topic of AIDS in South Africa.

The Rainbow Connection: LGBTQ Topics

- *Boy Meets Boy* (Levithan)
- *Don't Let Me Go* (Trumble)
- *Geography Club* (Hartinger)
- *Hard Love* (Wittlinger)
- *I Am J* (Beam)
- *Jumpstart the World* (Hyde)
- *Parrotfish* (Wittlinger)
- *Rainbow Boys* (Sanchez)
- *Tale of Two Summers* (Sloan)
- *The Mis-Education of Cameron Post* (Danforth)
- *Totally Joe* (Howe)
- *Will Grayson, Will Grayson* (Green and Levithan)

Beam, Cris *I Am J*. Little, Brown, 2011. 352p. $16.99. 978-0-316-05361-7. $8.99 Trade pb. 978-0-316-05360-0.

HOOK: His parents think he's a lesbian.

REVIEW: J has always felt misunderstood, and no wonder: His parents think he's a lesbian, his best friend Melissa think he's a girl, and his girlfriend Blue is pretty sure he's gay. But J knows that he is a boy, although he was born female. After doing some Google research, J learns about testosterone shots, and is convinced that taking "T" will fix everything in his life. But even after seeing a psychologist and starting hormone therapy, J learns that, as much as he loves them, the people in his life are still not perfect.

Recommended for readers age 14 and up.

Sex: 1; Cussing: 0; Violence: 0

bullying, gay friends, homosexuality, kissing, prejudice, sexual questioning, straight friends

READER REACTION: Readers will learn a lot about the lives of transgender teens, as J attends a support group, enrolls at a school for transgender teens, and does his best to become a man in a society that isn't quite sure how to define him. The book is obviously issue-driven; however, the convincingly multiethnic and gender-diverse characters salvage it from the "afterschool special" pile.

ALERTS: This book is almost squeaky-clean: no cussing, no sex; one scene of under-age drinking. References to body parts are polite. Sexual tension does not progress beyond a few exchanged kisses. This is a novel of hope.

Danforth, Emily M. *The Miseducation of Cameron Post.* Balzer & Bray, 2012. 480p. $17.99. 978-0-06-202056-7.

HOOK: Cameron kisses her best friend. Later that day, her parents die. It's a problem.

REVIEW: Cameron is twelve when her parents die in an automobile accident. She is already feeling guilty about kissing her best friend Irene. In fact, guilty would be a word to describe how Cameron feels about her yearnings for girls in general. She feels even *more* guilty when Aunt Ruth comes to take care of her and introduces Cammie to small-town conservative Christianity. Several loves enter and exit Cammie's life as she tries to understand who she is and who she loves, as well as who she should or shouldn't love. When at fifteen, she develops a relationship with a girl from church and Aunt Ruth finds out, Cammie is placed in "God's Promise," a school affiliated with the National Association for the Research and Treatment of Homosexuality.

Recommended for readers age 14 and up.

Sex: 2; Cussing: 2; Violence: 2

cussing, death, gay friends, grieving, homosexuality, kissing, prejudice, religious beliefs, sexual questioning, sexual situations, Star Trek *sex, straight friends*

READER REACTION: Cameron is a very likeable and well-drawn character, as are most of the characters in the book. Cameron's story is compelling and personal, giving it an autobiographical feel. This is a hefty tome, and the size is off-putting for some readers.

ALERTS: The story reaches back to Cameron at age nine, which could be a problem for some teen readers. It also takes place in the 1990s, and the political turmoil surrounding gay rights at that time is a major plot point. Although the Christian School and Center for Healing is fictional, the National Association for the Research and Treatment of Homosexuality and the events surrounding the Quake Lake earthquake are factual.

Hartinger, Bret. *Geography Club.* Avon/Tempest, 2004. 226p. $8.99 Trade pb. 978-0-06-001223-6.

HOOK: Talking about feeling alone in high school easily segues to an intro to this book. *Geography Club* has been hit by censors, supposedly *not* for homosexuality, but for unsafe use of the Internet. Do you believe that excuse? We don't either.

REVIEW: Russel knows what it's like to be different. He's convinced that he's the only gay kid at his high school. One night, while searching for kindred souls on the Internet, Russel chats with another gay kid from his town—in fact, this kid attends his school. Discovering the truth about Kevin leads to even more revelations: There are other gay kids in the school who are lurking below the student body radar. The gathering of this group eventually leads to the formation of a student club, which they name "The Geography Club" in order to dissuade others from joining. After all, what could be more boring than a geography club?

Recommended for readers age 14 and up.

Sex: 2; Cussing: 2; Violence: 2

abstinence, alcohol, bullying, cussing, drinking, gay friends, homosexuality, prejudice, sexual questioning, straight friends

READER REACTION: This is not just a book about gay kids and straight kids. This book is about being different and being afraid to be different. One of the best characters in the story isn't even homosexual— he's just an outcast: a poorly-dressed, unconventional nerd. There is no tidy ending, and not everyone emerges from his or her personal closet, but each character does grow and change in the course of the book. And that is what makes it a really good book. Hartinger personally answers emails to teens with questions and is a very approachable author.

ALERTS: No strong language or graphic descriptions, but frank discussions of possible sexual situations. The second book in the series (*The Order of the Poison Oak*) contains more explicit sexual situations.

Howe, James. *Totally Joe*. Atheneum, 2005. 208p. $5.99 Trade pb. 978-0-689-83958-0.

HOOK: The idea of an "alphabiography" assignments hooks lots of younger junior high students. Reading the first page and a half intro works well, too, to give a sense of the book's voice and to set up the plot.

REVIEW: Joe's English teacher has assigned the class to write an "alphabiography": an alphabetical review of their lives. Joe's alphabet begins with his best friend Addie, who knew him when they both liked to play with Barbie dolls. His story continues on towards Colin, the boy he has had a crush on since fifth grade, and finally ends with Zachary, the new boy in school. During the course of the book, Joe learns to use the word "gay" to describe himself, and his family is mostly supportive. However, the school jock torments Joe and spreads a false rumor that Colin and Joe have been kissing, which is hurtful to Joe and devastating to Colin, who is not ready to come out of the closet.

Recommended for readers age 12 and up.

Sex: 2; Cussing: 2; Violence: 2

bullying, cussing, gay friends, homosexuality, prejudice, sexual questioning, straight friends

READER REACTION: Most students feel that the situations are resolved too easily; however, Joe's funny, quirky voice is unique and strong as he relates the story of his seventh grade year. Any reader who has ever felt different from the rest of the crowd will find a friend in Joe, and those who loved his earlier adventures in *The Misfits* will be happy to see him again.

ALERTS: Some Christian families are seen in a very prejudicial and non-Christian light.

Hyde, Catherine. *Jumpstart the World*. Knopf, 2010. 186p. $16.99. 978-0-375-86665-4. $7.99 Trade pb. 978-0-375-86626-5.

> HOOK: Sixteen-year-old Elle's mom doesn't want her at home anymore—in fact, Elle's pretty sure that her mom doesn't want her at all anymore. Now Elle has an apartment, an ugly cat, and new neighbors including Frank, who is married but romantically interesting.

> REVIEW: Frank isn't what Elle imagined in her daydreams. Frank is a female-to-male transgendered person. When Elle learns the truth about Frank, she is angry with him, but more important, she questions the significance of her crush. Is Elle a lesbian? Or what? This book is full of people with problems, and it is also full of compassion. Fortunately, the characters shine beyond common labels, and even Elle's mom gets a tiny bit of redemption by the end.

> Recommended for readers age 12 and up.

> Sex: 2; Cussing: 1; Violence: 2

> *bullying, drinking, gay friends, grieving, homosexuality, kissing, prejudice, prostitution, religious beliefs, sexual questioning, straight friends*

> READER REACTION: The compassion towards misfits of all types is gentle and healing in this story. The author's empowering message is a reminder that each individual has the ability to make the world a better place.

> ALERTS: As found in other LGBTQ literature, some "Christian" characters are stereotypically intolerant. The violence level reflects bullying.

Levithan, David. *Boy Meets Boy*. Knopf, 2005. 192p. LB $17.95. 978-1-4352-8780-8. $8.99 Trade pb. 978-0-375-83299-4.

> HOOK: The author wrote this story for his friends as a Valentine's Day "card" that grew into a book. He still does this every year; they just don't all become books.

> REVIEW: At Paul's high school, the homecoming queen is also a cross-dressing quarterback, gay boys can walk through town holding hands, and the gay-straight alliance was formed to teach straight kids how to dance. Just because the "gaytopia" portrayed by David Levithan is completely unrealistic doesn't mean it isn't also completely charming. And it's refreshing to read a book where romantic troubles are equally distressing for gay and straight teens.

> Recommended for readers age 13 and up.

> Sex: 2; Cussing: 0; Violence: 0

> *kissing, gay friends, straight friends*

> READER REACTION: The very upbeat nature of the book lends itself to being unrealistic. Students who are very accepting of differences shrug and refuse to put this under the "gay literature" heading. It is just romance for all in every high school, full of tears and laughter.

> ALERTS: While the topic of love for everyone is a great quest, the totally optimistic, utopian setting may seem so unrealistic that other themes in the story will be overlooked.

Levithan, David and John Green. *Will Grayson, Will Grayson*. Speak, 2010. 336p. $9.99 Trade pb. 978-0-14-241847-5.

HOOK: Grab the audio version and play an excerpt of Tiny singing! Also tell students that both authors knew people with "exact same names" before writing this book.

REVIEW: Two people are both improbably named Will Grayson. One Will Grayson is the straight best friend of the ironically named Tiny, who is the most "out" gay student ever; the other Will is gay, but has a difficult time dealing with his sexuality. The story is told in alternating chapters (written by two well-known authors) through the eyes of the two very different Will Graysons, who ultimately answer the questions "What is a friend?" and "What is love?" The backdrop is the awful black hole known as high school. Although the book is named "Will Grayson," Tiny nearly steals the show. Tiny is producing a musical in high school based on his life and many loves. Tiny becomes best friend to both Will Graysons. Tiny is so over-the-top and so hard to forget.

Recommended for readers age for 14 and up.

Sex: 3; Cussing: 3; Violence: 3

alcohol, bullying, cussing, drinking, drugs, gay friends, homosexuality, masturbation, religious beliefs, sexual situations, Star Trek Sex, STDs, straight friends, violence

READER REACTION: Teens love this funny, quirky novel. The sexual language is explicit, although the story is needed for younger readers.

ALERTS: Reviews are mixed; while some readers have strong negative reactions, true fans will endlessly quote the passages that they love.

Sanchez, Alex, *Rainbow Boys*. Simon and Schuster, 2003. 272p. $9.99 Trade pb. 978-0-689-85770-6.

HOOK: Nelson is out. Kyle is in. Jason isn't sure.

REVIEW: Picture three high school guys from very different parts of the social map. Nelson has been out-and-proud for years, but he hasn't been able to tell that special guy that he wants to be more than friends. Kyle isn't sure he's ever going to be able to tell anybody *anything* about his secret crushes. And Jason has a steady girlfriend but he keeps thinking about sex with guys. Though full of social clichés, this book clearly fills a need for high school readers who want to read about other teens like themselves. The characters are not deep or thoughtful, but they are pretty typical. They don't always make good decisions, even when they've got good information, because that's another thing that teens do: They make mistakes sometimes.

Recommended for readers age 14 and up.

Sex: 3; Cussing: 3; Violence: 3

READER REACTION: When the book was newly published, it was something of a groundbreaker in teen literature. Alex Sanchez wrote about situations and characters that most other teen authors avoided at the time. With the passage of time (and the popularity of the television program *Glee*), homosexuality is no longer a topic that requires tippy-toes.

ALERTS: There are naked bodies. Together.

Sloan, Brian, *Tale of Two Summers*. Simon and Schuster, 2006. 256p. $15.95. 978-0-689-87439-0.

HOOK: The scene of Hal and Henri crawling out on a steel girder 50 feet above the ground is a great read-aloud.

REVIEW: Hal and Chuck have been best friends for ten years. This summer, before junior year, they are apart. Thus begins summer for two very different guys: Hal, gay, bored in Wheaton, Maryland, finally taking driver's ed. Chuck, straight, excited about drama summer camp. Both are looking for a summer romance and (they hope) sex. Chuck has devised a blog to which they both contribute, and this allows them to communicate more candidly with each other. The anonymity of the computer allows the two friends to talk about issues that sixteen-year-olds might not feel free to discuss face-to-face. Over the summer, their blog entries educate readers about gay issues in a very readable, witty, format. While all the characters are more than one-dimensional, the relationship between Hal and Chuck is the best part of the book; readers will cheer for the success of their friendship.

Recommended for readers age 15 and up.

Sex: 5; Cussing: 3; Violence: 2

alcohol, bullying, cussing, drinking, drugs, gay friends, homosexuality, nudity, prejudice, sexual situations, straight friends

READER REACTION: Some teens feel that the characters are far too mature for their age. The scenes with parkour and acrobatic antics are hugely popular with any male reader.

ALERTS: At times, the novel feels like a vehicle to educate the public on gay issues. Perhaps it is, but we forgive the author because these are just great characters. Straight people who are curious about the myths and realities of gay relationships will find good information here. This book lays it on the page in a way that teens will understand. Due to the frank talk and explicit actions, this book is for more mature readers. The sex scenes are very explicit, but tastefully done.

Trumble, J.H., *Don't Let Me Go*. Kensington Books, 2012. 344p. $15. Trade pb. 978-0-7582-6927-0.

HOOK: The T-shirt episode on p.112 is priceless.

REVIEW: Nate and Adam believe their relationship is forever, but Adam is graduating from high school and moving to New York to begin an acting career. Nate knows that he needs to discover himself without Adam, but the year is much harder than he anticipated. Last year the boys came "out." Last year Nate had Adam by his side. Now, entering his senior year, he is not sure if he has the courage to be without Adam. His best friend Juliet is still there to help, and Nate is also befriended by Danial, a student from Pakistan. Through flashbacks, readers are shown the circumstances surrounding a physical and sexual assault. Family relationships, friendships, and even sexual activities are brought out through the ensuing court trial, as the book skips back and forth in time.

Recommended for readers age 15 and up.

Sex: 4; Cussing: 3; Violence: 5

bullying, cussing, gay friends, homosexuality, nudity, prejudice, safe sex, sexual situations, straight friends, violence

READER REACTION: Students looking for books on "coming out" are hugging this book. The character of Danial seems too perfect, but the author says he is based on a real person. For the reader, learning the story in bits and pieces is much easier to absorb. The gradual reveal also helps readers deeply understand relationships and the horror of the assault.

ALERTS: The violence of the hate crime, even released in small bits, is difficult; however, the book is much more than a focus on hate crime. Emotions of the two boys run true, and these emotions are really the heart of the story.

Wittlinger, Ellen. *Hard Love.* Simon and Schuster, 2001. 224p. $9.99 Trade pb. 978-0-689-84154-5.

HOOK: Grab some student zines if you are in a city with a good bookstore or print some on-line zines.

REVIEW: John and Marisol come together over their zines. They find they like each other and appreciate the opportunity to discuss their families and problems. Marisol even talks about her possible feelings as a lesbian. John has trouble with emotions of any kind and he wants to "move Marisol into the heterosexual category." As the two mature as writers, and as people, they discover what friendship means and what honesty is.

Recommended for readers age 13 and up.

Sex: 2; Cussing: 2; Violence: 1

bullying, cussing, gay friends, homosexuality, prejudice, straight friends

READER REACTION: Teens like this book because the characters are intriguing, with honest teen reactions. Teachers like this book because it illustrates that writing can help students express their emotions and aid in understanding the world around them. Assignments to write and illustrate a zine often come from exposure to this book.

ALERTS: Although the themes of homosexuality appear in the book, the topic is really one of relationships, especially family relationships.

Wittlinger, Ellen. *Parrotfish.* Simon and Schuster, 2007. 294p. $16.99. 978-1-4169-1622-2. $8.99 Trade pb. 978-1-4442-0621-6.

HOOK: Have available a nonfiction book on parrotfish, or print out a picture of the fish to show.

REVIEW: At the beginning of her junior year, Angela changes her name to Grady. In fact, he has decided that he *is* a boy, although he was born a girl. Reactions run the entire gamut, from loss of friendship to complete understanding. New friends appear: gorgeous, popular, biracial Kira, and geeky Sebastian, who is studying the parrotfish, a creature capable of changing its gender. Bullying, harassment, and general disbelief abound. All of this "plays" on while Grady's family is staging a live-action *A Christmas Carol* through their dining room picture window (with speakers for outdoor spectators), an annual obsession for Grady's father, which is dreaded by the rest of the family.

Recommended for readers age 14 and up.

bullying, cussing, gay friends, homosexuality, prejudice, straight friends

READER REACTION: Teens, even those who do not understand or want to talk about transgendered people, find Grady understandable and accept him as a boy. This book has power. Partly thought-provoking, partly high school angst, and partly hilarious, this book begs to be discussed.

ALERTS: There are few books written for teens in the genre of transgendered persons. This story is told with sympathy and understanding for a complex situation, with a likeable protagonist.

Real Life, or Something Like It: Contemporary Realistic Fiction

- *Gingerbread* (Cohn)
- *The Espressologist* (Springer)
- *Flash Burnout* (Madigan)
- *The Misfits* (Howe)
- *My Life Next Door* (Fitzpatrick)
- *Nick and Norah's Infinite Playlist* (Cohn and Levithan)
- *Sky Is Everywhere* (Nelson)
- *Snitch* (Van Diepen)

Cohn, Rachel, *Gingerbread*. Simon and Schuster, 2002. 172p. $15.95. 978-0-689-84337-2. $8.99 Trade pb. 978-0-689-86020-1.

HOOK: The story of the doll, Gingerbread, is the best way to introduce teens to Cyd Charisse. Read that page or describe the incident in the airport, and then "fast forward" to today, just after her abortion.

REVIEW: If you were named Cyd Charisse, you might be rebellious too. Cyd is blessed with wealthy parents, a hunky boyfriend, an understanding step-dad, and an absent father who looms much larger because he has never been in her life. Cyd is sixteen, has just had an abortion, been left by her boyfriend, and fights constantly with her mother. Cyd knows her life will be perfect if she can only be with the dad she has never known. So mom ships her off to New York to be with her biological father. This is the story of a summer of self-discovery. Typical teen angst is ever-present; Cyd purports to be wild, but is in fact, a rule-follower. Her dad has a new family and they have problems of their own.

Recommended for readers age 14 up.

Sex: 2; Cussing: 2; Violence: 1

abstinence, alcohol, cussing, death, drinking, drugs, gay friends, kissing, nudity, pregnancy, prejudice, safe sex, sexual situations, Star Trek *sex*

READER REACTION: Teens love this selfish, spoiled brat who finds the route to change. Cyd's problems are not all solved by the end of the book. This is an honest portrayal: She is still a spoiled brat, although she is slightly less shallow. Change happens slowly, and readers know she will make many more mistakes, but now has a base on which to ground herself. Sequels include *Shrimp* and *Cupcake*.

ALERTS: Parents have a problem with this book, because of the abortion at the beginning. After reading the book, they may have a different reaction. This is one to discuss. This is a great series for conservative school libraries to share with less conservative institutions, as the sequels could be problematic.

Cohn, Rachel, and David Levithan. *Nick and Norah's Infinite Playlist*. Knopf, 2006. 192p. $16.95. 978-0-375-83531-5. $7.99 Trade pb. 978-0-375-84614-4.

HOOK: Slide into a chair next to an unsuspecting kid and ask her to do you a favor: Pretend to be some guy's girlfriend for the next five minutes.

REVIEW: Nick is onstage with the band, totally not prepared for his Evil Ex-Girlfriend to show up and prove how much his heart can hurt. Norah is watching the band and wondering what she's going to do now that she mailed her refusal to Brown University in favor of joining her Evil Ex-Boyfriend on a kibbutz in South Africa. In first-person chapters alternating between Nick and Norah, the two journey through the New York music scene, an all-night Korean grocery, an all-night Russian cafe, and eventually to the ice room of the Marriott. In twenty-four hours they cover a lot of territory, but are they getting any closer to love? Two eighteen-year-olds with musical passion have experienced infinite heartache. but are gonna survive.

Recommended for readers age 15 and up.

Sex: 4; Cussing: 4; Violence: 2

cussing, drinking, drugs, grieving, kissing, sexual situations

READER REACTION: Co-written by two exceedingly hip authors, David Levithan (voice of Nick) and Rachel Cohn (voice of Norah). The book is sweet, it's sexy, it's hip, it's cool, and it's true-to-life in New York. Readers who don't love it in the first two chapters will not enjoy the rest of the book—those who do love it will love it all the way through.

ALERTS: The language is honest, painful, and heavily strewn with cussing, showing the strength of tender feelings hidden within each character. The scene in the ice-room is steamy enough to melt the ice!

Fitzpatrick, Huntley. *My Life Next Door.* Dial, 2012. 394p. $17.99. 978-0-80373699-3. $9.99 Trade pb. 978-0-14-242604-3.

HOOK: Can two very different families really get along? Would you be able to keep a separate life a secret from your family?

REVIEW: Samantha lives alone with her sister and mother, the state senator. They live in an antiseptically clean, large, suburban home. Next door live the Garretts and their eight loud, very messy children. Sam surreptitiously watches them from her balcony. After Samantha is asked to babysit in an emergency, she returns to this outrageous family again and again, finding the family irresistible, especially Jase Garrett. Sam's mother is running a new campaign with an advisor-cum-boyfriend, leaving Sam available to become even more involved with the Garrett family. Sam feels conflicted about her mother's latest campaign, and especially mom's new boyfriend, but ignores the feelings until an accident that involves Jase's family. The side characters, especially the young kids, wonderfully round out the story.

Recommended for readers age 14 and up.

Sex: 4; Cussing: 1; Violence: 2

abstinence, alcohol, bullying, drinking, drugs, grieving, kissing, nudity, safe sex, sexual situations, Star Trek *sex*

READER REACTION: The lives of all the people in the book ring true. Teens are racing to get this book. Sam and Jase meet Romeo-and-Juliet style on her balcony in this accelerated romance.

ALERTS: Politics plays a role: Sam's Republican mother and boyfriend/campaign manager have ethical problems. While the large family next door is seen in a positive light, Sam and Jase discuss interesting points arising from the latest pregnancy.

Howe, James. *The Misfits*. Atheneum, 2003. 288p. $6.99 Trade pb. 978-0-689-83956-6.

HOOK: Presenters start by calling each other names: fatso; geek; fairy; beanpole. Ask the audience to supply epithets that they have heard.

REVIEW: After complaining that only the popular kids are elected to the student council, four middle school students decide to create a third party. They label it "The No-Name Party," and invite students to join if they have ever been called a bad name. This resonates with their classmates, as nearly everyone has been called a name. *The Misfits* has punchy humor and a fast moving plot.

Recommended for readers age 12 and up.

Sex: 0; Cussing: 0; Violence: 1

cussing, gay friends, straight friends

READER REACTION: Teachers love this book as a conversation starter. As a result of this book, there is now a National No-Name Week. To prove his points, the author allows his characters to become stereotypical. With one gay student, one fat student, one black student, etc., the book tries to hit a lot of points.

ALERTS: There is a tendency for this book to become too preachy. *Totally Joe,* the sequel, is a better book, although each book stands alone.

Madigan, L.K. *Flash Burnout.* Houghton Mifflin Books for Children, 2009. 336p. $16. 978-0-547-19489-9. $7.99 Trade pb. 978-0-547-40493-6.

HOOK: Blake likes to take gritty, realistic photos. Unfortunately, his best subject so far is Marissa's mom.

REVIEW: Marissa recognizes the subject of Blake's picture: The homeless woman passed out in an alley is her addict mother. While Marissa is initially upset by the image, the photo spurs the friendship to a new level, creating an obvious conflict with Blake's girlfriend. When they later believe that Marissa's mother is dead, the two find comfort together. Unfortunately, the resulting sex makes their lives even more complicated.

Recommended for readers age 15 and up.

Sex: 5; Cussing: 2; Violence: 2

cussing, death, drugs, grieving, kissing, nudity, prejudice, sexual situations, Star Trek *sex, violence*

READER REACTION: Blake's parents are wonderful and real and funny, His dad works as a coroner which sets the stage for many jokes. Blake also wants to be a comedian and is constantly trying his one-liners on everyone, often getting a laugh from readers as well as fictional characters.

ALERTS: This book has many mature themes. The addiction of Marissa's mother is well-handled and not graphic. The on-page sex scenes, while understandable, are problematic for some readers.

Nelson, Jandy. *The Sky Is Everywhere.* Dial, 2010. 288p. $17.99. 978-0-8037-3495-1. $8.99 Trade pb. 978-0-14-241780-5.

HOOK: You know those books where the older perfect sister dies suddenly and then you learn that she wasn't that perfect after all? This isn't that.

REVIEW: Lennie (named for John Lennon) is trying to recover from the sudden heart attack of her nineteen-year-old super-star sister, Bailey. She is also falling for the new kid in school, Joe. In trying to help Lennie and himself through the grieving process, Bailey's boyfriend, Troy, makes advances toward Lennie. This natural reaction to death leads both of them down a very guilt-ridden and ultimately destructive path, especially in the light of Lennie's new found romance. The main characters are believable, lovable, and quirky, as are Lennie's grandmother and "Uncle Big."

Recommended for readers age 14 and up.

Sex: 3; Cussing: 3; Violence: 1

abstinence, alcohol, cussing, death, drinking, drugs, grieving, kissing, nudity, pregnancy, religious beliefs, safe sex, sexual situations, Star Trek *sex, violence*

READER REACTION: Band geeks relate to Lennie; girls finding their way through romance relate to Lennie; teens who love poetry relate to Lennie; and anyone trying to work through their grief will love Lennie. Alternately serious and silly, teens love the journey they take with Lennie.

ALERTS: Lennie's grandmother helps her look at the consequences of sex; Lennie ignores this helpful information, creating problematic, but realistic, situations. The relationship between Lennie and Troy could have been an "eewwww" factor, but was handled so sensitively, it helps the reader understand the grief.

Springer, Kristina. *The Espressologist*. Farrar, Straus and Giroux, 2009. 192p. $8.99 Trade pb. 978-0-312-65923-3.

HOOK: What if you could find your perfect match by comparing coffees?

REVIEW: Barista Jane Turner has a theory: People's personalities are reflected by their coffee drinks. For example: *Medium Iced Vanilla Latte = Smart, sweet, and gentle. Sometimes soft-spoken but not a doormat.* It occurs to Jane that a person who drinks a medium iced vanilla latte would be a romantic match with a person who loves to drink a medium dry cappuccino (*Medium Dry Cappuccino = Smart and simple. A little timid and soft-spoken, but probably a powerhouse if ever tested*). Jane invents a new "science," which also leads to a terrific marketing tool for the coffee shop: Espressology. Soon, Jane is busy matching up hopeful singles by comparing their coffee preferences, with remarkable success. But will she ever find a romantic match of her own?

Recommended for readers age 13 and up.

Sex: 2; Cussing: 1; Violence: 1

coffee, kissing

READER REACTION: The story is cute and frothy. Teen readers recognize this and enjoy it for the fluff-piece that it is.

ALERTS: Only the caffeine-deprived would find something to object to in this book!

van Diepen, Allison. *Snitch*. Simon Pulse, 2007. 304p. LB $16.99. 978-1-4395-9237-3. $8.99 Trade pb. 978-1-4169-5030-1.

HOOK: Do you know any gang members? What would induce you to join a gang?

REVIEW: Julia and her friends have promised each other since grade school that they will not join one of the gangs that are so prevalent in their Brooklyn high school. But then Eric Valienté becomes the new student—and heart throb. Julia falls for him, even when he joins the Crips gang. Although she leaves him, she also warns Eric of an upcoming Bloods attack, earning her the title of "snitch," and snitches are dealt with violently by the girlfriends of gang members. For protection, Julia joins the Crips. Eric is harboring a secret that cannot be shared, even with another gang member.

Recommended for readers age 13 and up.

Sex: 3; Cussing: 3; Violence: 4

abstinence, alcohol, bullying, cussing, death, drinking, drugs, kissing, nudity, prejudice, religious beliefs, sexual situations, Star Trek *sex, violence*

READER REACTION: Teens looking to understand gangs, and teen who are looking for edgy thrillers love the van Diepen books.

ALERTS: Although a good story and romance, this is clearly a "gang story for suburban kids." The ending is too saccharine for the rest of the story.

Smokin' in the Boys' Room: The Male Experience

- *The Absolutely True Diary of a Part-Time Indian* (Alexie)
- *Be More Chill* (Vizzini)
- *Bluefish* (Schmatz)
- *Doing It* (Burgess)
- *Fly on the Wall* (Lockhart)
- *Half Brother* (Oppel)
- *King of the Screwups* (Going)
- *Little Brother* (Doctorow)
- *Seth Baumgartner's Love Manifesto* (Luper)

Alexie, Sherman. *The Absolutely True Diary of a Part-Time Indian.* Little, Brown, 2007. 230p. $18.99. 978-0-316-01368-0. $14.99 Trade pb. 978-0-316-01369-7.

HOOK: What's worse than being a reservation Indian? Junior is a weird-looking dork Indian with a huge head, gigantic feet, crazy eyes, a stutter, and a lisp.

REVIEW: Born with water on the brain, a talent for cartooning, and a brilliant sense of the absurd, fourteen-year-old Arnold Spirit "Junior" keeps a diary to chronicle, with words and pictures, his simultaneously tragic and outrageously funny attempt to escape from life on the Spokane Indian Reservation. Sherman Alexie's "semi-autobiography" is clearly based on real events and people near to the author's heart, and Junior's coming-of-age story will certainly appeal to adults as well as teens.

Recommended for readers age 14 and up.

Sex: 3; Cussing: 2; Violence: 3

alcohol, bullying, cussing, death, drinking, drugs, grieving, masturbation, prejudice, suicide, violence.

READER REACTION: This is a book made of awesome. Teachers like it, librarians like it, the National Book Award committee likes it, and even teens like it. This may be the only "required reading" book in the entire curriculum that almost all students will enjoy reading. We were thrilled when a school board in our home state removed the book from the high school curriculum after a parent complained . . . and then reinstated it when the school board members read the book and loved it.

ALERTS: Masturbation. It's there. There aren't any pictures, though. Bullying descriptions are off-page, as are accidental deaths and alcohol-inspired injuries on the rez.

Burgess, Melvin. *Doing It.* Henry Holt, 2004. 326p. $9.99 Trade pb. 978-0-312-55135-3.

HOOK: Dino, Ben, and Jonathon are obsessed with sex. Read the first pages aloud to a group (if you dare.)

REVIEW: Dino desperately wants to shag his girlfriend Jackie . . . or, you know, anybody. Jon thinks Deborah is beautiful, but he's afraid to date her because he worries that everyone else will say she's fat. Ben actually has *too much sex*, because he's the sexual partner of a predatory teacher. The boys talk about sex, fantasize about it, worry about it, and talk about it again in the raunchy, rude slang of British teens. What starts out as a "too-much-information" story about three teenaged sex fiends, actually becomes a very compassionate look into the lives and anxieties of three teen boys.

Recommended for readers age 16 and up.

Sex: 5; Cussing: 4; Violence: 1

abuse, bullying, cussing, drinking, drugs, kissing, masturbation, nudity, rape, sexual situations

READER REACTION: The book is intentionally strong and shocking. Many readers (especially adults) are horrified by the language and the frank obsession with sex. Aarene gave the book to a sixteen-year-old boy and asked for his reaction. He handed it back when he was done, saying that it was "pretty much right." Then she gave the book to a forty-five-year-old man and asked him if guys grew out of the obsession. He handed it back when he was done, telling her that, even for adult guys, the book was "pretty much right." Maybe that's more information than some people want, but it's good to know.

ALERTS: The language and sexual situations will be problematic in conservative institutions; still, the story is worthwhile and enjoyable. It perhaps helps that slang cuss words/sexual references are British and thus, cushion the impact for American readers.

Doctorow, Cory. *Little Brother.* Tor Teen, 2008. 384p. $17.95. 978-0-7653-1985-2. $10.99 Trade pb. 978-0-7653-2311-8.

HOOK: The author makes the text of *Little Brother* available for download at no charge on his website. If you read the book, you will understand why.

REVIEW: Marcus loves technology, delights in finding new ways to hack software, and especially likes flummoxing security systems. But Marcus is in the wrong place at the wrong time when the San Francisco Bay Bridge is bombed by terrorists. He and three teen friends are taken into secret custody by Homeland Security and interrogated mercilessly. Marcus and two of the friends are eventually released, but not the third boy. Is Darryl dead? A prisoner? They discover that while they were imprisoned, their beloved city has turned into a police state. Marcus decides to fight back, but will his efforts make the city safer? Or will Marcus become a different kind of terrorist? His girlfriend Ange joins him. What will happen when the DHS finally tracks down Marcus and Ange?

Recommended for readers age 14 and up.

Sex 3; Cussing 3; Violence 4

alcohol, bullying, cussing, death, drinking, drugs, dystopic, kissing, nudity, sexual situations, violence

READER REACTION: Set in the "near future," Doctorow's technological digressions and discussions are fascinating, especially after readers do a little research and discover that most of the story's "futuristic technology" already exists. This is dystopic science fiction, political commentary, teen fiction, and spy thriller writing at its best. Adult book groups and high school English teachers, we're talking to you: *Get this book, read it, and talk about it!*

ALERTS: The narrative contains violence (including a description of torture practices, specifically waterboarding), mild cussing, and some hot-but-tactful sexual situations between Marcus and Ange.

Going, K.L. *King of the Screwups.* Harcourt, 2009. 310p. $17. 978-0-15-206258-3. $7.99 Trade pb. 978-0-547-33166-9.

HOOK: Sixteen-year-old Liam takes after his retired-supermodel mom: He is athletic, good-looking, and has inherited her eye for fashion. According to his dad, Liam is a continual disappointment, a slacker, a screw-up.

REVIEW: When Liam is caught with a girl (on his dad's office desk), he gets kicked out of the house and goes to live with his "Aunt Pete," a cross-dressing glam-rocker who lives in a trailer park. Liam tries harder than ever to earn his dad's approval—working so hard that he cannot recognize his real strengths and talents until he nearly screws up his life for good. Awesome, quirky characters live in a small town where everybody knows the business of everybody else (at least, they think they do). Liam is likeable, Aunt Pete is terrific, the glam-rockers are supportive and fun, the class nerds are enjoyable, and even the school jocks and cheerleaders are people worth knowing. Only Liam's dad lacks virtues . . . or does he?

Recommended for readers age 13 and up.

Sex: 1 (the kids are interrupted on the desk); Cussing: 2; Violence: 2

bullying, cussing, drinking, gay friends, homosexuality, prejudice, straight friends

READER REACTION: Likable Liam is aggravating to many readers, because he obviously has so many talents, but he concentrates all his attention on trying to please his dad—a man who is steadfastly determined to be displeased. The UN-likable father character is also aggravating. In fact, the character easiest to love is Aunt Pete, who refuses to fit anybody's stereotypical expectations.

ALERTS: Don't read this on the bus. People look strangely at readers who keep giggling.

Lockhart, E. *Fly on the Wall.* Delacorte Press, 2006. 182p. LB $18.95. 978-1-4178-1260-8. $8.99 Trade pb. 978-0-385-73282-6.

HOOK: Sixteen-year-old comic book artist Gretchen Yee is kidding (in a desperate kind of way) when she makes a very unusual wish: to be a fly on the wall in the boys' locker room just so she could figure out what boys are all about! And then, her wish is granted.

REVIEW: Although Gretchen is alarmed to discover that she's turned into a fly stationed on the wall of the boy's locker room at school, she immediately starts examining—and critiquing—the various examples of male anatomy. In time, she discovers an unknown admirer, and is surprised to learn that guys have personal problems, too. The premise is ridiculous, but once you've discarded *that*, the narrative is actually quite fun and insightful. We gave this to a guy to read, so he could review the accuracy. He reported that the locker room at his school was a lot more boring, but that the information was not-too-far-off. Although the main character is female and the cover is pink, don't be surprised when boys pick up this book, too.

Recommended for readers age 14 and up.

Sex: 3; Cussing: 4; Violence: 2

bullying, cussing, drugs, homosexuality, masturbation, nudity, prejudice, sexual questioning, sexual situations.

READER REACTION: Who wouldn't want a "fly-on-the-wall insider perspective" sometimes? This is a quick—and surprisingly informative—read.

ALERTS: Male genitalia is tactfully referred to as "gherkins." How can we look at pickles anymore? Did we say it has a *pink* cover?!

Luper, Eric. *Seth Baumgartner's Love Manifesto.* Balzer and Bray, 2010. 293p. $16.99. 978-0-06-182753-2. $8.99 Trade pb. 978-0-06-182755-6.

HOOK: Seth doesn't understand love, relationships, or anything else. Except golf.

REVIEW: Seth's summer seems to be spiraling downward, with the exception of his golf game, which remains exceptional. While scheming to get back his girlfriend, Seth starts an anonymous podcast called "The Love Manifesto" to explain what love is—to himself and everyone else. His hilarious friend Dimitri is obsessed with the one thing he can't have: a girl, any girl. Dimitri also provides the smutty dialog that Seth could never deliver.

Recommended for readers age 13 and up.

Sex: 2; Cussing: 3; Violence: 1

abstinence, alcohol, cussing, nudity, prejudice, sexual situations

READER REACTION: The music listed as part of the sessions appeals to many readers. Anyone can predict how things will go awry, but it doesn't matter. It's funny enough to keep on reading—and laughing. Seth's podcasts will be dated because of the musical references.

ALERTS: It seems that dad escapes consequences, but this makes for a good discussion point.

Oppel, Kenneth. *Half Brother.* Scholastic Press, 2010. 384p. $17.99. 978-0-545-22925-8. $9.99 Trade pb. 978-0-545-22926-5.

HOOK: It's bad enough that Ben's parents don't ever ask his opinion about stuff. Now they're going to adopt another child—and it's a monkey.

REVIEW: Ben's parents are researchers with a very special project: examining the language and behavior of a chimpanzee who is adopted into their home and treated like a human child. Thirteen-year-old Ben isn't very enthusiastic at first. Gradually, however, teaching sign language to Zan becomes Ben's project. And then, the project funding fails. Thoughtful and sweet, the story explores the boundaries of scientific ethics, as well as the relationship between animals and people. The emotional sub-plot of Ben's experiences with his family and his first girlfriend are funny and pertinent as well. Sexual situations between young teens are tactfully addressed.

Recommended for readers age 13 and up.

Sex: 2; Cussing: 2; Violence: 1

sexual situations

READER REACTION: Many readers enjoyed the audiobook version of this story, read by Daniel diTomasso. The 1970s setting does not seem to be an obstacle.

ALERTS: Very few readers were alarmed the by sexual situations between Ben and his girlfriend, but those who were disturbed seemed to be *extremely* disturbed.

Schmatz, Pat. *Bluefish.* Candlewick, 2011. 240p. $15.99. 978-0-7636-5334-7.

HOOK: Travis figures the new school will be like the old place, except the old place had his dog Rosco and this place doesn't.

REVIEW: Travis is just starting to explore the possibilities of a relationship with a girl. He isn't ready for a girlfriend, but to his surprise, he makes friends with a girl: a smart, loud-mouthed girl called Velveeta. He also meets up with a savvy and persistent teacher who is not going to give up on Travis. Readers will enjoy the lovely writing, wonderful complex characters, and complex relationships between each of them. Be ready to cheer in triumph for at least one of them, and be ready to share the book with teens and adults who work with teens.

Recommended for readers age 12 and up.

Sex: 1; Cussing: 1; Violence: 1

bullying, death, drinking, grieving

READER REACTION: Adults may recognize that Travis has a learning disability (possibly dyslexia) that hinders his ability to read, but students may miss the early clues, because Travis is very adept at hiding his problems. His obvious intelligence and frustration at his own inability to master a "simple skill" are beautifully portrayed.

ALERTS: Adults are excellently portrayed in this book for younger teens. Share it with teachers—and parents, especially those who seem dispirited and feel like they make no difference. This is a "tipping point" book.

Vizzini, Ned. *Be More Chill.* Hyperion, 2004. 287p. $17.99. 978-0-7868-0995-0. $9.99 Trade pb. 978-0-7868-0996-7.

HOOK: Wanna be cool? Swallow this pill!

REVIEW: Jeremy is convinced that *some* people are born Cool—and he isn't one of them. He's desperate to be Cool, because he's sure that Coolness will guarantee him access to girls, especially Christine. When he gets the "squip" (a pill-sized computer device that advises him), he suddenly has access to all the tools that Cool people have: knowledge about what to say, what to wear, etc. But his squip is focused on the goal of getting the girl, and maybe that's not all that Jeremy wants. At first, the voice in Jeremy's brain is pretty funny—the reader even agrees with him: "First we need to fix your clothes, your body odor, and your work-out regime." The plot becomes unfunny when readers remember the single-purpose conquest. Still, it's a quick, quirky, fun read.

Recommended for readers age 14 and up.

Sex: 3; Cussing: 4; Violence: 1

cussing, drinking, drugs, masturbation, nudity, sexual situations

READER REACTION: Readers relate to Jeremy, though he isn't very likeable. We have all been in a situation where a "squip" would have been really nice to have as an advisor. There is always a waiting list for this book, even before the movie.

ALERTS: There are plenty of problems adults will dislike. The premise is silly, but funny, and real issues are addressed.

Truth or Dare: Nonfiction and Memoir

- *Changing Bodies, Changing Lives* (Bell)

- *Deal with It* (Drill)

- *It Gets Better* (Savage and Miller)

- *Pregnancy Project* (Rodriguez)

- *S.E.X. : The All-You-Need-to-Know Progressive Sexuality Guide to Get You through High School and College* (Corinna)

- *You: An Owner's Manual for Teens* (Roizen and Oz)

Bell, Ruth, and Alexander Page. *Changing Bodies, Changing Lives.* 3rd edition. Three Rivers Press, 1998. 432p. LB $33.95. 978-1-4352-7659-8. $24.95 Trade pb. 978-0-8129-2990-4.

HOOK: This is the back-up to all student questions relating to the real issues in fiction books. Help them access information from this reliable source.

REVIEW: Like its classic sister-book, *Our Bodies, Ourselves,* this teen-accessible book candidly discusses sexuality and the many physical and emotional changes that occur during adolescence.

Recommended for readers age 12 and up.

abstinence, alcohol, bullying, child abuse, death, drinking, drugs, gay friends, grieving, homosexuality, incest, kissing, masturbation, nudity, pregnancy, prejudice, prostitution, rape, religious beliefs, safe sex, sexual questioning, sexual situations, STDs, straight friends, suicide, violence

READER REACTION: Teachers, parents, students, and librarians all find this useful and easy to use.

ALERTS: This book contains the information that teens want, written in clear readable text. It isn't cute, it isn't colorful. It's just useful. We wish a newer edition was available.

Corina, Heather. *S.E.X. : The All-You-Need-to-Know Progressive Sexuality Guide to Get You through High School and College.* Da Capo Press, 2007. 332p. $17.95 Trade pb. 978-1-60094-010-1.

HOOK: Teens who want to know *everything* about sex: Here's your book.

REVIEW: Complete (and we do mean *complete*) information to answer all the questions you've ever had (and possibly some you never considered). Body image, relationships, masturbation, STDs, pregnancy (and prevention of STDs and pregnancy), as well as the "mechanics" of kissing, mutual masturbation, and various types of intercourse are discussed in frank, readable language. The author "translates" medical terms into slang terms (and vice versa) to make the information in this book as accessible as possible. She also addresses many topics that traditionally have been skipped over in sex information books: pornography, relationship skills, gender identity issues, and detailed information about the process and the physical and mental ramifications of abortion.

Recommended for readers age 14 and up.

abstinence, alcohol, bullying, death, drinking, drugs, gay friends, grieving, homosexuality, incest, kissing, masturbation, nudity, pregnancy, prejudice, prostitution, rape, religious beliefs, safe sex, sexual questioning, sexual situations, STDs, straight friends, suicide, violence.

READER REACTION: Teen and adult readers appreciate the no-nonsense writing and no-parts-skipped-over information. The author is authoritative, and the book is readable (even enjoyable!) Many readers consider this a "definitive" guide to teen and young adult sexuality.

ALERTS: Obviously, this book could be problematic in conservative institutions, and contains perhaps too much information for middle schools or junior high schools. The information is good, current, and needful. The book is a $17.95 investment that libraries should try to make wherever possible.

Drill, Esther. *Deal with It! A Whole New Approach to Your Body, Brain, and Life as a gURL.* Gallery, 1999. 320p. O.P. Trade pb. 978-0-671-04157-1.

HOOK: This is the book that began our *Sex in the Library* journey. We always use it at the beginning of the talk to illustrate the parameters of our program. The cover is fun and engaging—flip the "trench-coat" back and forth tantalizingly as you talk about the book.

REVIEW: The creators of the award-winning website *http://www.gURL.com,* present a hip, no-non-sense resource book for girls. Totally non-judgmental, the advice is geared toward anything teen girls might want to know, from frank sex talk to acne problems.

Recommended for readers age 15 and up.

abstinence, alcohol, bullying, child abuse, death, drinking, drugs, gay friends, grieving, homosexuality, incest, kissing, masturbation, nudity, pregnancy, prejudice, prostitution, rape, religious beliefs, safe sex, sexual questioning, sexual situations, STDs, straight friends, suicide, violence

READER REACTION: The book is somewhat dated now, but still very popular. While technically correct, this book contains information on "swallowing" and other topics that schools and conservative institutions may consider "too much information" for young teens. Students love the hip layout and easy reading style.

ALERTS: Read it before placing it on your shelves. Ask us how we know.

Rodriguez, Gaby. *The Pregnancy Project.* Simon and Schuster, 2012. 224p. $17.99. 978-1-4424-4622-9.

HOOK: What would your friends say if you told them you were pregnant? What would your family do? Gaby Rodriguez decided to find out.

REVIEW: Gaby Rodriguez' mother got pregnant for the first time when she was fourteen years old. Her older sisters were pregnant in high school; her older brothers were fathers before they turned twenty-one years old. Although she was a straight-A student and a member of the leadership class at school, and often lectured her peers about the need for safe sex, Gaby was often told by family, friends, teachers, and others that she would very likely end up as a teen mother. In 2011, eighteen-year-old Gaby decided to study what being a pregnant teen was *really* like: She pretended to be pregnant and took notes on how other people responded to her.

Recommended for readers age 12 and up.

Sex 1; Cussing 1; Violence 1

abstinence, pregnancy, prejudice, religious beliefs, safe sex

READER REACTION: This book is an excellent quick-read for students and adults interested in the topic. Interspersed with the narration are plenty of statistics about teens, pregnancy, and education, and the description of life for teens in a small rural town is spot-on.

ALERTS: Gaby was trying to disprove stereotypes, but her own research supported many of the stereotypes she was fighting against. The social implications of this project are worthwhile discussion topics.

Roizen, Michael F., and Mehmet C. Oz. *YOU: The Owner's Manual for Teens: A Guide to a Healthy Body and Happy Life.* Free Press, 2011. 464p. $16.99 Trade pb. 978-0-7432-9258-0.

HOOK: Dr. Oz is online, and showing his website to students will give them an idea about this book and also point them to an additional information source.

REVIEW: This basic anatomy book also provides information on keeping fit and healthy. Both authors have been on "Health Radio," and the website gives advice to both teens and adults. Their hip, no-nonsense approach to healthy lifestyles is probably already being accessed by teens in your library via the Internet!

Recommended for readers age 13 and up.

abstinence, alcohol, bullying, death, drinking, drugs, gay friends, grieving, homosexuality, incest, kissing, masturbation, nudity, pregnancy, prejudice, prostitution, rape, religious beliefs, safe sex, sexual questioning, sexual situations, STDs, straight friends, suicide, violence.

READER REACTION: Because of the emphasis on staying healthy, parents have flocked to this book for their children. Celebrity author doctors appeal to parents and students.

ALERTS: This book might be considered "too much information" in some conservative institutions, but the information is important—make it available wherever possible.

Savage, Dan, and Terry Miller. *It Gets Better: Coming Out, Overcoming Bullying, and Creating a Life Worth Living*. Dutton, 2011. 352p. $21.95. 978-0-525-95233-6. $15. Trade pb . 978-0-452-29761-6

HOOK: Read the pledge from the website *http://www.itgetsbetter.org*: "Everyone deserves to be respected for who they are. I pledge to spread this message to my friends, family, and neighbors. I'll speak up against hate and intolerance whenever I see it, at school and at work. I'll provide hope for lesbian, gay, bisexual, transgender, and other bullied teens by letting them know that it gets better."

REVIEW: This is a compilation of the narrative of some of the thousands of videos from the "It Gets Better Project" freely available on Youtube. Only one hundred three narratives were included in the book, some from famous gay people like Ellen Degeneres and Gregory Maguire; some with recognizable names like Randy Roberts and Ronnie Roberts, grandson and son of Oral Roberts, the TV evangelist known for his intolerant views. Others are not well-known, but offer ways to not hate yourself, but "hate the forces that made you hate yourself." The book is not only written by gay, lesbian, or transgendered folk; there are many stories from straight people as well, the most notable being Barack Obama, president of the United States. His message: "No one should be bullied. Period. Not in the United States." It's a goal devoutly to be sought.

Recommended for readers age 13 and up.

Sex 1; Cussing 3; Violence 5

abstinence, alcohol, bullying, child abuse, cussing, death, drinking, drugs, gay friends, grieving, homosexuality, kissing, nudity, prejudice, rape, religious beliefs, safe sex, sexual questioning, straight friends, suicide, violence

READER REACTION: This book belongs in every school where there is bullying of LGBTQ kids. In other words: It belongs in every school. While the narratives are powerful, the book and website also allow straight people to stand against bullying. Dan Savage says he wrote this book, because kids in middle and high school need to know that if they are gay, there are people out there who went through what they are going through and survived; if they are straight, there are people out there who stand against bullying. It's a message that is "simple, loud, and clear."

ALERTS: As with other books about LGBTQ teens, conservative communities may have strong feelings. Perhaps the anti-bullying message will override other fears.

Resources

Bildner, Phil, "Texas: If You Can't Ban Books, Ban Authors." *Time U.S.* Sept. 29, 2010. Available: *http://www.time.com/time/nation/article/0,8599,2022356,00.html*.

APPENDIX

Great Sources for Booktalking

Agosto, Denise E., and Sandra Hughes-Hassell, ed. *Urban Teens in the Library: Research and Practice.* American Library Association, 2010.

Cyrus, Ann-Marie, and Kellie Gillespie. *Something to Talk About: Creative Booktalking for Adults.* Scarecrow, 2006.

Edwards, Kirsten. *Teen Library Events: A Month-by Month Guide.* Greenwood, 2002.

Flake, Sharon. *Library Loft.* Available: http://www.libraryloft.org.

Gorman, Michele, and Tricia Suellentrop. *Connecting Young Adults and Libraries: A How-to-Do-It Manual, 4th Edition.* Neal-Shuman, 2009.

Heller, Mary Jo, and Aarene Storms. Sex in the Library. Available: *http://Sexinthelibrary.blogspot.com.*

Jones, Patrick, Maureen L. Hartman, and Patricia Taylor. *Connecting with Reluctant Teen Readers: Tips, Titles, and Tools.* Neal Schuman, 2006.

Koelling, Holly. *Classic Connections: Turning Teens on to Great Literature.* Libraries Unlimited, 2004.

Langemack, Chapple. *The Booktalker's Bible: How to Talk about The Books You Love to Any Audience.* Libraries Unlimited, 2003.

Mahood, Kristine. *Booktalking with Teens.* Libraries Unlimited, 2010.

Martin, Hillias J., and James R. Murdock. *Serving Lesbian, Gay, Bisexual, Transgender, and Questioning Teens.* Neal-Shuman, 2007.

Public Libraries, Young Adults, and Children (PUBYAC) Discussion List. http://pubyac@lists.lis.illinois.edu to register.

Washington Young Adult Reviewer's Group (WASHYARG) Available: *http://www.kcls.org/evergreen/about_washyarg.cfm.*

Welch, Rollie James. *The Guy-Friendly YA Library: Serving Male Teens.* Libraries Unlimited, 2007.

BIBLIOGRAPHY

American Library Association. Available: *http://www.ala.org*

Bott, C.J. "Why We Must Read Young Adult Books that Deal with Sexual Content." *ALAN Review.* Summer 2006: 26-29. Available: *http://scholar.lib.vt.edu/ejournals/ALAN/v33n3/*

Cornog, Martha and Timothy Perper. *Graphic Novels beyond the Basics*: *Insights and Issues for Libraries.* Libraries Unlimited, 2009.

Elliott, Sinikka. "Parents' Constructions of Teen Sexuality: Sex Panics, Contradictory Discourses, and Social Inequality." *Symbolic Interaction*, 33(2), 191-212. Available: *http://people.wku.edu/steve.groce/Parents%20and%20Teen%20Sexuality.pdf*

First Amendment First Aid Kit. Available: *http://www.firstaidfirstamendment.com.*

Girmscheid, Laura, and Rebecca T. Miller, "It Takes Two." *School Library Journal* (May 2012): 26.

Guide for Developing and Evaluating School Library Programs. Nebraska Educational Media Association, 2010.

Hartzell, Gary. "Why Should Principals Support School Libraries?" *Teacher Librarian, Vol. 31, No. 2.* (November 2002).

Heins, Marjorie. *Not in Front of the Children: "Indecency, Censorship, and the Innocence of Youth.* Hill and Wang, 2001.

Levine, Judith. *Harmful to Minors: The Perils of Protecting Children from Sex.* University of Minnesota, 2002.

McDermott, Jeanne T. "Getting It On: An Examination of How Contraceptives Are Portrayed in Young Adult Literature." *Young Adult Library Services* 9, (4): 47-53. June 2011

McFann, Jane. "Boys and Books." *Reading Today*, 22(1), 20-21.

Wickens, Corrine M, and Linda Wedwick. "Looking Forward: Increased Attention to LGBTQ Students and Families in Middle Grade Classrooms." *Voices from the Middle.* 18, (4): 43-51.

INDEX

CPSIA information can be obtained at www.ICGtesting.com
Printed in the USA
BVOW00s0427230114

342718BV00005B/14/P